W9-BZX-072

"I wish that all business leaders would struggle
with the cases presented in this book, their principles and their rationale.
It is an excellent tool for managers who struggle with how to apply
Christian ethics in the marketplace. *Just Business* is full of challenge and
hope—well-written, balanced and informative."
HOWARD BUTT
author, *Renewing America's Soul*

"Business practicioners are in sore need of an ethical framework
which applies eternal principles to everyday
marketplace decisions. Based on the scriptural norms of holiness,
justice and love, *Just Business* provides such a
framework. I highly recommend it."
JACK McMILLAN
former co-chair of the board, Nordstrom's

"Alec Hill has crafted an unusual volume.
This book is solidly based on a biblical theological foundation
(*why* questions are more important than *how to* questions);
it is richly spiced with case studies and illustrations
(there is both heat and light); and it offers a most welcome concordance
of Scripture references. Hill places the business
enterprise in the expansive context of vocation or calling, that liberating
summons of God to live first for Someone and then for something."
PAUL STEVENS
Regent College

JUST BUSINESS

CHRISTIAN ETHICS FOR THE MARKETPLACE

Alexander Hill

InterVarsity Press
Downers Grove, Illinois

InterVarsity Press® is the book-publishing division of InterVarsity Christian Fellowship®, a student movement active on campus at hundreds of universities, colleges and schools of nursing in the United States of America, and a member movement of the International Fellowship of Evangelical Students. For information about local and regional activities, write Public Relations Dept., InterVarsity Christian Fellowship, 6400 Schroeder Rd., P.O. Box 7895, Madison, WI 53707-7895.

ISBN 0-8308-1886-3

Printed in the United States of America ♾

Library of Congress Cataloging-in-Publication Data

Hill, Alexander D.
   Just business: Christian ethics for the marketplace/Alexander D. Hill.
      p.   cm.
   Includes bibliographical references.
   ISBN 0-8308-1886-3 (alk. paper)
   1. Business ethics.   2. Christian ethics.   3. Business—Religious aspects—Christianity.   4. Truthfulness and falsehood.   I. Title.
   HF5387.H55   1997
   174'.4—dc21
                                                    96-39118
                                                      CIP

20	19	18	17	15	15	14	13	12	11	10	9	8	7
13	12	11	10	09	08	07	06	05	04	03	02	01	

To four very special people in my life:

Mary, my content editor, best friend and life partner;
Helen, my grammatical editor, adviser and life-giver;
Laura, my Mariner-loving, quick-witted eldest daughter;
Carolyn, my lap-sitting, infectiously humorous eight-year-old.

And special thanks also to
Randy Franz, Dwight Van Winkle, Randy Rowland
and Scott Bryant for their input
into the manuscript.

PART 1: CONCEPTS 9

  1 A Christian Ethic for Business *11*

  2 Holiness 22

  3 Justice *34*

  4 Love *47*

PART 2: FALSE EXITS *59*

  5 Dual Morality *61*

  6 Law *74*

  7 Agency *90*

PART 3: TOPICS *105*

  8 Honesty & Deception (Part 1) *107*

  9 Honesty & Deception (Part 2) *118*

  10 Concealment & Disclosure *133*

  11 Employer-Employee Relations *148*

  12 Employee Rights in Termination & Privacy *163*

  13 Discrimination & Affirmative Action *174*

  14 The Environment *184*

  15 Property *199*

Epilogue: A Theocentric Approach to Business Ethics *217*

Notes *220*

PART 1
CONCEPTS

1

A CHRISTIAN ETHIC FOR BUSINESS

An ethical man is a Christian holding four aces.
MARK TWAIN

Man is too complicated. I would have made him simpler.
FEODOR DOSTOYEVSKY

You must be perfect as your heavenly Father is perfect.
JESUS

Christianity has not so much been tried and found wanting, as it has been
found difficult and left untried.
G. K. CHESTERTON

M*ARIA MANAGES A SMALL DIVISION WITHIN A MANUFACTURING corporation. Roughly 60 percent of the division's annual $250,000 budget is allocated to the salaries and benefits of Maria and her three subordinates, Abe, Barb and Carl. Maria's supervisor informs her that $40,000 to $50,000 needs to be cut from next year's budget. Since nonpersonnel expenses constitute only $100,000 of the budget, Maria is inclined to lay off one of her employees.*

Before the company moved Abe to Seattle from Chicago last year, Maria told him over the phone that his employment would "no doubt be a long-term arrangement." This was not written into his contract and is, Maria thinks, quite ambiguous. Abe has not worked out as well as Maria had hoped. His work product is mediocre at best, and his interpersonal skills are poor.

A long-term employee, Barb was divorced by her husband two years ago. She is now a single parent of three small children, and it is evident that her work performance has suffered.

Carl works hardest of the three and regularly receives the highest annual evaluations. Another employee has informed Maria that Carl recently inherited a substantial sum of money from his parents' estate. Maria believes that Carl would have a much easier time finding employment elsewhere than either Abe or Barb.

What should Maria do?

Is a Christian Ethic Possible in Business?

Managers regularly confront such nerve-wracking, heart-wrenching and (often) guilt-producing scenarios. In their quest to do the "right thing" for both shareholders and subordinates, they may experience a deep sense of uncertainty. Why? Because when the "shoulds" of life are dealt with, values and relationships are brought to the forefront. Ethics—the study of "shoulds" and of doing the "right thing"—attempts to provide a value-laden framework, a grid through which real-life decisions can be made.

Christian ethics is the application of Christian values to the decision-making process. What counsel does this perspective have for Maria? Does it provide a simple solution to her dilemma? One approach is to view Scripture as a book of rules to be applied to specific situations. Simply find the right rule and match it with the current problem and, bingo, the two pieces fit like a puzzle!

While this strategy works fine in relatively simple situations such as when a worker is tempted to steal or an executive considers slandering a competitor, what about more complex situations like the one confronting Maria? If Abe approaches her first seeking to keep his job, must she heed Jesus' admonition to "give to the one who asks you" (Mt 5:42)? What if Barb and Carl then make similar requests? Or what if Abe assaults Maria when he learns of the possible layoff? Is she to "turn the other cheek" (Mt 5:39), or should she demand restitution and even bring criminal charges against him (Ex 21:23— 22:14)? Taking this line of reasoning a step further, is there a scriptural rule that provides guidance to Maria's company in deciding how many units to produce or in which geographical areas to seek expansion?

Attempts to find easy answers to such enigmatic situations has led one philosopher to label Christian ethics "infantile." He compares the "rule book" approach to the types of absolute commands typically given to children between the ages of five and nine—for example, don't talk to strangers and no singing at the dinner table.[1] While this criticism misunderstands the heart of Christian ethics, it should give pause to those who would take a rules-based approach. In ambiguous cases, it is clearly deficient in its capacity to give precise answers in every situation. Ironically, recent studies indicate that corporations with strict codes of ethics actually are cited more often for breaking the law than their counterparts without such spelled-out rules.[2] Perhaps either human nature rebels against minute regulations or a rule-keeping perspective provides little guidance in morally ambiguous situations. German ethicist Dietrich Bonhoeffer was bluntly uncharitable toward such an approach, labeling it "naive" and those who practice it "clowns."[3]

Other critics attack the idea of a Christian business ethic from a different angle, arguing that Scripture has nothing relevant to say about business today. After all, they point out, the Bible was written between eighteen hundred and three thousand years ago largely in the context of an agrarian economy. Israel's entire gross national product under King Solomon was no doubt less than the net worth of General Motors. What significant insights, they ask, can Scripture give Maria in deciding the fates of Abe, Barb and Carl? Indeed, is the Bible relevant to leveraged buyouts and software copyright infringement situations? Using Scripture as a business rule book, they contend, would be like using ancient medical scholars such as Galen and Hippocrates to train modern doctors.[4]

If the critics are correct in arguing, first, that the Bible is rule-bound and, second, that it lacks relevance, then we need not proceed any further. If they are right, Scripture has minimal applicability to modern business practices. However, if it can be demonstrated that Christian ethics is rooted in something much deeper, then they are wrong.

God's Character

The foundation of Christian ethics in business is not rules but the changeless character of God. Scripture describes God as being the creator of all things, perfect, preceding and superseding all things. It also tells how we as human beings were originally created to emulate God. Christianity operates on the notion that ethics (the study of human character) logically follows theology (the study of God's character). Behavior consistent with God's character is ethical—that which is not is unethical. This approach is quite different from human-based ethical systems, which generally focus on either egoism (promotion of individual pleasure via material goods or career success), utilitarianism (the option that best maximizes pleasure and minimizes pain for all involved), or deontological reasoning (the keeping of moral rules such as "Don't harm others").[5]

This is not to say that Christian ethics rejects all of these values. To the contrary, there is much overlap between Christian ethics and many human-centered ethical systems. The major difference rests in its central priority. While concerned with human happiness and the fulfillment of ethical obligations, Christian ethics does not see these as its ultimate goal. Rather, it prizes the life that seeks to emulate God's character. Thus, the great Catholic saint Ignatius Loyola was eulogized as follows: "The aim of life is not to gain a place in the sun, nor to achieve fame or success, but to lose ourselves in the glory of God."[6] In a similar vein, Reformer John Calvin wrote:

> We are not our own: in so far as we can, let us therefore forget ourselves and all that is ours. Conversely, we are God's: let us therefore live for him and die for him. We are God's: let his wisdom and will therefore rule all our actions. We are God's: let all the parts of our life accordingly strive toward him as our only lawful goal.[7]

Holiness-Justice-Love

If being ethical in business is reflecting God's character, then the critical question becomes "What is God like?" Christianity's answer includes such common responses as God's orderliness and artistry in creation. It also goes much further, focusing on God's self-revelation as recorded in Scripture and through his Son Jesus Christ.

Three divine characteristics that have direct bearing on ethical decision-making are repeatedly emphasized in the Bible:

1. God is holy.[8]
2. God is just.[9]
3. God is loving.[10]

Each of these qualities will be explored in much greater depth in the following three chapters. Here it suffices to say that a business act is ethical if it reflects God's holy-just-loving character. Such hyphenation is appropriate because the three qualities are so intertwined that it would be just as accurate to describe God as being loving-just-holy or just-loving-holy.

The human body provides a helpful illustration. If holiness is comparable to the skeleton in providing core strength, then justice is analogous to the muscles ensuring balance, and love is similar to the flesh emanating warmth. Obviously, all three are needed in equal measure. Just imagine a body with only a skeleton (or a business with only a code of ethics)—it would be rigid and immobile. Or picture muscles without a skeleton and flesh (or a business steeped in detailed procedures and policy manuals)—they would be cold and improperly focused. Finally, consider flesh unsupported by any infrastructure (or a business trying to meet every need)—it would be undefined and undisciplined.

Christian ethics requires all three characteristics to be taken into account when decisions are made. Holiness, when untethered from justice and love, drifts into hypercritical legalism. Likewise, justice that loses its anchor in holiness and love produces harsh outcomes. And finally, love when it is orphaned lacks an adequate moral compass. Each of the three contains a vital ethical ingredient. Christian ethics does not involve "either/or" analysis—as if we could chose between holiness, justice and love—but rather a synthesis in which all three conditions must be met before an action can be considered moral. Each, like a leg on a three-legged stool, balances the other two (see figure 1.1).

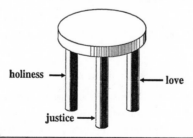

Figure 1.1

Highly respected clothing maker Levi Strauss & Co. has six core values. Interestingly, three of these—integrity, fairness and compassion—directly mirror the biblical principles of holiness, justice and love. The company's remaining values of honesty, promise keeping and respect for others are also important secondary principles to be discussed later. Significantly, CEO Robert Haas has discarded the corporation's thick ethics rule book because "it didn't keep managers or employees from exercising poor judgment and making questionable decisions." Instead, the company now focuses on the core principles and conducts extensive employee training.[11]

Flawed Humanity

Unfortunately, being holy-just-loving is easier said than done. A quick glance at the deception and broken promises common in the marketplace indicates that something is fundamentally wrong. Why is it that, despite our noblest intentions, we seem so incapable of living as we ought? Why do employers feel compelled to give "honesty tests" to job applicants? Why do American employees steal billions of dollars worth of goods from their companies annually? Why did executives at Kidder-Peabody brokerage firm claim $350 million in fake profits?[12]

Scripture labels the fundamental human flaw "sin." At its core, sin is the refusal to emulate God and to instead set our own independent agendas. This attitude of self-sufficiency, of elevating self to godlike status, results in spiritual alienation. The apostle Paul goes so far as to call us "enemies" of God in a state of rebellion (Rom 5:10). Analogous to cancer, this moral disease infects our entire being, clouds our moral vision, and alters our very character. J. I. Packer describes it as "a perverted energy . . . that enslaves people to God-defying, self-gratifying behavior."[13] The result is a chasm between us and God. He remains holy-just-loving, but we have become dirty-biased-selfish.

An important distinction must be made at this point between the dual concepts of "sin" and "sins." While the former term describes our defective moral character, the latter includes actions that naturally follow—lying, promise breaking, stealing and so on. Two sports metaphors describe our situation. First, like archers with poor vision, sin has affected our ability to properly focus. The bad shots that follow—we often fail to even hit the target!—are like sins in that they are the natural outcome of our bad eyesight. Second, we are comparable to high jumpers with broken legs. Try as we may, we cannot even come close to clearing the standard. As theologian Reinhold Niebuhr wryly observed, "The doctrine of original sin is the only empirically verifiable doctrine of the Christian faith."[14]

Our fallen natures are like petri dishes in which sinful actions flourish. This is particularly problematic in the marketplace where financial stakes are high, career destinies are decided and the temptation to rationalize unethical behavior is strong. How else can one explain the bribes American Honda executives demanded from their dealers in exchange for preferred treatment[15] or the substandard parts manufactured by many defense contractors? Why did senior managers at the Wall Street firm of E. F. Hutton engage in "check kiting"—writing checks for an amount greater than the balance on deposit in order to take advantage of the time lag between credit and collection? What caused a college president, who had earlier been honored as one of the nation's top eighteen college presidents by the Exxon Foundation, to embezzle three million dollars?[16]

Lest the finger of accusation be pointed too quickly, we must all acknowledge our own susceptibility to the temptation of justifying unethical or imprudent behavior. The former chief financial officer of Greyhound Lines provides an apt illustration for Lewis Smedes's observation: "Self-deception is a fine art. In one corner of our mind we know that something is true; in another we deny it. . . . We know, but we refuse to know."[17] Refusing to accept the recommendation of a subordinate that a computer-driven reservation was faulty, the Greyhound executive denied that problems existed. As a result of this and other forms of self-delusion, the company's stock value plunged from nearly twenty-three dollars a share to just over two dollars in less than sixteen months.[18] Psychologists have a label for such behavior—"denial."

A Mixed Moral Bag

Imagine a society operating entirely under the paradigm of sin. Sellers and purchasers could never trust each other, so deals would be difficult to transact. Managers would constantly spy on subordinates to prevent theft and laziness. Slavery, child labor and bribery would be common. Since "might makes right" would be the guiding principle of business, companies would hire armed personnel to protect and pursue their interests. Prisons would be full and new ones would be needed at an accelerated pace. Society would so distrust business that government regulators would be assigned to every company. These bureaucrats would in turn be inept and corrupt. As a result of all these factors, the costs of doing business would skyrocket and the very foundations of capitalism would be undermined. While some pessimists view this as an accurate description of the direction in which our culture is heading today, it is clearly a bleak picture.

Thankfully, as Henry David Thoreau chided his generation, this paradigm is not the complete story of Christian ethics: "Men will lie on their backs, talking about the fall of man and never make an effort to get up."[19] At least three factors encourage us to arise from the moral muck.

First, despite our sinful nature, our spiritual core has not been erased—we retain the "image of God." We continue to aspire for wholeness and regret when we fall short of our ideals. Our conscience, though less reliable than originally designed, is still operative. We also remain capable of reciprocal kindness—of providing for those who in turn give something to us. Hence we ought not be surprised by acts of managerial benevolence toward hard-working, loyal employees.

Second, God has established social institutions such as government, the legal system, family and business to check human sin, preserve order and provide accountability. Human authority and tradition provide the frame-work necessary for communal living: government punishes wrongdoers, law requires fair play, parents discipline their children, and businesses provide societal order. Without such institutions, anarchy would reign. Reformed scholars call this "common grace" because these protections extend to all members of society regardless of whether they acknowledge God. Of course this is not to say that all governments, parents and employers are ideal. To the contrary, authority figures often abuse their power; they too are infected by sin. Rather, common grace merely affirms the general principle that human authority is necessary in an imperfect world and should ordinarily be respected.

The third force for good are those whom Jesus identifies as the "salt and light" of the world (Mt 5:13-16). As salt prevents decay and light illuminates the darkness, so Jesus expects his followers to positively affect their sur-roundings. Corruption is to be confronted and high moral standards are to be set. Examples of business leaders who serve as salt and light in the marketplace include Bruce Kennedy, former CEO of Alaska Airline, who led his company to the rarest of feats in the airline industry—twelve successive profitable years while maintaining a strong Christian presence. He contends that his faith enabled him to maintain his integrity in the turbulent era following deregulation.[20] William Pollard, former administrator at Wheaton College and current CEO of ServiceMaster, has created a billion-dollar company on the belief that every individual, including every janitor and launderer, is an image-bearer of God. By bringing this value to the marketplace, he has enabled thousands to find dignity in their work. Likewise Edward Land, founder of Polaroid, told shareholders at an annual meeting that "the bottom line is in heaven."[21]

These business leaders, while realistic about human nature, did not base their careers on a half-empty-glass paradigm of sin. Rather, they saw the glass as being at least half full, with opportunities to be holy-just-loving in one of the most challenging arenas of all—the marketplace. This book is an exploration of how we might follow their lead in wrestling with tough, real-world issues.

Creative Morality in an Imperfect World

To summarize, Christian ethics recognizes that the vast majority of humans are neither "wicked" nor "angelic" but fall somewhere in between on the moral continuum. Christian ethics also acknowledges that it is difficult to be holy-just-loving not only because of human foibles but also because worldly institutions and systems are marred. Thus we are often forced to struggle between what is "realistically attainable" and what is "ideal."

This brings us back to the case involving Abe, Barb and Carl. Economic realities require that the budget be cut. In God's original plan for a perfect world, such a decision would no doubt have been unnecessary. But since humanity and its various systems, including the market, are imperfect, difficult choices must be made. It is quite probable that the final solution for Abe, Barb and Carl will be less than ideal but may represent what is possible under the circumstances. Like an optometrist during an eye exam, Maria's task is to line up the three lenses of holiness, justice and love so that they align as much as possible.

It is imperative that Maria not constrict her range of possible choices too hastily. While it would be simple to frame the problem as having only three options—fire Abe, Barb or Carl—she should opt to emulate God's creativity instead. Rather than abandoning us in our moral failure, God lovingly devised a plan for our restoration. What is important to note here is that in doing so, neither holiness nor justice was sacrificed. In a stunningly creative move, God took the radical step of substituting his own Son for us, casting our punishment on him. The roughly analogous act in the situation involving Abe, Barb and Carl would be for Maria to fire herself!

A more modest integration of holiness, justice and love might lead to some type of job sharing, joint reduction in hours, a deferral in capital spending or, at minimum, a severance package for the dismissed employee. In any event, Maria should explore all options before acting and choose the one that is most pure, fair and benevolent to all involved.

Questions for Discussion

I. Case for Discussion
1. What do you think Maria should do? Why?

2. What guidance does the holiness-justice-love model provide for her?

3. Of holiness, justice and love, which would be the most difficult for Maria to apply? Which is generally most lacking in the marketplace?

II. Workplace Application
1. Have you witnessed unethical behavior in your work environment? Explain.

2. What has been the prevailing value/ethical system in the companies where you have worked?

III. Concepts to Understand
How might each passage be applied to a business context?

1. Rule Book Approach to Ethics

Luke 6:1-11: Why do Jesus and the religious leaders conflict? What two ethical systems are at play?

Matthew 23:16-22: Why does Jesus criticize the religious leaders' approach? With what would he replace it?

2. God-Based (Theological) Ethics

Ephesians 5:1: What does it mean to be "imitators of God"?

1 Peter 1:15-16: What does it mean to "be holy as God is holy" in business?

1 John 4:16-21: How are divine love and human love interconnected? Is there a tension between justice and love?

3. Image of God

Genesis 1:26-31; 2:4-9, 18-25: How are humans different from the rest of creation? What responsibilities and privileges does this bring in those engaged in business?

4. Self-Delusion

Genesis 3:1-13: What rationalizations do Adam and Eve make?

Genesis 4:1-9: How does Cain deal with temptation?

Matthew 4:1-11: How is Jesus tempted to rationalize? How does he deal with it?

Luke 22:54-62: How is Peter tempted? What is his response?

James 1:22-24: What warning is given?

5. Sin and Sins

Genesis 6:5-6: Why is God "grieved"?

Romans 3:9-18, 23: How does "sin" differ from "sins"?

Romans 7:14-24: Why does Paul feel tension between the ideal and reality?

6. Conscience

Genesis 3:7: How do Adam and Eve display conscience?

Romans 2:14-15: What is the role of conscience?

7. Common Grace

Romans 13:1-7: Why does God establish government? By what standard should government be measured?

Ephesians 6:1-9: How do the concepts of authority and reciprocity interact in family life and in superior-subordinate relationships?

8. Salt and Light

Matthew 5:13-16: How can salt "lose its saltiness" in the business world? How can light be hidden?

9. Creative Morality

Romans 3:21-26: How do holiness, justice and love interact in God's plan to restore relationship with us?

10. Holiness-Justice-Love

Leviticus 19:1-4, 9-18, 33-37: How do holiness, justice and love interact?

Matthew 22:35-40: Are the concepts of holiness and justice present in the "love command"? If so, how?

2

HOLINESS

You cannot stop the birds from flying over your head, but you can keep them from building a nest in your hair.
MARTIN LUTHER

Make every effort . . . to be holy; without holiness no one will see the Lord.
HEBREWS 12:14

Our progress in holiness depends on God and ourselves—on God's grace and on our will to be holy.
MOTHER TERESA

Lord, please let the bad people be good and the good people be nice.
ANONYMOUS CHILD'S PRAYER

H OLINESS—THE CONCEPT OF SINGLE-MINDED DEVOTION TO GOD AND absolute ethical purity—is a predominant theme in Scripture. Cited over six hundred times in the Old Testament, it is also strongly emphasized in the New Testament, particularly by Jesus, Paul and Peter. John Wesley, father of the Methodist movement, considered it to be the linchpin of Christian ethics.[1]

During the Middle Ages, holiness was understood to mean separation from ordinary life for otherworldly contemplation. Hence business—perhaps the most fleshly of all human enterprises—was viewed as being antithetical to holiness. Though this attitude is less prevalent today, many still consider the marketplace to be "dirty."

Is this perspective fair? Holiness is, after all, an ideal standard, whereas business is conducted in the rough and tumble environment that beckons players to think in terms of "survival of the fittest." In the midst of this

Darwinistic competition, is it really possible to be simultaneously holy *and* successful in the marketplace?

Holiness is composed of four primary elements: zeal for God, purity, accountability and humility.

Zeal for God

CHURNING AND YEARNING. Last year Jill was hired as a stockbroker. Working seventy-hour weeks, she was under great pressure to make more sales. Her manager motivated her with promises of a yacht, expensive cars and a lakeside home. Affluence was the name of the game, and she was determined to succeed. She saw less and less of her husband and permitted her spiritual life to atrophy.

When a dry spell came, Jill decided to conduct unneeded trading on some of her accounts, "churning" as the practice is known. Her sole purpose in making these sales was to increase daily performance. Her manager congratulated her and asked no questions about methodology. However, three months later, when one of Jill's clients questioned why she had been advised to sell high-performing stock, Jill's manager immediately fired Jill and held her up to other brokers as an example of "what not to do." Jill was devastated and felt betrayed.[2]

At its center, holiness calls us to zealously make God our highest priority. It demands that all other concerns—such as material goods, career goals, and even personal relationships—be considered of lesser importance. The Old Testament compares God to a spouse who demands faithfulness from his mate and who is understandably jealous when rivals are entertained (Hos 1:2). This theme is echoed in the New Testament when Jesus warns that we cannot serve two masters at the same time (Mt 6:24) and that our greatest duty is to "love the Lord your God with all your heart and with all your soul and with all your mind"—clear calls to holiness (Mt 22:37-38). He illustrates this single-minded passion by chasing exploitive moneychangers from the Jerusalem temple: profit must not be permitted to gain priority over piety (Mk 11:15). Indeed, Jesus' focus on holiness is so intense that his followers must "hate" all competing loyalties by comparison (Mt 10:34-39).

Are we to conclude from this that Christianity opposes business success?

By no means. The crucial point is that holiness is fundamentally about priorities. So long as business is a means of honoring God rather than an end in itself, the concept of holiness is not violated. What holiness abhors is when business, or any other human activity, becomes an idol.

Unfortunately, Jill does not fare well against such expectations. By permitting career, wealth and desire to please others to become her primary concerns, God has been displaced. There is simply no time for reflection, thanksgiving or rest. She never intentionally rejected God—no, she merely permitted him to drift to the outer fringe of her life. But negligence is no defense. "We live in the age of God-shrinkers. For many, God is no more than a smudge."[3]

Like the Greek traveler Ulysses who was tempted by unseen voices to land his ship on the rocks, financial and career ambition can lure us to destruction. The marketplace is replete with now well-known names—Nick Leeson, Ivan Boesky, Michael Miliken—who later regretted listening to temptation. Holiness is a competing voice, beckoning us to honor God, to praise him in good times and to be prayerful in the bad. Though subject to the same ill winds, individuals who choose holiness have a secure moral mooring.

Purity

HONESTY IS THE BEST POLICY? Last week Vantha went on a business trip with two coworkers—James and Charlie. After they returned, James and Vantha had the following conversation.

JAMES: *Charlie and I have been talking. Since we worked so much overtime on the trip, we figure that the company owes us a little something extra. We're going to add twenty dollars each to our meal expenses and fifteen dollars each for taxi rides. But we need you to go along so that those darned accountants don't figure it out.*

VANTHA: *But that's not right. We didn't eat that much, and we borrowed my cousin's car.*

Purity, the second ingredient of holiness, reflects God's moral perfection and separation from anything ethically unclean. It contains two components—ethical purity and moral separation.

Ethical purity reflects God's moral perfection and aversion to anything impure. In the Old Testament, priests are instructed to be physically and morally clean before entering God's presence (Lev 21:1-24). Likewise, in the New Testament, Jesus encourages his followers to be "perfect as your heavenly Father is perfect" (Mt 5:48). The apostle John directs his readers to emulate the purity in Jesus' character, and Paul charges Christians to be "holy and without blemish" (2 Pet 3:11, 14). This is consonant with a recent survey in which business executives listed moral integrity as one of the top three qualities sought in managers (along with competence and leadership).[4]

Moral separation follows naturally from ethical purity. In an impure world, ethical gold ought not to be mingled with moral dross. Scripture constantly warns the people of Israel not to assimilate with other cultures lest they imitate their behavior.[5] Similarly, Jesus chides his followers "not to be like them" (Mt 6:8) and, no doubt with a degree of hyperbole, teaches that it is better to be blind or lame than to accommodate lower ethical standards (Mt 18:7-9). These twin principles of integrity apply to business today in at least three ways.

1. *Purity in communication.* Jill's willingness to breach her client's trust illustrates the triumph of expediency over integrity. When personal benefit is valued over ethical purity, the result is a host of predictable consequences—financial reports are skewed, contract language is manipulated, and innuendo is used to undercut others. One case involved over thirty travel agents accused of setting up dummy companies, ordering airplane tickets on credit, and then going out of business. Such behavior is most unholy. When holiness is valued, people communicate without guile, saying exactly what they mean. No hidden agendas exist.[6]

2. *Purity in sexuality.* Scripture is replete with warnings against sexual immorality. Base sexual conduct is common in many offices—lewd comments, offensive jokes, not-so-innocent flirting and harassment. Employees who distance themselves from such behavior are often labeled "prudes." Ethical purity frequently comes at a social price.

3. *Purity in purpose.* A recent college graduate achieved national attention with his book *Cheating 101*. The work, basically a composite of the best cheating techniques, is illustrative of impurity in purpose.[7] Vantha, in the expense-reporting case, illustrates the opposite principle. Rather than putting his finger to the social wind to determine which course of action to take, he

resolves to follow the holy path whatever the personal consequences. His integrity will not permit him to go along with James and Charlie even though a measure of ostracism will no doubt follow. The alternative—deception and theft—is simply unacceptable as a viable option. Integrity has its cost, but then so does unethical behavior.

Accountability

WHAT GOES AROUND COMES AROUND. Bill is the marketing director for a corporation that manufactures ski clothing. To discover more about a competing company, he secretly paid Anne, one of its employees, to give him information. In this manner he learned of its manufacturing and marketing plans for the upcoming year. As a result, Bill was able to make adjustments, and his company's sales increased.

Last week, however, Anne's supervisor discovered the secret arrangement and fired Anne immediately. Bill was also dismissed when his CEO was informed. Anne and Bill now face civil lawsuits by their respective companies and possible criminal charges by the state.

Holiness holds us accountable by rewarding moral purity and punishing impurity. Biblical examples include Abraham being blessed for his virtues (Gen 15:6) and the people of Sodom being destroyed for their vices (Gen 19:24-25). While it is tempting to relegate the doctrine of divine accountability to the Old Testament, it is important to note Jesus' many threats of judgment (see, for example, Mt 11:20-24; 25:46). The early church certainly had not lost its sense of reward and punishment: when Ananias and his wife Sapphira died after lying about money, the narrative concludes that "great fear seized the whole church" (Acts 5:11).

The analogy may be rough, but accountability is both a theological and economic concept. For while the market does not credit righteousness nor sanction sin per se, it does tend to reward companies that keep their promises and to punish enterprises that regularly miss deadlines or manufacture substandard products. In the case above, Bill and Anne discovered this principle the hard way. Accountability is built into the moral universe—all actions have consequences. Bill and Anne's misbehavior not only displeased a holy God but also undermined the trust of their employers. Holy living not only honors God but also enables the creation of long-term relationships.

Successful businesses know that earning the trust of their employees, suppliers, dealers and customers is critical.

Intelligent Electronics, the largest American reseller of computers, provides another example of how unholy behavior ruins relationships. IBM, Apple and Hewlett-Packard recently discovered that the company had been overcharging them for advertising costs. Over a period of several years, these overbillings were so significant that they constituted half of the company's annual earnings. The resulting fallout may mean a significant loss of business and possible lawsuits.[8]

While some might object to using the threat of punishment, whether human or divine, as a motive for ethical behavior in business, the human propensity for self-delusion makes fear a legitimate motivator. As Dietrich Bonhoeffer points out, holy fear limits the risk of "cheap grace"—that is, of accepting God's forgiveness but not changing our behavior.[9] The apostle Paul echoed this sentiment: "Let us purify ourselves . . . perfecting holiness out of reverence for God" (2 Cor 7:1).

Humility

I DID IT MY WAY. Juanita, the owner of a janitorial service company, rarely listens to the ideas of her employees. After all, she reasons, she has an MBA and they are mostly immigrants without any higher education. While giving lip service to "empowering" them and soliciting their advice, she generally does what she thinks best.

Humility is the natural outcome of seeking to imitate God's holiness. If we honestly measure ourselves by divine standards, we are forced to recognize how far short of the ideal we fall. Pride evaporates and despair envelops even the greatest of saints. Take Jonathan Edwards, seventeenth-century Puritan leader: "When I look into my heart and take a view of my wickedness, it looks like an abyss infinitely deeper than hell."[10] The gap between God's holiness and our impurity only seems to expand the more we attempt to bridge it. No wonder the apostle Paul calls himself the "worst" of sinners (1 Tim 1:15).

One of the deepest insights of Christian ethics is that we are incapable of making ourselves holy. Holiness gives us a correct self-assessment, deflating our balloon of pride and self-reliance.[11] Paradoxically, Scripture instructs that the way to rise in holiness is first to sink, to admit our moral inadequacy.

Jesus labels such an attitude as "poverty of the spirit." He further commends those who "mourn" their loss of innocence and praises those who become meek (Mt 5:3-5). The road to the mountain of holiness first passes through the valley of humility.

Is there a place for humble people in the corporate world today? Or are they victims-in-waiting, the next roadkill on the capitalist highway? Max De Pree, retired CEO of the Fortune 500 furniture maker Herman Miller, takes umbrage with such thinking. Humility, he argues, is not synonymous with weakness, but is rather a prerequisite to accurate self-assessment.

In the case above, Juanita fails in this regard. Her overinflated ego makes her relatively unapproachable, hierarchical and arrogant. Humble leaders, on the other hand, listen to their subordinates, build strong teams and are not embarrassed to admit mistakes.[12] They reach out to others, hesitate to criticize and are effective listeners.

Potential Abuses of Holiness

As discussed in chapter one, holiness, justice and love are like three legs on a stool. When imbalances occur, holiness becomes distorted and falls into error. As one author notes: "Partial views of holiness—half-truths—have abounded. Any lifestyle based on these half-truths ends up looking grotesque rather than glorious; one-sided human development always does."[13]

Three erroneous views of holiness are legalism, judgmentalism and withdrawal from society.

Legalism. Legalism reduces holiness to rulekeeping. Its primary adherents in Jesus' day were the Pharisees, a group of religious leaders. On the surface Pharisees appeared to be models of piety—regularly attending the temple, possessing vast theological knowledge, donating 10 percent of their income (including even their food!) and strictly observing the sabbath. Unfortunately, most were also cold and aloof, caring more for the keeping of petty rules than for people. Focusing on minutiae, they missed matters of great ethical importance.

MIND YOUR P'S AND Q'S. Sergei was stunned his first day on the job to receive a two-page memo from Meg, his new manager, detailing how to shut down the office at the end of each day. It included such tasks as "place a cover on your computer, empty your wastebasket, recycle all paper, account for paper clips, turn off all lights, make sure all phone messages are off your voice mail. "

Sergei did not feel that this was an appropriate way to treat professional staff. As time passed, he found Meg to be quite formal and difficult to get to know. He trusted her but did not particularly like her. When he requested time off without pay to visit his best friend who was quite sick, she said that company policy permitted absences only for family emergencies. Besides, she noted, he had not worked long enough yet to accrue any time off.

Meg is obviously a legalist. She treats subordinates fairly and is honest to an extreme but is relationally anemic. She follows policies and keeps promises but shows very little emotional sensitivity to others. Companies operated by legalists often become rigid and institutionalized, since procedures and manuals cannot produce a committed work force. Workers learn all too quickly not to invest too much emotional capital in their jobs but merely to follow the rules. Tragically, Sergei may well be on his way to becoming a clock puncher.

Unfortunately, legalism is worming its way into corporate ethics offices. Many such programs owe their existence to the Federal Sentencing Guidelines Act, which promises to reduce fines for illegal corporate behavior if internal ethics programs are in place. Surely this is not the right reason to institute top-down reform. Too often the result is a set of moral rules disconnected from higher principles: "Too many companies just write up a code of ethics and display it for public relations."[14]

Legalism is both self-defeating and morally wrong. It misses what is truly important: it cannot tell the forest from the trees. A ludicrous example involves a cadre of legalistic Christians who fought in the German army during World War II. While refusing to dance or imbibe alcohol, they participated in the execution of thousands of Jews in Nazi death camps.[15]

Judgmentalism. When legalists fail, they justify themselves by pointing out even greater moral lapses in others. The classic example is found in Jesus' parable of a proud Pharisee who attempts to justify his actions by comparing himself to thieves, adulterers and tax collectors—not exactly tough competition. He concludes his "prayer" by alluding to his strict tithing and fasting twice a week (Lk 18:9-14).

Judgmentalism is a ghastly imitation of holiness. That the two are linked when we call self-righteous individuals "holier than thou" is most unfortunate. Operating on the basis of pride and self-reliance (rather than on humility and grace), these smug individuals criticize others in order to inflate their own self-opinions. By contrast, holy people refuse to cast stones at others and are careful to put their own moral houses in order before confronting others (see Mt 7:1-5; Jn 8:1-11).

Judgmental employers like Meg have long memories, refusing to forget errors committed by their subordinates. Like precise accountants, they carefully log each mistake and then keep the offender on a short leash. Ironically, judgmentalists are doomed to hypocrisy, because they are unable to live up to their own standards. As a result, pride forces them to become masters of deception in covering up their own failures.

Withdrawal from society. False asceticism is another bastardization of holiness. As noted at the beginning of this chapter, many well-meaning people have concluded that withdrawal from "the world" is the only way to attain holiness. Most extreme were medieval hermits such as Simeon Stylites, who lived alone on a small tower for thirty years, and an Irish saint who remained suspended by his armpits over an open hole for seven years.[16] These men would scoff at the notion of a "holy businessperson," regarding it as a wicked oxymoron. For them business was indeed a dirty, worldly profession, staining all who touched it.

BUSINESS IS CRASS. When Rose was a college student, her parents encouraged her to major in business. Rejecting this advice, she focused on education instead, reasoning, "I would rather deal with people's brains and character than with their pocketbooks. In business you always have to think about money. It's so crass."

Just out of college, Rose married a social worker named Don. When Don tired of that line of work, he successfully launched several service companies. Rose took very little interest in Don's activities, preferring to read the classics and work with the poor. "Business is so exploitive," she complained, "and the Bible says that you can't honor God and money." When her daughter later decided to major in business, Rose was irate: "How could you make such a compromise? And for what? So that you can get a job when you graduate?"

Todd Putnam, editor of the *National Boycott News,* represents an updated secular version of the false ascetic approach. He refuses to wear leather shoes because that would be cruel to animals. Nike products are out of the question because of past complaints of exploitation from the African-American community. Rubber and plastic shoes don't recycle well, and Chinese thongs are not an option because of that nation's poor human rights record.[17]

While well-intended, this perspective is simply incorrect. By confusing moral separation with physical separation, a primary point is missed: holiness is acceptance of, not flight from, responsibility. True holiness involves incarnation into the world and its troubles, not abdication from it. Jesus did not pray that his followers be removed from common life, but that they might discover holiness in the midst of it (see Jn 17:15). Holiness does not convert us into hothouse plants that can grow only in artificially controlled environments.[18] Jesus certainly did not live in such an antiseptic manner and, if physically present today, would no doubt feel quite comfortable befriending sales representatives, IRS agents and defense attorneys. Indeed, nearly a quarter of his parables dealt with business situations.[19]

Unclean, messy and full of opportunities for good or ill, the marketplace provides a forum in which responsible holiness can grow. Like the apostle Paul, who wrote positively about his own business experience, we should use the marketplace as an opportunity both for testing our character and for bringing light into darkness. It is certainly an environment in which zeal for God, purity, accountability and humility are sorely needed.

Questions for Discussion

I. Case for Discussion

Jonah works as an auditor for a big-six accounting firm. After two years he is finally given the opportunity to lead an audit team. Unfortunately, the client operates a chain of pornographic movie theaters. Jonah strongly believes that such films degrade women, tempt men and dishonor God. However, when he expresses his reservations about the assignment, his fellow team members tell him to "get off his high horse."

1. What do you think Jonah should do?

2. If Jonah follows the guidelines of this chapter, what should he do?

II. Workplace Application

1. Identify holiness concerns in your workplace.

2. Have these concerns been properly resolved? Discuss.

III. Concepts to Understand

How might each passage be applied to a business context?

1. Zealous for God

Exodus 20:1-4: What are some modern-day idols? What does it mean that God is "jealous"?

Matthew 10:34-38: What does Jesus mean by saying that he came not to bring peace but a sword? Does he really expect us not to love our family members?

Matthew 13:44-46: What is the main point of these two short parables?

James 4:4-10: What warnings and advice are given?

2. Purity

Genesis 39:1-23: In what ways does Joseph display purity? What motivates him?

Leviticus 18:1-5: Why are the Hebrews told to not pattern their behavior after these groups?

Romans 6:11-14, 19-23: What rather stark options are provided?

Ephesians 5:1-12: Why are these behaviors inappropriate? What virtues are lauded?

3. Accountability

Leviticus 26:1-46: What conditions does God put on his relationship with the people of Israel? How does God hold them accountable?

Matthew 13:24-30, 36-43: What does this parable tell us about accountability?

Hebrews 10:26-31; 12:14, 28-29: What characteristics of God are emphasized? How does modern society tend to react to these divine qualities?

2 Peter 2:4-22: What is the common theme of all these Old Testament stories?

4. Humility

Matthew 5:3-5: What does it mean to be "poor in spirit," to "mourn" and to be "meek"? How might these qualities apply to business?

Luke 18:15-17: Why does Jesus hold this little child up as an example?

Luke 5:1-8: Why does Peter react this way?

Luke 18:9-14: Who is humble? Who is judgmental? Is there a sense of irony in the parable?

5. Legalism

Matthew 15:1-20: How does Jesus criticize the religious leaders?

Galatians 3:19-25: According to Paul, what is the purpose of the Old Testament law?

Colossians 2:16-23: What sorts of moral rules are criticized? Why?

6. Judgmentalism

Matthew 9:10-13: Is Jesus being sarcastic? Who is really sick?

Luke 6:37-42: Is judging others always wrong?

John 8:1-11: What does Jesus' handling of this situation tell us about holiness and judging others?

Romans 2:1-3: Why should we be careful not to criticize others?

7. Withdrawal from Society

Matthew 4:1-17; Luke 6:12-13: Why does Jesus withdraw from others?

Matthew 5:13-16: What do the metaphors of salt and light say about withdrawal?

John 17:13-19: How can a person be "not of this world" and yet not be "taken out of the world"?

1 Corinthians 5:9-13: What is Paul saying about withdrawal? About judging others?

3

JUSTICE

A society without justice is no better than a band of thieves.
AUGUSTINE

Follow justice and justice alone.
DEUTERONOMY 16:20

We know what justice is when we feel the wounds of injustice.
ARISTOTLE

Christianity preaches "love your neighbor" while Judaism
preaches justice. I think that justice is the big thing we need.
SAMMY DAVIS JR., ON HIS CONVERSION TO JUDAISM

COMPLEX AND MULTIFACETED, JUSTICE (OR ITS EQUIVALENT) APPEARS
over eight hundred times in Scripture.[1] At its core, justice provides order to
human relationships by laying out reciprocal sets of rights and duties for those
living in the context of community—business partners, employees, neighbors and family members. The marketplace, an arena abuzz with human
interaction, is a hot spot for justice concerns.

The concept of rights is central to justice. By virtue of being God's
image-bearers (Gen 1:27) we have been endowed with two fundamental
rights: the right to be treated with dignity and the right to exercise free will.
Therefore, any action that attacks our dignity—such as sexual harassment or
invasion of privacy—or that severely impairs our freedom of choice—such
as pervasive regulation or prohibition of expression—is morally suspect.
Rights serve as "no trespassing signs" to others, protecting us from harmful
intrusions.

Duties, the flip side of the justice coin, are inextricably linked to rights.

One person's right becomes another's duty. For example, a CEO's right to maintain her good name creates a corresponding obligation not to defame her. Likewise, a Hispanic's right to nondiscriminatory treatment creates a reciprocal responsibility in others to behave in an unbiased manner. A community's right to clean air and water imposes a duty on manufacturers not to pollute the environment.

Just how far such duties extend is a matter of serious disagreement among ethicists and politicians. While it is universally agreed that we are obliged not to injure others—*negative injunctions*—there is little unanimity about responsibilities toward those whom we have not harmed—*affirmative duties*. By way of illustration, a clear duty exists not to run other motorists off the road, and if we do, compensation must be provided. It is less clear, however, what affirmative duties, if any, we have toward strangers whose vehicles simply stall on the freeway. Likewise, while we are obliged to fill in our own golfing divots, must we replace those created by others as well?

In the marketplace, the distinction between negative injunctions and affirmative duties is helpful but also controversial. Few would disagree with the notion that businesses are obliged not to harm others via price fixing, false advertising, defective products or industrial espionage. Breaches of these duties require compensation to those injured. However, what of the affirmative duties of businesses toward those they have not harmed? For example, should American Airlines contribute to charities working with the homeless? Is IBM obliged to loan money to a supplier (or extend credit to a dealer) who is in financial difficulty? Should the owner of a small dry-cleaning shop support the local school levy?

We will return to these questions in later chapters. For now, it suffices to conclude that rights and duties exist in tension, providing a necessary counterbalance to each other. If a society overemphasizes individual rights, people become selfish, thinking only of their own freedoms. Many Asians, Africans and Europeans perceive the United States in this light. On the other hand, if duties are overemphasized, people lose their sense of dignity and freedom to choose: the community dictates what they must do. Many Americans view Asian, African and European nations in this light. Biblical justice rejects both perceptions—egoism and collectivism—and supports a more balanced approach.

Four basic aspects of justice are procedural rights, substantive rights, merit and contractual justice. If any of these rights are breached, compensation is owed.

Procedural Rights

Procedural rights focus on fair processes in decision-making. They include two legal-sounding terms: due process and equal protection.

Due process. Due process has three components. First, it requires decision makers to be *impartial,* to have no conflicts of interest.

FAMILY FIRST. In a family-owned business, Joe, the vice president of finance, promotes his nephew over another equally qualified employee.

THE VELVET TOUCH. A local CPA firm is hired by a manufacturing company first to provide financial consulting and later to conduct its annual audit. The firm has had a difficult time securing new businesses, so the partners tell their audit staff to "go soft whenever possible and not to lose the consulting business."

Impartiality forbids decision-makers from having preexisting biases or from reaping personal gain from their decisions. Perhaps the most blatant abusers of this principle in Scripture were Samuel's sons, who while serving as judges accepted bribes (1 Sam 8:3). Jesus' judges were no better. In order to protect their own political power, they issued a death decree *before* his trial had even begun (Mt 26:1-5). Similarly, Paul was left in jail for more than two years—not in the interest of justice—but so that a corrupt governor might stroke potential political allies (Acts 24:25-27). Though the Bible generally applies impartiality to the judicial process, its logic of fair and equal treatment extends to the marketplace as well. Paul makes this very point when he calls for masters to do "what is right and fair" vis-à-vis their subordinates (Col 4:1).

In the "Family First" case above, the uncle may very well have violated the due process rights of the nonpromoted employee by being biased toward his nephew. Even if he was entirely impartial, suspicion of nepotism now clouds his nephew's rise in the company. No doubt the process would have been cleaner if a nonfamily member had made the final decision. Likewise, the recent decision of a leading software company's CEO to direct his company's business toward a second company he owns has created the impression of partiality.[2]

In the second case above, the accounting firm's attempt to "go soft" on its client's audit to protect its consulting business illustrates the danger of permitting self-interest to affect supposedly objective analysis. If the audit staff follow orders, the due process rights of the client's creditors will be infringed. The result—as was so evident in the poor audits conducted on savings and loan institutions in the 1980s—is not only great financial loss to creditors but four thousand pending lawsuits against accountants.[3]

Second, due process mandates that *fair and adequate evidence* be presented. Decision-makers must be careful to collect sufficient information before rendering decisions. To do otherwise is to invite both ethical and legal danger. Richard Chewning wisely warns: "Be cautious in the use of isolated evidence. . . . And always be careful with secondhand evidence concerning a person."[4] Jesus, Stephen—the church's first martyr—and Paul were all incriminated by the use of fragmentary or inaccurate information (Mt 26:59; Acts 6:13; 25:7).

In the business realm, auditors must be thorough, able to authenticate all findings. Likewise, supervisors should hesitate before dismissing employees for theft, disloyalty or incompetence solely on the word of a coworker or on circumstantial information. For while Scripture's standard of requiring at least two witnesses—for criminal cases in the Old Testament and church discipline in the New Testament (see Deut 19:15; 1 Tim 5:19)—is not applied directly to workplace situations, the principle of substantiated evidence is.

Finally, due process provides those accused of wrongdoing with the *opportunity to tell their side of the story* before a decision is reached.

GONE WITH THE WIND. Late one Friday afternoon Mary is told to empty her desk and leave work immediately. After nearly a decade of employment, she is neither informed why she is being fired nor given a chance to defend herself. Since no one else is being terminated, it appears that her dismissal is not being made solely for economic reasons.

Mary's abrupt dismissal strips her of the right to give her version of the facts. Had she been permitted to present an explanation to an impartial decision-maker, she might have been able to clarify a misunderstanding or to address other causes for her firing. Perhaps she was the casualty of a petty vendetta by a nefarious supervisor or the victim of an internal turf battle between two managers. Without due process, she will never know.

This aspect of due process was violated on several occasions in Scripture. Nicodemus, an expert in law and ethics, confronted his fellow civic leaders for condemning Jesus "without first hearing him to find out what he is doing" (Jn 7:50). Likewise, Paul was punished without having the opportunity to defend himself. He later complained that this infringed on his rights as a Roman citizen and received an apology from government officials (Acts 16:37-39).

Equal Protection

Equal protection flows logically from the concept of due process. Simply stated, it prohibits discrimination by decision-makers. The law of Moses instructed its judges to "not show partiality to the poor or favoritism to the great" (Lev 19:15). True justice is blind, particularly in regard to race and socioeconomic status.

The ideal of equal justice is deeply embedded in Western civilization. It is an ideal that is easily violated because the temptation to favor the powerful is ever present. In the business context, equal protection requires human resource managers to take the complaints of their janitors as seriously as those of their CEOs. It forbids protecting executives charged with sexual harassment merely because of their status, and it requires managers to be open-minded when resolving disputes between employees of different genders or ethnic backgrounds. Equal protection ensures that each individual is treated according to the merits of his or her claim, not on the basis of group membership.

Substantive Rights

BLOOD FOR SALE. Plasma Inc. has identified a very inexpensive source of clean blood in a Third World nation. In light of transmittable diseases such as AIDS and hepatitis B, untainted blood is in relatively short supply. Plasma Inc. charges top dollar—more than 100 times what it pays for the blood—selling mostly to private hospitals. The poor, both in North America and overseas, are unable to afford its prices.[5]

Substantive rights are what procedural rights seek to protect. They may be universal—such as the rights to own property, to bodily safety, to prompt payment for work completed, and to be told the truth—or they may be unique to each society—the right to citizenship, to copyright or patent protection, to go bankrupt and to "appropriate" tax rates.

Employers often rely heavily on the concept of property rights in stating their moral and legal positions. Since their company belongs to them, they reason, they are free to hire and fire, set compensation rates, provide benefits and determine the nature of the work environment. They expect their subordinates to steal neither time nor material goods. Further, they contend that so long as they do not cause harm to the community, they are free to use their land as they see fit. Employees, on the other hand, point to their rights to form unions, to work in a safe environment, to have their privacy respected and to receive worker's compensation when injured. Likewise, communities argue that they also have significant substantive rights vis-à-vis employers—for example, to set reasonable zoning restrictions on private property, to require environmental impact statements for construction projects and to be given several months' notice prior to factory closures.

In the medical field, government investigators recently accused several doctors of violating patients' rights to informed consent. Instead of providing the best care possible, the U.S. Department of Health and Human Services contends that the physicians regularly referred patients to a home health care provider in exchange for substantial kickbacks—reaching up to $100,000 per year. If true, not only were the patients' substantive rights infringed, but the procedural notion of impartial decision-makers was also violated. The doctors were engaged in a classic conflict of interests.[6]

The "Blood for Sale" case is problematic in regard to substantive rights. Plasma Inc. has acquired its blood supply without engaging in fraud or any illegal behavior. According to general capitalist thought, it has the right to sell its property at whatever price the market will bear. The question remains, however, whether the poor also have substantive rights in regard to life-sustaining blood. If they do not, then no reciprocal duty to provide aid is created. If, however, blood is considered to be a basic human right, then an affirmative duty exists. Would this oblige Plasma Inc. to substantially drop its prices? Or should the burden fall exclusively on the governments involved? What role, if any, do impersonal market forces play in this ethical debate?

Such a conflict of substantive rights is not uncommon, particularly if affirmative duties are involved. Do workers have a right to their jobs? To medical insurance? To leave when family members are ill? Viewed from another perspective, what obligations do companies owe their employees, society and the poor? In the Old Testament, farmers—the business leaders of that day—were instructed to leave unpicked crops for the disenfranchised; to contribute a tenth of their income to, among other things, supporting the needy; and to extend no-interest loans to less affluent neighbors (see Deut 15:1-11). Are these principles of affirmative duties still valid today? Discussion of property rights and duties continues in chapter fifteen.

Merit

EARNING POWER. Joan Phan is CEO of Airbot Inc., an aerospace robotics manufacturing firm. Last year she earned over two million dollars in salary and stock options. This is nearly one hundred times more than Airbot line employees received and contrasts sharply with Japanese CEOs, who typically earn no more than seventeen times their line workers' salaries.

Merit links the concepts of cause and effect. If Joan has worked very hard for Airbot Inc. (cause), she may be entitled to the high salary (effect). If, on the other hand, line employees have not been diligent in upgrading their skills (cause), they deserve to be paid less (effect). The moral issue involved is not whether Joan should be paid more but whether she has really "earned" her full salary. It is quite possible that a review based on merit may conclude that she deserves less and her subordinates more.

Merit justifies unequal distribution in many areas of life. Professors give a wide variety of grades, but if the evaluative process is fair, there is no perception of unfairness. Likewise, certain professional basketball teams regularly make the playoffs, while others rarely do. Is this unjust? No. If everyone is given an equal chance to succeed, then those who exert greater effort or make better choices will achieve. While we deem it unfortunate that one teenager becomes a concert pianist while his twin does not, we attach no unfairness to the outcome if the former practiced and the latter did not. Merit is like the law of gravity—ignore it at your own peril.

The author of Proverbs concurs: "He who works his land will have abundant food, but he who chases fantasies will have his fill of poverty" (Prov 28:19). In a similar vein, Jesus says that "with the measure you use, it will be measured to you" (Mt 7:2), and Paul advises his readers, "A man reaps what he sows" (Gal 6:7). The apostle applied the concept of merit negatively by denying church welfare to those who refuse to work and positively by opening church leadership positions only to those with strong character (see 2 Thess 3:10).

Critics of merit argue that this approach is not entirely fair because it favors those with natural talents. Not all of us, they point out, are born with Michael Jordan's body, Bill Gates's brain or Mother Teresa's temperament. Our genes and childhood environment, they contend, are more significant factors than merit in who succeeds and who fails. Admissions to medical school and promotions to senior management positions, they insist, are based more on the luck of the lottery of birth—good DNA and caring parents—than on hard work.

Defenders of merit counter with two arguments. First, if the critics are correct, then our free will is extremely limited and we have little moral responsibility for our actions. Failure in business can be conveniently blamed on our parents or on government regulations. A condescending attitude toward the disabled can be dismissed as part of the baggage carried to adulthood from our youth. A second response is that merit provides an incentive to improve our lives. There are many men with Michael Jordan's physique, but few who worked so hard to improve their game. Bill Gates is certainly bright, but does this fact somehow mitigate his accomplishments? Mother Teresa was not born a saint; she had to develop her spiritual qualities through much sacrifice and self-discipline.

Christian merit permits disparity in the distribution of wealth and accolades so long as procedural rights (due process and equal protection) are protected and substantive rights (such as basic provision for the poor and fair compensation for efforts) are honored. It is within this context that the huge differential between Joan Phan's salary and the wages received by her subordinates should be critiqued. While a higher salary is no doubt in order, a one-hundred multiplier may be difficult to justify.

Contractual Justice

ALMOST, BUT NOT QUITE. Fred, a recent college graduate, obtains his first "real" job selling insurance. Along with nine other trainees, he agrees to

a six-month term contract that requires him to meet his sales quota in five
of the six months. He succeeds in four of the first five months but, unfor-
tunately, barely fails in the final month. As a result, he is terminated along
with six other trainees.

Contractual justice is limited to three concurrent duties. First, we must not
violate a negative injunction by causing harm to others. Second, we must
respect procedural justice. Third, we must fulfill our contractual promises.
Following this logic, Fred's firing is not unjust. He is not injured by his
employer but has simply failed to meet expectations. Due process and equal
protection have apparently been afforded, since he was clearly informed of
the conditions of his employment and is not being treated differently than
others. Finally, his employer has fulfilled his contractual obligation and, since
Fred failed to meet his sales quota, is no longer bound to employ him.

As Fred has discovered, contractual justice can be rather severe. Consider
the following extreme example. If a baby buggy is rolling off a pier, does a
disinterested bystander have any obligation to rescue the child from certain
death? When the situation is viewed solely from a contractual justice point
of view, the answer is probably negative. She did not cause the harm
(passivity generally does not qualify as a breach of a negative injunction),
has not violated any form of due process (she does not appear to be
discriminating against this particular buggy) and is not under contract to
provide care. Of course the case would be quite different if she was hired to
serve as the infant's nanny.

Thankfully, Christian ethics does not rest its entire weight on contractual
justice. Isolated, contractual justice results in extreme individualism. Only
when integrated into a fourfold concept of justice—including procedural
rights, substantive rights and merit—does it find its proper role. In the buggy
case, for example, the baby's substantive right to life creates a reciprocal duty
for the adult to act, regardless of the existence of a contract. An ethical floor
is set, beneath which we ought not venture. This does not mean, however,
that the concept of contractual justice is without value. What if the baby is
in no danger but merely needs a diaper change? Clearly the nanny has a
greater obligation to act than does the stranger. Why? Because she has
voluntarily assumed affirmative duties that the ordinary citizen does not owe.

Thus, while contractual justice is inadequate in setting an ethical floor, it does permit the ceiling of reciprocal rights and duties to rise. For example, business partners take on the affirmative duty to divide their income; neighbors do not. Employers discipline their subordinates; friends do not. Husbands and wives establish joint bank accounts; casual daters do not. Of course neighbors may become partners, friends may hire staff, and couples may invest together. But until they do, their rights and obligations are on a lower level. Contractual justice permits people to take on additional duties not owed to the general populace.

This aspect of justice abounds with theological implications. When God exchanged reciprocal promises with Abraham—and subsequent addenda via Jacob, Moses, David and Solomon—a special relationship was established. This agreement granted extraordinary rights to the patriarch and his descendants but also imposed additional responsibilities on them. Like all contracts, these covenants were conditioned on the other party's performance. If Abraham's offspring remained true to their promises, peace and prosperity would follow. However, if they breached the covenant, severe sanctions would surely result (see Lev 26 and Deut 30).

Compensatory Justice

When any of the four rights discussed—procedural rights, substantive rights, merit and contractual justice—are violated, justice demands compensation. We deem it only fair that polluters are required to pay damages to "down winders" harmed by noxious fumes. Likewise, manufacturers of defective products are expected to make reasonable restitution to injured consumers. In a similar vein, executives who steal trade secrets or defame rivals should make restoration to their victims. Indeed, without the notion of compensatory justice the very notion of rights would be rendered meaningless.

Potential Abuses of Justice

Although justice is a cornerstone of Christian ethics, serious problems arise when it is isolated from holiness and love.

Harsh results. As Fred and his six fellow ex-trainees can attest, justice is often harsh. It gives people what they deserve and generally permits no second chances. A case in point is the apostle Paul's treatment of a junior associate in the early church. When John Mark failed to complete an assignment, Paul dismissed him. This so infuriated Barnabas, John Mark's mentor, that he dissolved his long-standing partnership with Paul (Acts 15:37-40). Paul acted justly, but was he holy-just-loving? (It is interesting that late in his life Paul reversed his attitude and spoke highly of John Mark; see 2 Tim 4:11.)

Justice tends to be cold and dispassionate, lacking the emotional heat and relational passion of holy love. None of us would like to be employed by a company that fires staff for minor breaches of corporate policy. Who would want to be associated with a firm that reacts in knee-jerk fashion with a lawsuit for every noncompliance by a supplier or dealer? Or, imagine working for the older brother in Jesus' parable of the prodigal son. He illustrates sterile justice at its worst. In a narrow sense, he was correct when complaining about the welcome given his wayward sibling. After all, the latter had contracted with their father to take his money and run. And since actions have consequences, he deserved to be treated as a servant at best. In the larger picture, however, the elder brother showed no compassion, granted no second chances (Luke 15:25-31). Lewis Smedes describes such ice-hearted justice: "Suppose your family specialized in fairness . . . all the kids were left equally far out in the cold. Perfect equality. You were all starved for affection at the table full of fairness."[7]

This raises several interesting questions relevant to the commercial sector. Should employees with alcohol problems be fired immediately? Or might companies permit (perhaps even fund) rehabilitation programs? Must sick leave policies always be rigidly enforced? Or may exceptions be made for special cases? Biblical justice does not give easy answers to such questions. It does, however, call for a greater degree of flexibility and neighbor love than mere justice standing alone.

Condemnation. Justice also requires compensation for duties left unper-formed. While this principle is relatively easy to apply in the marketplace—where monetary damages can generally "patch up" incomplete performance—it is much more problematic in our relationship with a holy God. How do we compensate for moral failure? How do we set the books right with the Almighty? Surely money is not sufficient.

When combined, holiness and justice condemn us. Why? Because they are evil? To the contrary, they reflect the very character of God. No, the problem rests solely with us. Our moral imperfections separate us from a holy God, and our unfulfilled duties demand compensation. In frustration, we join the apostle Paul: "What a wretched man I am! Who will rescue me . . . ?" (Rom 7:24). Clearly a third element—love—is needed to provide forgiveness and hope.

Questions for Discussion

I. Case for Discussion

Acme Chemical Corporation owns fifty acres of land, thirty-five of which are currently used for manufacturing. The other fifteen acres are undeveloped and zoned for commercial use only. This means that while office buildings may be built on the fifteen acres, manufacturing facilities may not. Acme has been very successful over the past decade and now wishes to expand its manufacturing facilities. It claims that over three hundred new jobs will be created.

The zoning plan was formulated over twenty years ago after lengthy discussion among all interested groups. Acme has applied for an exception, but local residents oppose it due to the added chemical pollution that would result. They contend that their neighborhood is poor enough already and that Acme's expansion will only further drive down the value of their homes.

The county's land use commission, which must make the decision, consists of five elected members. All are elected at large, and none live near the Acme plant. Three members are up for election and want to impress the general public by being "pro-growth" (that is, promoting the creation of jobs and an increase of the tax base). One member lives next door to Acme's CEO and often socializes with her.

To expedite Acme's application, the commission permits two hours of public discussion and then takes a vote. The application is approved.

1. In your opinion, is this action just? Why or why not?

2. Analyze the commission's action in light of this chapter's definition of justice.

3. Does the concept of holiness provide any additional insights?

II. Workplace Application

Identify a situation in your work environment that raised justice concerns. Was it resolved justly?

III. Concepts to Understand

How might each passage be applied to a business context?

1. Impartial Decision-Maker

Exodus 18:13-26: What qualities should decision-makers possess? Why?

Proverbs 18:5; 24:23-25: Why is impartiality so important?

Acts 24:1-27: Analyze Felix's decision-making process.

2. Adequate Evidence

Exodus 20:16: What is the primary concern of the Ninth Commandment?

Leviticus 5:1: What affirmative duty is imposed?

Deuteronomy 19:15-21: What applicability, if any, does this Old Testament law have for business today?

1 Timothy 5:19: Why is more than one witness required in these situations?

3. Opportunity to Tell One's Side of the Story

Matthew 18:15-17: How should disputes be resolved?

Acts 16:16-40: How are Paul's due process rights violated? Remedied?

Acts 22:22-30: How does Paul exercise his rights?

4. Equal Protection

Exodus 23:6-9; Leviticus 24:22: What groups are assured of equal protection? Why are they included?

Romans 2:9-11: How does God demonstrate the concept of equal protection?

Galatians 2:11-14: Why does Paul confront Peter? Is he justified in doing so?

Galatians 3:28: What groups does Paul add to the lists of Exodus 23:6-9 and Leviticus 24:22?

James 2:1-6: What form of discrimination is condemned? Why?

5. Substantive Rights

Jeremiah 22:13; Malachi 3:5: What substantive rights are protected? How are violators to be punished?

Exodus 20:15; Ezekiel 22:29: What right is protected? What reciprocal duty does this create in others?

Leviticus 25:35-43: What substantive rights and duties are described?

1 Corinthians 9:1-23: What rights does Paul have vis-à-vis the church? How does he exercise these rights?

6. Merit

Matthew 25:14-30: What does this parable teach about the concept of merit?

Romans 2:5-8: On what basis will God judge humanity?

Galatians 6:7-9: Why should we be virtuous?

Revelation 20:11-13; 22:10-15: How will God conduct the final judgment?

7. Contractual Justice

Genesis 23:7-20: Analyze Abraham's land purchase according to principles of contractual justice.

Joshua 24:1-27: What is the nature of the agreement entered into between the people of Israel and God? What reciprocal affirmative duties does it impose?

Romans 7:1-6: How does Paul use contractual justice analysis?

8. Harsh Results

Matthew 18:21-35: In the parable of the unforgiving servant, is justice done? Is the punishment too harsh?

Acts 17:22, 30-31: What does Paul anticipate the result of God's judgment to be?

James 2:13: When is mercy not appropriate?

9. Condemnation

John 8:1-11: What action does the crowd initially want? Why do they change their minds?

Romans 7:7-24: Why is Paul so upset?

4

LOVE

While justice is the equivalent to fairness, love
is closer to foolhardiness.
DONALD BLOESCH

What is more harmful than any vice? Active sympathy for the
ill-constituted and weak. . . . Christianity is mankind's
greatest misfortune.
FRIEDRICH NIETZSCHE

Many have learned how to offer the other cheek
but do not know how to love him by whom they were struck.
AUGUSTINE

What's love got to do with it? It's just a second-hand emotion.
TINA TURNER

MANY CONSIDER LOVE TO BE THE CENTERPIECE OF CHRISTIAN ETHICS. The apostle Paul identified it as the greatest human virtue (1 Cor 13:13), and Martin Luther thought it best described the essence of God's character.[1] Ethicist Lewis Smedes characterizes love as "the hinge for every other moral rule to swing on."[2] When Jesus was asked which Old Testament law was the most important, he responded by ranking love for God first and love for neighbor second (Mt 22:37-39). Parenthetically, it is important to note that his definition of love includes both holiness—making God our highest priority—and justice—taking others' interests into account in all our decisions.

Love's primary contribution to the holiness-justice-love mix is its emphasis on relationships. By way of example, imagine an embezzler who now regrets what she has done. While holiness causes her to feel unclean and justice creates a fear of getting caught, love produces a sense of grief over the harm she has caused others. This is because while holiness focuses primarily on purity and justice on rights, love concentrates on relationships. It creates bonds between people, the breaching of which causes pain.

While it may be tempting to define love as a "soft" virtue, concluding that it has no place in the rough-and-tumble of the marketplace, we need only note that business history is littered with companies ruined by fractured relationships. Crown Books, a large family-dominated corporation, nearly imploded when the elderly father expelled his CEO eldest son from the company.[3] It is no exaggeration to observe that successful commercial ventures depend more on cooperation than competition. Without a solid relational foundation, no group effort can succeed in the long term. Partners must get along, supervisors must engender loyalty among their subordinates, and suppliers and distributors must be brought into a supportive network. Love provides the relational framework in which such cooperation flourishes. Without it, our sinful tendency to exploit each other takes over and group endeavors die.

Christian love has three prominent characteristics—empathy, mercy and self-sacrifice.

Empathy

> *OLD FRIEND. The first problem confronting Deon when he takes over his family's business is what to do with Thomas. Thomas, a childhood friend of Deon's deceased father, has been employed by the company for more than thirty years. However, his incompetence has become so glaring that it can no longer be ignored. Rather than firing Thomas directly, Deon does so indirectly by reorganizing the company. In this manner Thomas is "laid off" (the only employee so affected), and shortly thereafter Deon is able to help him find work with another employer. Deon informs her that Thomas is a "competent and dependable" worker.*

This case illustrates love's first characteristic—it empathizes with others, celebrating their joys and shouldering their pain. The impulse of love is to make Thomas feel good, to create a positive situation for him.

Scripture portrays God as being empathetic, comparing him to a husband loving his wife, a mother nursing her infant, a doctor ministering to the sick and a shepherd binding the wounds of an injured animal (see Is 49:15; Ezek

34:15-16; Hos 2:1-23). Jesus' concern for others is also stressed: "his heart went out" to a widow whose only son had just died (Lk 7:13), and he wept at the funeral of a close friend (Jn 11:35).

Charles Swindoll captures this quality nicely in a story about an American soldier in England after World War II. Spotting a hungry orphan salivating at a bakery window, the G.I. bought a bag of doughnuts and handed them to him. Unaccustomed to such generosity, the little boy called out, "Mister, are you God?"[4] The orphan was at least partially correct—empathy for others reflects the divine character.

Does the marketplace value traits such as empathy, kindness, flexibility and sensitivity? Management experts such as Tom Peters certainly think so, stressing the value of sincere concern for others—customers, suppliers, distributors, employees.[5] These qualities make long-term business relationships possible.

Of course it would strain credibility to argue that modern capitalism operates primarily on the basis of empathetic love. Among the general populace, backs are scratched to mutual advantage, and perhaps achieving reciprocal respect is the best that can be expected. Christian empathy goes far beyond this, however. It encourages corporate executives to demonstrate heartfelt concern for the less fortunate, to take a personal interest in the fate of severely ill associates and to sympathize with sales staff who miss quotas due to unexpected personal problems. In the case above, Deon rightly shares Thomas's pain and seeks to ameliorate it. This is not to say, however, that empathy is the sole focus of Christian ethics. This case raises other ethical concerns that will be discussed in greater detail below.

Mercy

BACKSTABBER. Marcin and Linda were hired by Acme Inc. at the same time. It soon became apparent that both were young managers with tremendous potential. Sensing the competition, Linda has begun to undercut Marcin's relationship with a vice president. Marcin becomes furious when made aware of her tactics and vows to retaliate in kind.

Mercy is empathy with legs. While empathy feels for others, mercy takes action on their behalf. If a relationship is broken, merciful love takes the initiative in forgiving, redeeming and healing. As Martin Luther observed,

"To love is not to wish good for another person; it is to bear another's burden, that is, to bear what is painful to you and which you do not bear willingly."[6]

God sets the standard in this regard by repeatedly seeking reconciliation with us. Jeremiah noted, "His compassions never fail . . . they are new every morning" (Lam 3:22-23). David, who had much personal experience with moral failure, lauded divine forgiveness: "As far as the east is from the west, so far has he removed our transgressions from us" (Ps 103:12). The basic Christian story—that Jesus died on a cross so that we might be forgiven—speaks reams about the merciful character of God and the lengths to which he will go to restore broken relationships.

What does Christian mercy require of Marcin in the above case? Is he justified in taking revenge on Linda for attempting to undermine his career advancement? As difficult as this may seem, Marcin is instructed to be nonretaliatory and to be merciful toward her (Mt 5:38-44). The concept of "enemy love" distinguishes Christianity from other ethical systems. Aristotle and Confucius, for example, refused to go so far, teaching that the duty to love is conditioned on the other person's response.[7] The Christian position demands much more, requiring Marcin to "live not according to the golden rule but beyond it."[8] Or as another author puts it: "To return evil for good is devilish; to return good for good is human; to return good for evil is divine."[9]

This is not to say, however, that Marcin must be naive in his dealings with Linda. Jesus warned against being overly vulnerable to those who abuse (Mt 7:6). Neither is Marcin to be passive in his response. Rather, he is to actively seek reconciliation. This will no doubt involve face-to-face meetings with Linda, prayer for her and unsolicited acts of kindness. It may also include setting the record straight with the vice president. At no time, however, should Marcin sink to Linda's ethical level. He must neither demean nor hate her. Of all Jesus' moral teachings, his enemy-love command may be one of the most difficult to obey.

Sacrifice of Rights

TO GIVE OR NOT TO GIVE. Esther is a humanitarian who invests wisely in the stock market. Among other civic activities, she serves on the board of a shelter for battered women. On the very day she receives an unexpected $2,350 dividend check, the shelter's executive director calls regarding an *emergency need of $2,000. Esther contemplates the request.*

The final characteristic of love is its willingness to give away the very rights that justice bestows. For example, an employee motivated by love may decide to relinquish her office space in order to accommodate a disabled peer. Or a spouse may consent to move so that his wife's career may be enhanced.

Esther has justly earned her dividend check. Her rights are based on both meritorious justice (a wise choice produces a reward) and contractual justice (taking on affirmative duties and rights). While the substantive rights of the poor may slightly reduce the dividend check through taxation, Esther has the right to pocket the bulk of it. Justice is satisfied. But is love? A great need has been brought to her attention that asks for more. How much self-sacrifice does love require in this case? Two thousand dollars? One thousand? Two hundred? Nothing?

Sacrificial giving frightens us because it appears to be a blank check with no limits. While we may honor soldiers who jump on hand grenades to save their comrades and we admire Jesus for voluntarily dying so that others might live, we understandably balk at being so vulnerable ourselves.

So how much should Esther give? What measure of self-sacrifice is appropriate in the marketplace? No precise standard exists. If business were to follow the example of St. Francis of Assisi, the outcome can barely be imagined. Francis took the love command so seriously that he regularly gave his clothes away to the poor. This led his disciples to complain that they had difficulty keeping him dressed.[10] Self-sacrifice was embraced, self-interest renounced. While we greatly admire Francis, we are left to ponder whether his model is normative. What limits, if any, do justice, holiness and love itself place on self-sacrifice?

Potential Abuses of Love: Narrow Focus

A FRIEND IN NEED. Alice rushes up to Kien, a member of her work team, in desperation: "Last week I reported more overtime hours than I actually worked. I could get fired for this. I know that you've been working a whole lot of overtime lately. If you'll just tell payroll that you saw me work the extra hours, I'll make it up to the company real soon. I promise. No harm done, right? Well, will you cover for me?"

In 1966 clergyman Joseph Fletcher penned his now famous book *Situation Ethics*.[11] According to Fletcher, love and love alone is the Christian's guiding moral star. "Right" and "wrong" no longer have meaning, only that which is "fitting" and "not fitting." Fletcher wrote: "No principle or value is good as such—not life or truth or chastity or property or marriage or anything but love."[12] In this light it is "fitting" for a woman to seduce a man in order to cure his desire for young girls and for a prostitute to disprove a soldier's doubts about his manliness.[13]

So what advice would Fletcher give Kien? He would no doubt focus on her relationship with Alice. Refusal to vouch for Alice could result in irreparable harm to their friendship and possibly lead to Alice's dismissal. On the other hand, a lie in this situation might cement their relationship, and since Alice has pledged to make up the extra hours, there would be no real cost imposed on the employer.

If lying is so loving in this situation, what could possibly be wrong with it? At least two things. First, it completely ignores holiness concerns such as truth telling and promise keeping. What may appear at first to be a virtuous "cover" for Alice is in reality nothing but a lie to her supervisor. Fletcher describes all other ethical principles as "servants of love to be quickly kicked out of the house if they forget their place and try to take over."[14] Thus in the name of love Fletcher casually discards fundamental holiness values such as zeal for God, ethical purity and moral accountability. In doing so he neglects the fact that holiness provides the necessary moral boundaries within which love must act. Likewise, Deon's benevolent deception of Thomas's next employer in the first case is immoral whatever his loving intentions might be. Biblical love operates within the bounds of holiness.

Second, Fletcher's narrow definition of love not only degenerates holiness but flaunts justice as well. What good are the shareholders' property rights when Alice's theft of time can be willy-nilly disregarded in the name of love? What about the substantive rights of Kien's supervisor and Thomas's new employer to be told the truth? Due process is also clearly impaired if Kien's supervisor, the decision-maker, is not given full and accurate evidence. Finally, the principle of meritorious justice suffers if Alice does not reap (disciplinary action or reduced pay) what she has sowed (deception and theft).

Potential Abuses of Love: Ambiguity

A second problem with Fletcher's perspective is that it provides little guidance as to which action is the most loving. Consider a hospital administrator
who must decide what to do with a donated heart. Should she disregard the
list of potential recipients (many of whom have waited for years) to save the
life of her suddenly ill brother? Which is the more loving act? Should a pizza
driver speed to make a home delivery within the acceptable time limit? While
the customers certainly appreciate eating a hot pizza and shareholders enjoy
increased profits, what about the safety of other drivers? or of the pizza
drivers themselves? To which group is more love owed? Likewise, should
Kien be more concerned about loving Alice, her supervisor or the company's
owners? How do her fellow employees factor into the equation? Fletcher's
definition of love is so ambiguous that any of the above might be acceptable.
His approach is not nearly as self-explanatory as he thought it to be.[15]

Love is also a poor predictor of outcomes. Would Alice really fulfill her
promise to make up the extra hours? She hasn't exactly been a stellar
truth-teller to date. It is also doubtful that Kien would be able to verify Alice's
compliance. Further, what if the supervisor already has sufficient evidence
to dismiss Alice? If such were the case, Kien's lie would not benefit her friend
and in addition would erode her supervisor's trust.

One writer wryly observes that Fletcher's love paradigm would "be the
perfect ethics if all men were saints."[16] Of course, such is not the case. By
ignoring our sinfulness and propensity to self-delusion, Fletcher conveniently erased half of the human nature equation. His concept of love certainly
did not provide much guidance to the Lockheed executive who paid bribes
to Japanese government officials to preserve jobs and reward shareholders.[17]
Such reasoning reminds one of the advice given by King Solomon several
millennia ago: "There is a way that seems right to a man, but in the end it
leads to death" (Prov 14:12). Sin easily clouds our moral vision, permitting
selfishness to be rationalized in the name of service to others. Or as the old
saying goes, "The road to hell is paved with good intentions." How can we
be sure that we are doing the loving thing in every situation?

Potential Abuses of Love: Doormats

Finally, Fletcher's weak definition of love invites abuse. If Kien acquiesces to Alice's request, will it be the last moral compromise made in the name of friendship? Will she next ask her to keep quiet regarding her lying about sick days? about stealing inventory from the company? What starts as sacrificial love often becomes warped and unbalanced. Love that produces doormats is not Christian love.

To answer a question raised earlier in the context of St. Francis of Assisi's life, Scripture places three limitations on self-sacrificial love. First, holiness frowns upon altruistic sinning. Altruistic sinning is the laying aside of ethical conduct to please another. While Christian ethics generally praises those who sacrifice rights for others, it is reluctant to endorse such actions. For instance, insider trading on the stock market cannot be justified merely because the goal is to aid a friend. Likewise, lawyers ought not lie to benefit their clients. Such self-sacrifice violates holiness concerns.

Second, justice grants everyone the substantive right of dignity. Based on our unique status as image-bearers of God, no one can give or take our right of dignity away. Each of us has an inner core that is inviolable. When Alice asks Kien to compromise a small measure of her Godlikeness, Kien's personal integrity is being subtly attacked. Dignity sets a base line beyond which self-sacrifice is not permitted.

Finally, love places limits on itself. Would it really be loving for Kien to cover for Alice? Perhaps Alice has a serious problem with lying to her family as well. Getting caught at work might force her to clean up her total life. As we have seen, love certainly isn't clairvoyant. Actions taken for the best of reasons often end in disaster. Likewise, would it be loving for Marcin to ignore Linda's byzantine maneuverings to pretend that nothing is happening? No. Avoidance permits such behavior to continue, and that is of no ultimate service to Linda. Acting as a doormat may actually cause more long-term harm to the person being "helped." King David's slavish devotion to his son Absalom produced a selfish and ultimately self-destructive personality (2 Sam 15:1-37). Doormat love eventually ruins all involved.

Further, biblical love calls us to "love our neighbors *as ourselves.*" Self-love is healthy, reflecting our status as God's image-bearers. Balanced self-love can be lost in two ways. At one extreme it becomes narcissistic. As Lewis Smedes notes: "It is not love of self, but love of self alone, which is

sinful."[18] We all know people who are too full of themselves; many find their
way into the marketplace. At the other extreme, when self-love is ignored it
becomes completely subordinated to neighbor love. Employees who lack
self-confidence often become servile. They never stand up to the boss, don't
expect promotions and rarely state their values.

A proper understanding of self-love sets both a ceiling and a floor. While
the ceiling prevents us from thinking only of ourselves, the floor prohibits us
from thinking nothing of ourselves. The result is an inverted Golden Rule: If
we would feel ethically uncomfortable asking another to do a particular act,
then we ought not consent to do it for others.

Sacrificial love should never compromise the concepts of holiness, justice, neighbor love or self-love. In this regard we learn from St. Francis rather
than Joseph Fletcher. The former did not sin altruistically, compromise his
dignity or succumb to playing the doormat. Rather, his love was full of
integrity and wholeness. And it changed his world.

Love That Is Holy and Just

A balanced view of biblical ethics requires holiness, justice and love to be
respected equally. Like pulling apart a tightly woven tapestry, analysis that
separates them is somewhat risky.

Without holiness, love degenerates into permissiveness. Nearly anything
can be justified in the name of unholy love—defamation, price fixing,
industrial espionage. Inversely, holiness without love produces unforgiving
perfectionism. Who would want to work for a supervisor who embodied such
an ethic? When merged, "holy love" produces the highest and purest form of
love. This ideal love burns brightly with integrity and compassion. It calls
for the highest ethics but makes provision for forgiveness as well. It reacts
sharply against social injustice and calls for absolute purity in business
relationships. Jesus clearing the temple of usurious money lenders provides
a vivid image of holy love (Jn 2:13-22).

Likewise, love without justice lapses into favoritism and a very short-term
perspective. Imagine an employee being given a day off with full compensation without regard to the perception of partiality by other staff. Justice
without love is equally unacceptable. Turning the facts of the prior example,
how do we react to supervisors who always "go by the book," never

acknowledging exceptional individual circumstances? Such a harsh approach leaves us feeling cold. Only when combined do justice and love form "tough love," a disciplined balancing of long-term interests.

Finally, holiness without justice drifts toward a privatized form of religion. Purity is stripped of its social ramifications. Inversely, justice without holiness results in an amoral form of procedural fairness that lacks moral substance. Decision-makers become absorbed in procedural details—for example, time lines, required signatures, waivers—and fail to focus on the deeper moral issues involved. Only through "holy justice" can both personal ethical integrity and social justice be ensured. Figure 4.1 summarizes these points.

	Combined with Justice	Without Justice	Combined with Holiness	Without Holiness
Love	Tough love	Favoritism Short-term perspective	Pure love Hatred of injustice Necessitates forgiveness	Permissive Altruistic sinning
Justice			Integrity in social institutions	Fairness without purity
Holiness		Privatized purity		

Figure 4.1

Questions for Discussion

I. Case for Discussion

Dora manages the pharmacy department of a large retail store. Over the past few months, small quantities of a very expensive prescription heart medication have been disappearing on a regular basis. After setting up a hidden camera, she catches her technical assistant pilfering. As she is about to call the police, she asks him why he has turned to crime. He explains that his niece will die without the drug and that her parents cannot afford medical insurance. His request for understanding leaves Dora pondering what her next step should be.

1. What do you think Dora should do?

2. What is the "loving" thing for Dora to do?

3. Analyze the case through all three moral lenses—holiness, justice and love.

When combined, what guidance do they give Dora?

II. Workplace Application

Identify a situation in your work environment that raised issues discussed in this chapter.

III. Concepts to Understand

How might each passage be applied to a business context?

1. Empathy

Ezekiel 34:1-31: How does God display holiness? justice? empathy? mercy?

Matthew 14:13-21: In what ways is Jesus empathetic and merciful toward the hungry crowd?

Luke 7:11-17: What does Jesus' reaction to the widow tell us about his character?

John 11:1-3, 32-36: Why does Jesus weep at his friend's funeral?

2. Mercy

Genesis 4:1-16: How does God show holiness to Cain? justice? mercy?

Genesis 27:1-45; 32:3-8; 33:1-9: How is Esau merciful to his brother?

Matthew 18:21-35; Luke 17:3-4: Must we forgive only those who apologize?

Romans 12:17-21: How far should our mercy extend? Are there limits?

3. Sacrifice of Rights

Matthew 5:38-42: Jesus gives four short illustrations. What is their common theme?

Philippians 2:3-11: What rights does Jesus give up? What is the application to us?

Romans 14:1-21: Why does Paul expend so much energy discussing vegetarians and carnivores?

1 John 3:16-20: What should motivate us to sacrifice our rights?

PART 2
FALSE EXITS

ARE THE ETHICAL STANDARDS SET BY HOLINESS, JUSTICE AND LOVE TOO high for the marketplace? Can we really expect advertisers to be as ethical as nuns? In the highly competitive world of business, aren't workers entitled to an ethical respite, a bit of moral leeway?

The next three chapters will attempt to address these questions. Chapter five ("Dual Morality") responds to the contention that "business culture" establishes its own definition for what is acceptable behavior in the marketplace: "When on Wall Street do as the Wall Streeters do." The logical result of this approach is to separate personal and professional ethical standards. Chapter six ("Law") addresses the question whether businesses should do more than merely comply with the letter of the law. Chapter seven ("Agency") deals with the assertion that employees must lower their personal ethical standards when serving as corporate agents.

The primary deficiency of these three arguments—dual morality, law and agency—is that each relies on an external force to define what is ethically acceptable. They are false exits because they deposit ultimate ethical authority in human instrumentalities—business culture, government and corporate management—rather than in God's character. In doing so, they create "moral sanctuaries" in which the demands of holiness-justice-love are minimized.

5

DUAL MORALITY

The trouble with the rat race is that even if you win, you are still a rat.
LILY TOMLIN

Trying to be Christian in the business world is like jumping
on two horses which then ride off
in different directions.
ANONYMOUS

Work is a thing so good and godlike. . . . In this life, the
worker is most like God.
ULRICH ZWINGLI

Do right and risk the consequences.
HARRY TRUMAN

THE FIRST FALSE EXIT, A SPECIES OF CULTURAL RELATIVISM, REJECTS THE notion that universal principles of right and wrong exist. Instead each culture is responsible to define what is moral and immoral. While, for instance, it would be inappropriate for Americans to lie on a tax return or to be polygamous in the United States, these actions would be permissible if the Americans were to move to other nations where such practices are common. Likewise, while it might be considered wrong to lie, steal or break promises in one's personal life, it may be permissible behavior in the business world. Why? Because the marketplace, like any other culture, is morally self-defining. Business—not religion or personal ideals—determines what is acceptable within its own environment. The result is a separation of personal and professional ethics—"dual morality."

Another way to express the same idea is to compare business with a poker game. Both, it is argued, require distrust, nondisclosure and deception to succeed. Mark Twain's observation, cited in chapter one, that "an ethical man is a Christian holding four aces" reflects the widely held notion that personal Christian ethics is a luxury few can afford in competitive professional environments such as the marketplace.

KILLED BY CONSCIENCE? For five years Eli Black was CEO of United Fruit, a large multinational corporation. He was also an ordained rabbi, the descendant of ten generations of rabbis. Among other things, he used his executive role to improve the lot of poor farm workers in Third World nations by raising their wages to nearly six times that of competitors and by significantly upgrading their housing. He was also regarded by his New York City staff as a kind and highly principled manager.

After initial success during Black's tenure as CEO, United Fruit experienced a series of unexpected problems. A major hurricane caused significant crop damage and several Latin American nations sharply increased their banana taxes. Nevertheless, it came as a great shock when Eli Black jumped forty-four floors to his death. A writer for the Wall Street Journal *queried: "Can a sensitive person with high moral standards survive in an uncompromising financial world?"*

Three days later two senior vice presidents disclosed that Eli Black had approved a $2.5 million bribe to a Latin American official in an attempt to reduce the banana tax. At the time such payments were not illegal.[1]

Would Eli Black be alive today if he had accepted the notion of dual morality? If he hadn't tried so hard to integrate his personal and professional lives, perhaps he would have accepted the fact that the marketplace tolerates nasty choices such as the payment of bribes. Did his sense of biblical ethics so contradict business necessity that he cracked under the pressure?

Three writers—Albert Carr, John Ladd and Milton Friedman—answer these questions affirmatively. Carr contends that so long as one plays within the accepted "rules of the business game," his or her actions are morally acceptable.[2] These "rules" are often unwritten and reflect the lowered moral expectations in the rough-and-tumble "real world." Carr pities religious employees like Black who misguidedly attempt to bring their spiritual values to work. Not only is such quixotic integration hopeless, but he fears that these well-intentioned (but naive) individuals will ultimately suffer by attempting to do the impossible.

Ladd echoes Carr's thesis from a slightly different perspective. By comparing corporate employees to "cogs-in-the-machine," he argues that workers bear no individual responsibility for acts done while pursuing company interests. If, for example, they contribute to the production of harmful goods such as cigarettes or unsafe automobiles, the marketplace exonerates them from any moral responsibility.[3] Ladd would no doubt conclude that Black acted appropriately in paying the bribe and that he should have slept well at night rather than taking his own life. As a cog in a larger corporate machine, he should not have let personal ideals interfere with his workplace responsibilities.

Economist Friedman presents a somewhat softer version of dual morality. He advises corporate managers to lay aside personal values and focus solely on generating profits for shareholders. Their duty is to do everything possible—except break the law or commit fraud—to enhance the bottom line.[4] As such, corporate employees have no right to interject personal values into such matters as environmental concerns or fairness to fellow workers if shareholder wealth is threatened. Since the bribes approved by Black were made before such payments were declared illegal and were made for the purpose of enhancing corporate earnings, Friedman would probably have supported the decision.

Businessman Dan Drew, founder and namesake of Drew Theological Seminary, smartly summed up this philosophy a century ago:

Sentiment is all right up in the part of the city where your home is. But downtown, no. Down there the dog that snaps the quickest gets the bone. Friendship is very nice for a Sunday afternoon when you're sitting around the dinner table with your relations, talking about the sermon that morning. But nine o'clock Monday morning, such notions should be brushed aside like cobwebs from a machine. I never took any stock in a man who mixed up business with anything else.[5]

A soulmate of Drew was oil baron John D. Rockefeller. On the one hand, influenced by his devout Baptist mother, Rockefeller developed a strong personal religious ethic. On the other, his shrewd father taught him to win at any cost in business, once boasting: "I cheat my boys every chance I get. I want to make them sharp."[6] John D. resolved this apparent contradiction by compartmentalizing his life into two separate realms.

Ruthless in business, Rockefeller gave kickbacks to railroads, violently suppressed labor unrest and bribed competitors' employees to give him inside information.[7] In his personal life, however, he donated nearly half a billion dollars to a countless variety of worthy causes—missionaries in China, the University of Chicago, a retreat for migratory birds and relief for war victims. As one author observes, Rockefeller was a "conscientious Christian who struggled to end the livelihood of his every rival."[8] Carr, Ladd and Friedman would no doubt have recommended this approach to Eli Black.

A Christian Response

AN INTEGRATED LIFE. By the age of fifty-two, Bruce Kennedy achieved what most businesspeople only dream about. As CEO of a billion-dollar airline, he had operated the company in the black for twelve straight years and was highly regarded for his integrity and stewardship of corporate resources. During this time, his tight-knit family hosted a series of Southeast Asian refugee families in their home. "They're friends," he said. "We feel closer to those people than we do to my peers in business."

As a deeply committed Christian, Kennedy refused to accept a separate business ethic, telling a reporter: "Your faith has to come down to the way you live. . . . CEO is what I do. It's not who I am."[9]

Bruce Kennedy provides a moral counterpoint to Drew and Rockefeller. Is he correct in rejecting dual morality? Is dual morality inherently unchristian? If so, why?

Dual morality should be rejected because it subtly attacks each of the three undergirding principles of Christian ethics—holiness, justice and love. First, it violates the principle of holiness by idolizing business success. Money-making is so important, it is presumed, that the marketplace must be permitted to play by lower moral standards. Implicit in this position is the assumption that achieving financial success is a higher priority than pleasing God. Scripture has a label for such a reversal of priorities—idolatry.

Holiness also condemns dual morality because it justifies ethical impurity. The fact that "everyone else is doing it"—for example, regularly exaggerating advertising claims, shortchanging customers or copying software without permission—does not legitimate an action. To the contrary, Old Testament Jews were warned not to conform to the customs of their neighbors lest they become morally unclean and unacceptable to God. Likewise, Jesus exhorted his followers "not to be like" others, and Peter admonished his readers not to imitate the behavior of their neighbors (Mt 6:8; 1 Pet 2:11-12).

Perhaps most important, holiness rejects dual morality because it challenges Christ's lordship over all things by carving out a special niche that is somehow exempt from his rule. The apostle Paul counters such thinking by pointing out that all things were created "by him," "for him" and "in him" (Col 1:16-17). No human activity, such as advertising or negotiations, or physical location, such as the stock exchange or a lawyer's office, is outside his jurisdiction. To believe otherwise is not just bad ethics, it is also bad theology. Any teaching that so denigrates Christ's lordship is, bluntly stated, heresy.

Better is the approach taken by Abraham Kuyper, former prime minister of the Netherlands. He suggested that while a Christian may play many different roles during the course of a week—business leader, family member, churchgoer, neighbor—Christ remains Lord of each sphere.[10] This perspective avoids the sacred-secular split as embodied in the lives of Drew and Rockefeller, which relegates Christian ethics to part-time status.

Second, dual morality undercuts justice. If textile manufacturers regularly ignore employee due process and privacy rights, for instance, dual moralists conclude that such behavior must be morally acceptable in that industry. The ethical reference point is fixed by common practice. The danger of this approach is that justice concerns that may cost employers profits—such as full disclosure to creditors, promised funding of employee pension funds or ensuring workplace safety—can be conveniently discarded because "everyone else is doing it." The Christian model of justice is not so easily and unilaterally ignored. Reposed in the character of God, it demands that basic rights—dignity and free will being primary—not be ignored. It provides a moral trump card that supersedes common business practices.

Third, dual morality ignores the principle of love. Rather than applying the Golden Rule—"Do to others as you would have them do to you"—the opposite is promoted: "Stick it to the other guy before he sticks it to you." The marketplace is viewed as a dog-eat-dog environment where authentic caring for others is inappropriate. All business players are expected to watch their own backs.

Unfortunately, not everyone understands the unwritten rules of the game in business. Many—including immigrants, elderly, children, friends and family members—do not have their guards up. When promised a particular product or service, they expect fair play and as a result become prey to the unscrupulous. Greed is legitimated as being part of the culture. Cooperation and trust are disdained. Further, it must be noted that business is no mere poker game but a major social institution. To compare it to a game is to trivialize its importance. Bruce Kennedy utilizes a different image—that of the steward—to describe the proper role of business in society. He argues that corporations have the responsibility to marshal their resources carefully for the benefit of others.[11]

A Christian Alternative: Vocation

Dual morality doubts that Christian ethics can be effectively integrated into the workplace. A second, and more holistic view, is that of vocation.

BROTHERS THREE. John, Pete and Harry are brothers. John majors in religious studies and becomes a pastor. He tells his brothers that this is the highest and most important task in life. Pete rejects his advice and heads into business instead, claiming, "I can do more good for humankind in manufacturing than as a cloistered cleric. I'll make my impact on life through my job." Harry, now eighteen, is confused by his brothers' rhetoric. He wants to be a software designer but ponders whether one job is morally better than another.

Harry's confusion is understandable. His brothers have presented him with two distinctively different views of work. John believes that jobs that encourage wholehearted service to God and humanity are most important. In this category he would probably include clergy, social workers, teachers and health care professionals. The second group represents the remainder—for example, accountants, lawyers, mechanics and contractors—who supposedly work for the less noble ideals of personal self-fulfillment and the acquisition of material goods.

John's view parallels that taken by the medieval church, which taught that only religious professionals were regarded as having been "called by God" to have a special vocation.[12] Merchants and bankers, on the other hand, were highly suspect because their motives were presumed to be selfish. The marketplace was viewed as a dangerous place for the soul, and holiness was equated with withdrawal from its temptations.[13] "Spiritual" things required total focus.

This sacred-secular split continues to have unintended negative consequences today. When the first category of jobs is elevated to "God-preferred" status, the not-so-subtle implication is that careers in the second group—including business—are somewhat less than holy. No wonder people like Rockefeller and Drew bifurcated their lives: the church had already unwittingly initiated the process. The split is also evident today in those who view their secular daytime "jobs" as being completely separate from their evening or weekend "ministries." The marketplace is a place to earn an income, a necessary semi-evil. Ministry and work never mix. This model is represented in figure 5.1.

Calling of
God
(sacred)

Work
(secular)

Figure 5.1

Pete, rejecting John's approach to ranking jobs based on the percentage of their overt religious orientation, believes that all work has equal value. In taking this position he follows the lead of Martin Luther, who declared that all worthwhile work is a "calling" of God. Luther was quick to point out that most of the biblical figures were not professional religious workers but lived in the real world—farmers, doctors, shepherds, lawyers and tax collectors.[14] Pete is correct in asserting that one's vocation need not be expressed through full-time Christian service but may include any task that honors God. Luther taught:

> A cobbler, a smith, a farmer—each has the work of his trade, and yet they
> are all alike consecrated priests and bishops. . . . We should accustom

ourselves to think of our work as sacred, not on account of the position, but on account of the faith on which the obedience and work flow.[15]

While Pete's approach to vocation is more sound than John's, it is not without potential problems. Like Luther (and ironically John, too), Pete tends to regard *work* and *vocation* as synonyms. This blurring is dangerous because, as will be discussed in greater detail below, vocation is a much larger concept. To equate the two is to run the risk of giving work too central a place in our lives. A job is never to be an end in itself, but a means of service to God and others. "Workaholics" run the risk of violating this principle by deifying their careers. Figure 5.2 represents this view.

Figure 5.2

For Harry to have a proper view of vocation—to avoid the implicit dual morality of model 1 and the risk of idolizing work in model 2—a third approach must be identified. To do so, Harry must redefine vocation not just as work but as the decision to live his whole life in submission to God's will. This includes the choice about which job to take but focuses more broadly on which master to serve. In this framework, work is treated as but one of many means—for example, friendship, family, community activities, politics, volunteering—through which one lives out his or her vocation. A Christian writer nicely captures this distinction:

> The really crucial decision comes, not when a person decides to be a foreign missionary rather than a farmer; the really crucial decision comes when a man decides that he will live his whole life in holy obedience; whether that leads to farming or banking or evangelistic work in Africa is then wholly secondary. The major decision has already been made.[16]

This approach is antithetical to dual morality because it presumes that the marketplace can serve as a vehicle through which spiritual values can be transfused.

A secular expression of this sentiment was voiced by former U.S. Supreme

Court Justice Louis Brandeis:

> In the field of modern business, so rich in opportunity for the exercise of man's finest and most varied mental faculties and moral qualities, mere money-making cannot be regarded as the legitimate end. . . . Nor can a man nobly mindful of his serious responsibilities to society view business as a game, since with the conduct of business human happiness or misery is inextricably interwoven. Real success in business is to be found in achievements comparable rather with those of the artist or the scientist, of the inventor or the statesman.[17]

In this light, Harry should feel quite secure in choosing to become a software designer. So long as he is fulfilling his vocation—humbly submitting to God's will and serving humanity—this career decision would be every bit as acceptable as those made by his brothers. As a designer, he would have an excellent avenue through which to reflect God's creativity and to help others. Figure 5.3 illustrates this model.

Figure 5.3

Faithfulness to Vocation May Result in Financial Loss

DOES GOD WANT US TO BE RICH? Melissa and Juan work as managers for Toxic Waste Services (TWS). TWS specializes in the disposal of chemicals. The company is owned and operated by three Christian partners.

MELISSA: *I believe that TWS is making so much money because God is blessing us. He always rewards those who honor him.*

JUAN: *I'm not so sure about that. I recently read about an Egyptian man who, upon becoming a Christian, stopped selling alcohol out the back door of his store. As a result, his business failed and his wife left him.*

MELISSA: *Oh, I'm sure that God will take care of him.*

Is Melissa correct in arguing that Christians have a significant financial advantage in the marketplace? Or is Albert Carr closer to the truth when he contends that religious employees stand at a disadvantage vis-à-vis less conscience-bound counterparts? While both views contain an element of truth, each misses the mark for different reasons. Carr fails to take into account that ethical behavior—promise keeping, truth telling, property respecting—engenders trust and builds a solid foundation for long-term business relationships, and Melissa naively presumes that those who view work as a means of serving God always succeed financially.

Ironically, Carr and Melissa make the same ultimate mistake of overfocusing on bottom-line profitability. Vocation rejects the notion that "winning" financially is business's primary goal, emphasizing instead its role as a vehicle through which God is honored and others are served.

	Win financially	Lose financially
Make ethical choice	#A No tension ("Justly blessed")	#B Tension ("Good guys finish last")
Make unethical choice	#C Tension ("Crime pays")	#D No tension ("Justly cursed")

Figure 5.4

Figure 5.4 illustrates four possibilities when Christian ethics and profitability intersect. Box A represents those situations in which no tension exists between profitability and ethical behavior. For example, if revenues increase because Melissa treats her subordinates fairly, both common sense and biblical ethics encourage her to continue to act in this manner. A similar "no brainer" exists in box D. It is irrational to intentionally select an immoral option that incurs economic loss. For example, if Juan cheats a supplier and this results in financial loss via a lawsuit or lost business, it is imprudent to conduct himself in this manner. In the vast majority of situations, good ethics pay and, conversely, bad ethics cost.

This is not the complete story, however. Boxes B and C represent situations in which making money is pitted against doing the right thing. In box

B, for example, if the partners of TWS decide not to take on the account of a cigarette company because they believe it wrong to facilitate smoking, they will be sacrificing potential profits. Or if, in box C, the partners calculate that the financial upside of secretly dumping toxic waste in a river far outweighs the financial downside (bad publicity, government fines), they may be sorely tempted to compromise their ethical principles. As in the cigarette company example, high moral standards would cost revenue.

Vocation shifts the focus of discussion. Honoring God and serving neighbor, not profitability, become the chief criteria for making business decisions. Financial losses suffered in box B and avoided in box C situations are accepted as the price paid for valuing integrity and wholeness. While Melissa might argue, with some justification, that TWS could more than make up for such losses by the profits generated in box A situations, her argument is misdirected. Vocational fulfillment, not financial success, is the true bottom line.

In short, a Christian version of business ethics accepts no artificial division between work and life. We are to be the same wherever we go, whatever we do. Within this framework, we are to follow Harry Truman's advice: "Do right and risk the consequences."

Questions for Discussion

I. Case for Discussion

Two good friends, Christy and Joan, got into an argument over coffee before church.

CHRISTY:	*There are certain jobs that Christians should never take.*
JOAN:	*Ah, come on. You're being too rigid. All jobs have some value.*
CHRISTY:	*What about prostitution and drug dealing?*
JOAN:	*That's unfair. I mean all legal jobs. I challenge you to come up with a list of jobs that you think Christians should never take.*
CHRISTY:	*Okay, I will.*

The next week Christy brought her list. Under the heading "Unchristian Jobs" she wrote the following:

1. State executioner (operator of the electric chair)
2. CIA spy
3. Bartender
4. Cigarette manufacturer
5. Owner of adult video store
6. Psychic hotline receptionist
7. Gun shop owner

8. *Potato chip manufacturer (junk food)*
9. *Mercedes-Benz dealer (luxury goods)*
10. *Nerve gas manufacturer*
11. *Liquor retailer*
12. *Nuclear plant operator*

Joan was stunned: "How in the world did you come up with these? I particularly don't understand how you could include the Mercedes dealer and potato chip company."

1. What do you think of Christy's list? Do you agree more with her or with Joan?

2. How does the concept of vocation apply to this list?

II. Workplace Application

1. Have you ever worked with someone who treats business like a poker game? Do you envy or pity this person?

2. Are you able to apply the concept of vocation to your job? What barriers limit your ability to live out your vocation at work?

III. Concepts to Understand

How might each passage be applied to a business context?

1. Poker Game Ethic

Genesis 27:1-46: How did Rebecca and her son Jacob "play poker" in this situation? What was the outcome of their disregard for "normal ethics"?

Genesis 29:15-27; 30:25—31:2: How do Laban and Jacob treat each other? What is the end result for both?

1 Samuel 16:1-3: Is Samuel being dishonest with King Saul? Is this an acceptable example of poker playing?

2. Dual Morality

Leviticus 6:1-7: Does this passage apply to personal or business situations, or both? What is its implicit message about dual morality?

Proverbs 5:22; 10:9; 20:17; 21:6; 28:18; Isaiah 29:15-16; Micah 2:1-3; 6:10-15: What is the ultimate fate of the person who applies a low ethical standard in business?

Isaiah 5:20-21: Is the marketplace ethically self-defining? Do business leaders have the moral authority to define what is ethical and what is not?

Jeremiah 7:1-11; Amos 5:21-24; 1 John 1:6-7: How do these warnings and promises apply to the ethical perspective of Dan Drew and John D. Rockefeller?

3. Ethical Separation

Leviticus 20:23, 26; 1 Peter 2:11-12: For a Christian businessperson, what does it mean to be different from the surrounding culture?

Proverbs 5:21: Is business activity exempt from God's accountability?

Matthew 5:13-16; Philippians 2:15: What do the salt, light and star metaphors teach us about dual morality?

Matthew 5:33-37; 23:16-22: Is promise-breaking acceptable in the marketplace?

Romans 6:11-14: How can we act as "instruments of righteousness" in the business environment?

Colossians 1:13-23; 3:17: How should our transfer of citizenship from the "dominion of darkness" to the "kingdom of the Son" affect our business conduct? What impact should the lordship of Christ have on our commercial dealings?

1 Timothy 3:7: Why should church leaders have good reputations with the non-Christian community? Does this apply to business practitioners? If so, why? How?

4. Consequences of Righteous Business Practices

Deuteronomy 28:1-11: Are material blessings guaranteed to the righteous?

Proverbs 19:1 and 28:6: Of what practical value is integrity?

Titus 2:11-14: Is prosperity ensured to faithful Christians? What is the chief measure of "success"?

5. Vocation

Exodus 35:30—36:5: How do Bezalel and Oholiab use their jobs as a means by which to fulfill their vocations?

Jeremiah 1:4-5; Acts 18:1-4; Galatians 1:15: Are vocation and profession synonymous? How do the lives of Jeremiah and Paul answer this question? Are they the exception or the rule?

1 Corinthians 5:9-11: Must we all become priests and nuns in order to escape the corruption of the world? How should Christians behave in the marketplace? not behave?

1 Corinthians 7:17-24: Martin Luther concluded that *vocation* and *work* are synonymous in this passage. Do you agree or disagree with his analysis? Why?

6

LAW

Two things I contemplate with ceaseless awe: the stars of heaven
and man's sense of law.
IMMANUEL KANT

A society with no other scale but the legal one is not quite
worthy of man. . . . The letter of the law is too cold and formal an
atmosphere of moral mediocrity, paralyzing man's
noblest impulses.
ALEKSANDR SOLZHENITSYN

The better the society, the less law there will be. In heaven there
will be no law, and the lion will lie down with the lamb. In hell
there will be nothing but law, and due process will be
meticulously observed.
GRANT GILMORE

When Gentiles [non-Jews], who do not have the law, do by nature things
required by the law, they are a law for themselves, even though they do
not have the law, since they show that the requirements of the law are
written on their hearts, their consciences also bearing witness.
THE APOSTLE PAUL

T HE SECOND FALSE EXIT LOOKS TO THE LAW TO DEFINE WHAT IS ACCEPT-
able business conduct. It presumes that if an action is legal, it is morally
permissible as well. In the marketplace, the concepts of "legal" and "ethical"
are merely two ways of saying the same thing. Like dual morality, business
behavior is benchmarked not to holiness-justice-love, but to an external
human standard.

This perspective is particularly appealing because law has a strong moral bent,
asking such fundamental ethical questions as "What is fair?" and "What obligations do we have toward one another?" Taken to an extreme, law can even

become a substitute for organized religion. Legislation, not the Sermon on the Mount, becomes our moral compass. Judges, not clergy, make the hard moral decisions. Court procedures, not common notions of fairness, define justice.

This is not to say, however, that the business community has high regard for the legal system. To the contrary, law is often viewed as an invasive arm of governmental control. Whether the subject is workplace safety, taxation or environmental impact statements, law is regarded as an encroaching pest. Government regulators, hearing examiners and bureaucrats are certainly not among society's most admired individuals.

Is this evaluation fair? Not entirely. The law contributes to the marketplace by ensuring predictability and by providing a level playing field for all competitors. Predictability is vital because it enables companies to effectively plan for the future. For instance, defining delivery terms such as "cash on delivery" and "risk of loss" permits businesses to allocate compensation for goods damaged in transit. Likewise, law provides a line demarking acceptable and unacceptable behavior. Since each business— be it a pharmaceutical company, defense contractor or advertising agency—must play by the same set of rules, fair play is encouraged and the general public protected. It is no exaggeration to suggest the marketplace would quickly grind to a standstill if the legal system ceased to function. Just imagine the New York Stock Exchange attempting to operate outside a legal framework.

The interrelationship between law and ethics has generated much academic ink over the years. Two distinctly different approaches to this interaction are positivism and an integrated Christian approach.

Positivism

FUZZY CHOICE. Mark, age thirty, is looking to make his first foray into the stock market. Barb, a close friend, encourages him to invest in Mobile Traffic Industries (MTI), an electronics company. MTI manufactures a high-quality "fuzz-buster," a product that uses sensors to warn drivers of upcoming speed traps.

When Mark questions whether such a device is ethical, Barb explains: "Look, it's all legal, and my stock values increased by 17 percent last year. You need the money. Don't always be such a goody-two-shoes."

Positivism, the dominant legal theory in the world for the past two centuries, has three elements. First, it completely divorces law from the realm of ethics. Focusing on what the law is, not what it ought to be, positivism is "a concept of law that has no moral connotations whatsoever."[1] From this perspective, Mark should not worry about what is right or wrong in buying MTI stock, but focus solely on what the law permits. Since the investment is not illegal, he is free to do as he pleases. Legal compliance, not an idealistic search for truth, is his only civic obligation.

Second, positivism accepts the law as being whatever the government says it is, never questioning its rightness or wrongness. If Congress were to pass a law forbidding fuzz-busters tomorrow, Mark would be ill-advised to invest in MTI. Perhaps more important, he would have no basis for complaint. Just as university officials (not college athletes) determine the distance of the three-point shot line in basketball, so government leaders (not individuals such as Mark) define what behavior is appropriate and inappropriate in society. They alone have the power to make such decisions. Therefore "no law can be unjust."[2]

Third, positivism assumes that law can be studied scientifically. Its advocates believe that law must be based on quantifiable facts, not "soft" theology or philosophy. As they would say, we "have no knowledge but phenomena [natural sciences]. . . . Their ultimate causes are unknown and inscrutable to us."[3] Put another way, the study of law is not deductive, starting with universal standards, but rather inductive, starting with tangible information at hand. From this perspective, the goal of law is not to promote high-minded ideals but to reflect reality. If Congress were to decide to regulate fuzz-busters, it should first secure solid empirical evidence of the product's social and economic impacts.

Criticisms of Positivism

TOXIC MILK. James and Rikki Pomerenke of Yakima, Washington, are a husband-wife team who used to operate their own independent long-haul trucking company. About six years ago, a client wanted them to haul liquid fertilizer one direction and milk on the return trip. At the time, state law required only a modest soap cleaning of the truck's interior container. The Pomerenkes felt that this provided inadequate protection for the milk and, concerned particularly with the health of young children, refused to back haul it.

As a result, the client had them "blacklisted"—other companies also refused to do business with them. Within a year, the Pomerenkes were unable to repay the bank loan for their truck and were forced to live on disability insurance. Two years later, largely in response to the Pomerenkes' story, Congress passed a law forbidding the hauling of toxic chemicals and consumable liquids in the same interior containers.[4]

Critics point to four flaws in positivism. First, they contend that law is an imperfect product of an imperfect political process. As demonstrated in the Pomerenkes' situation, the process operates slowly, resulting in significant time lags between the identification of social needs and the implementation of new laws.[5] Despite strong public support, Congress still took two years to respond to the Pomerenkes' concern. Legislative wheels grind slowly. For positivists to argue that law is the exclusive guide for business behavior is to ignore the rightness of the Pomerenkes' position during the two-year interim period preceding enactment of the federal legislation.

Further, corporate lobbying often defers (or even kills) needed legislation. Take the automobile industry's success in postponing for a decade the mandatory installation of air bags. Does the fact that prospective laws are stalled by lobbyists make corporate behavior that is technically legal during the interim—such as not installing air bags—morally acceptable? This line of reasoning is particularly problematic because of the obvious self-interest of the corporations that hire the lobbyists. Positivism implicitly legitimates such egoistic political maneuverings by focusing solely on the letter of the law. If an airplane manufacturer contributes financially to a politician's reelection campaign in order to significantly alter a pending piece of legislation, the positivist would have no basis to criticize such behavior.

The second criticism of positivism is that it justifies immoral behavior. Consider the following situation.

PROMISE BREAKER. Ricardo agrees to sell Mona his computer for $750. They even shake hands on the deal. Two days later Ricardo sells it to Bob instead for $820. Visibly upset, Mona threatens Ricardo with a lawsuit. Ricardo responds: "Fine, go ahead and make my day. I just took a business law class and learned that contracts for the sale of goods over $500 must *be in writing. Ours wasn't, so you lose." Assume that Ricardo is correct in his legal analysis.*

Positivists would have no basis for questioning Ricardo's conduct. Legal standards set by the government cannot be reviewed by such abstract concepts as holiness, justice and love. The law permits Ricardo to renege on the deal—end of discussion.

Positivism provides no outside reference point by which to evaluate law. Taken to an extreme, human sacrifice, slavery, torture and apartheid—all considered legal at different times in various cultures—would be acceptable. In a similar vein, Lockheed Aircraft's payments of millions of dollars in bribes to Japanese government officials was permissible because no law yet prohibited such behavior. Conceivably, a company could purchase the patent from an inventor for the sole purpose of keeping it from competing with its existing product lines. According to positivism, so long as the act is legal, no questions could be raised about the transaction, even if society might greatly benefit from the invention.

The third criticism of positivism follows logically from the second. When we make human law the final word on what conduct is acceptable and unacceptable, God is dethroned as the ultimate moral authority. With no external ethical reference point or accountability, government alone determines what is right and wrong. While this variant of idolatry is frightening enough in democratic nations, it is downright terrifying in countries headed by tyrants. It certainly brings little solace to Chinese human rights activists being held in government-controlled labor camps or to multinational corporations that have their properties expropriated by host nations. Positivism simply provides no moral accountability for governmental action: "Such a command can be given by a man with a loaded gun, and law surely is not the gunman situation writ large."[6]

It seems self-evident that the simple possession of power does not always equate with its proper usage. If, as the old saying goes, "power corrupts and absolute power corrupts absolutely," what confidence should we place in government to always wield its power appropriately? For instance, take the infanticide and cruel slavery practiced by the Egyptian pharaoh (Ex 5:6-9). Or note Adolf Hitler's declaration after having seventy Nazis murdered during a 1934 intraparty dispute that "the supreme court of the German people [has acted] . . . and it consists of myself."[7] The vacuousness of this position is clear.

The fourth problem of positivism is that it leads to more government regulation of business. This is the logical result of the theory, because if law is the sole determinant of business behavior, its importance is magnified. If business leaders operate at the margins of the law, citizens who are affected by their decisions will respond by demanding tighter government controls. If, for example, several large corporations exploit an unintended loophole in a state water-pollution statute, voters will clamor for more strictly defined regulations. Likewise, if companies are insensitive to consumer complaints, employee safety issues or stockholder concerns, the democratic process will inevitably lead to more governmental oversight. What then results is over-regulation, a form of legalism, the pitfalls of which are discussed in chapter two.

Integrated Christian Approach

ALL KEYED UP. Two decades ago, Ace Key Company (AKC) manufactured and legally sold keys via mail orders. It did so despite the fact that it had been informed that several of its customers were automobile thieves.[8]

Unlike positivism, an integrated Christian approach does not separate law and ethics. Predicated on the sovereignty argument made in chapter five, this view argues that God's moral principles supersede and overshadow human law. No realm of human activity—neither the marketplace nor the law—is exempt from divine authority. This approach would not excuse AKC's management merely because it was acting within the bounds of the law. Rather, its behavior would be evaluated against a higher and more universal set of values.

Such values flow from the principles of holiness, justice and love. They include, though are by no means limited to, the following:

Duties
□ Keep promises.
□ Tell the truth.
□ Make restitution for harm done.
□ Respect legitimate human authority.

- ☐ Respect the rights of others.
- ☐ Be responsible stewards of natural resources.
- ☐ Show concern for the poor.
- ☐ Maintain healthy family relationships.

Rights to
- ☐ freedom of choice
- ☐ equal protection
- ☐ dignity
- ☐ due process
- ☐ own property
- ☐ life
- ☐ be told the truth

Universal norms are predicated on the premise that we are all created in God's image and that despite our moral flaws, everyone possesses a general sense of right and wrong. In this light, all societies—whatever their religious views—are expected to protect fundamental rights and to encourage the fulfillment of basic duties via their legal systems. As the apostle Paul observed: "When Gentiles [non-Jews], who do not have the law, do by nature things required by the law, they are a law for themselves, even though they do not have the law, since they show that the requirements of the law are written on their hearts, their consciences also bearing witness" (Rom 2:14-15).

In essence, Paul taught that God imprinted certain values in all of us through our consciences. Lying to a business partner or stealing from a boss is wrong not just because law or custom says so but because we intuitively know that such behavior is immoral. While it is possible to sever this ethical nerve through repeated abuse, a basic sense of right and wrong is encoded deeply within us.

The Reverend Martin Luther King Jr. captured this call for consistency between ethics and law when he wrote: "A just law is a man-made code that squares with the moral law or the law of God."[9] In like manner, Gustav Radbruch, a German legal philosopher who was a positivist prior to Hitler's ascent, reversed his position and concluded that law and ethics must not be separated. After World War II he articulated his support for a universal ideal

and was instrumental in bringing criminal charges against members of the
Third Reich in the Nuremberg War Trials.[10]

Criticisms of the Integrated Christian Approach

*SELLING THE BIRD. Pedro owns and operates a small food store in a poor
section of Chicago. Many of his customers are alcoholics who live down
the block in government-subsidized housing. One of Pedro's top-selling
products is Gallo Thunderbird, a product with twice the alcohol content
of a regular bottle of table wine (the maximum percentage permitted by
U.S. law) and which sells for less than half the price. Some drinkers claim
that Thunderbird's sweet, fruity taste makes them thirstier for more.
Pedro's son is upset with him, claiming that he has become "a dope pusher
for the wine industry." Pedro responds that such sales are not illegal and
that the profits keep his family fed and housed.*

Critics point to three perceived weaknesses of the Christian approach to law
and ethics. First, they charge that it is neither scientific nor precise. How do
concepts such as dignity, life, free will, property ownership and concern for
the less fortunate get transposed into legal guidelines applicable to Pedro's
situation? These values are, it is argued, too vague and subjective to provide
much guidance. Pedro has no simple solution.

Second, they contend that no one has the authority to designate a list of
universal ethical values and that to attempt to do so ignores cultural particu-
lars. When compared to the dynamic character of positivism, this static view of
the law is most unappealing. Positivism, on the other hand, adjusts itself to every
culture, affording wide latitude to formulate policies on such issues as patents,
securities and real estate law. Why, they query, should the antitrust laws of
Vietnam and England be the same? Must the sale of Thunderbird be regulated
the same in Chicago as in Iran? Each culture should decide for itself.

Third, and perhaps most significant, critics charge that the Christian
approach would impose a religious standard on society. Do we really want
the high ethical standards of Christianity imposed on business through the
legal system? Didn't Prohibition (making the sale of alcohol illegal in the
1920s) teach us to avoid such religious control? Certainly Pedro should be
free to sell his products as he sees fit. Wouldn't an expanded Christian ethic
invite more government intrusion into our private lives? If Jesus' interpreta-

tion of the Ten Commandments were codified into law, wouldn't greed, pride and coveting be declared illegal? Do we really want to have "covet cops" and "lust police" evaluating our motives and reading our magazines?

Defenses of the Christian Approach

These legitimate concerns merit serious responses. First, to the charge that the Christian position is not scientific or precise, no direct defense is offered. Rather, a series of counterquestions are asked. How do positivists quantify values such as honesty, disclosure and neighbor love? Does the fact that they cannot be measured really make them worthless? Of course not. What would life be like without ideals such as human dignity and equal protection? We are regularly enriched by that which is not scientifically verifiable. Where would we be without such "soft" items as music, literature, philosophy, art and faith? The inductive scientific method, while certainly an important contributor in defining human experience, is limited in its ability to capture our essence.

The second criticism, that universal principles are inflexible, is more problematic. Clearly it would be ludicrous to impose a single set of particular laws on all nations. Should we be surprised that Canada and Mexico have different bankruptcy codes? Of course not. It is certainly reasonable to expect differences in the time limits creditors have to file and the amount of property debtors are permitted to exempt from being taken. What is needed is a two-tiered system that contains both universal principles and particular cultural applications. In regard to bankruptcy law, this "flexible absolutism" would, on the one hand, expect all nations to reflect universal values of promise keeping, compensation for harm and respect for legitimate property rights. On the other hand, it would grant broad discretion to each nation to determine just how these principles are best applied in its context.

An interesting illustration of this approach can be found in the Mosaic code. In the mostly agrarian Hebrew culture of that period, thieves were required to give five animals to their victims for every one stolen (Ex 22:1). While this particular solution was quite reasonable in that culture, it would be woefully inappropriate in most urban societies today. This ought not surprise us. For while the universal principle on the first tier—restitution for harm done—must be observed by all societies, its application on the second tier will vary from culture to culture. In our culture, the stolen goods may be cars or credit cards rather than sheep, but the underlying principle remains the same. Wrongdoing triggers the need for compensation in one form or another.

Thomas Aquinas couched this distinction in terms of "primary" law and "secondary" law. Primary law, he argued, is based on unchangeable values— such as dignity and truth telling—while "secondary" law—how each society applies these universal values—will vary depending on local circumstances and needs.[11] In making this distinction Aquinas relied on Aristotle, who labeled the two components of law "natural" and "conventional."[12] Both men recognized that this two-tiered approach provides both a strong moral base and, simultaneously, significant local flexibility. See figure 6.1.

Universal values	Honor due process	Make restitution	Promote sexual purity	Protect life	Rest from work
Local applications	Two or three years to file lawsuit Face-to-face meeting or arbitration 60- or 90-day filing period	Compensate in damages or criminal penalties	Limit certain products Restrict TV ads Rely on peer pressure	Ban cigarettes Limit advertising Test legal drugs	Day of week Definition of "rest"

Figure 6.1

FAMILY TROUGH. A local bank permits its executive officers and their families to temporarily overdraw on their accounts with no additional penalties. When some shareholders discover this, they complain that it is an unsound and unfair business practice. The executives respond that they are not acting illegally.

The final criticism of the Christian integration of law and ethics is that it attempts to impose religious standards on society. While this concern has already been partially addressed, three additional points need to be made.

First, forcing religious ethics down an unwilling electorate's throat is highly unlikely where voters determine the content of their laws through elected representatives. If anything, the opposite is more likely to occur: social compromises inherent in the political process will lower the law's ethical content. Truth-telling standards are relaxed in sales to facilitate commerce, environmental stewardship is compromised to save jobs, employee privacy rights are diminished by the use of drug tests to increase productivity, and bank executives are permitted to engage in small amounts of self-dealing to avoid overregulation. "Pluralism"—the political reality of divergent interest groups pushing and shoving for influence—forces the moral pointer down to an ethically bland median. The lowest common denominator—not holiness, justice and love—is the de facto determinant of law in a democratic society.

Second, Scripture is reluctant to cede too much power to government. For while it may be a necessary instrument of God's common grace, it must never become a substitute for God. Scripture warns that all-powerful governments tend to usurp God's sovereignty, becoming idols to be feared and opposed (Rev 13:1-10). Witness the former Soviet Union, which attempted to control every aspect of its people's lives. Even lesser forms of governmental control are to be viewed with a degree of suspicion. Paternalism—when government plays the role of parent over its citizens—should not be stretched so far that it dramatically infringes on individual free will. We must recognize that government's ability to serve as a vehicle through which holiness, justice and love are transmitted is limited.

The integrated Christian approach therefore does not endorse "covet cops" and "pride police." While ethical standards are to remain high, little confidence is placed in government to enforce them. As exemplified in the parable of the wheat and the weeds—where the two are permitted to coexist until harvest—God's final verdict will wait until judgment day (Mt 13:24-30). In the meanwhile, the good and the bad live side by side, and the law must not be overly controlling of our lives. As one author notes, the proper role of government is "somewhere between blue-nosed Salem and everything-goes Sodom."[13]

Finally, the Christian approach recognizes that law has a limited purpose. While it may attempt to perform some affirmative duties (for example, redistribute wealth via taxation), its primary function is to enforce negative injunctions—punish lawbreakers, require compensation for breached contracts and mandate restitution for negligent actions (Rom 13:1-7). The former Soviet Union attempted to create the perfect "Soviet person" via the law and failed miserably.[14] For while law can effectively regulate visible behavior, it can neither create saints nor usher in the kingdom of God.

Figure 6.2 illustrates the difference between the standards of holiness-justice-love, on the one hand, and human law on the other. Whereas the former emphasizes internal motives and a higher standard of righteousness, the latter focuses on outward deeds.

Standard of Holiness-Justice-Love	Greed/ Coveting	Judging others	Deceit	Hate/Anger	Moral purity
Standard of Human Love	Theft	Slander	Fraud	Murder	Harm caused to others

Figure 6.2

Human law focuses on what we ought not do—for example, steal patents, engage in industrial espionage or lie on tax forms. Holiness-justice-love, on the other hand, reflects the affirmative character of God. Adam Smith, the father of modern capitalism, compared this difference with two types of grammar. Human law is like the basic rules of composition (for example, punctuation and proper sentence structure), while Christian ethics is comparable to that which is "sublime and elegant" in writing (for example, prose, poetry and drama). Merely obeying the rules of grammar does not make our writing "good." Neither does minimal compliance with the law make us morally good.[15] Does the fact that neither Mother Teresa nor Donald Trump has ever committed a felony place them on the same ethical plane? Of course not. As one scholar wryly notes: "Standing before the law, scoundrels, stinkers and triflers who do nothing illegal are at one with the most industrious humanitarians."[16]

It may be helpful to picture the law as an invisible moral pointer that operates somewhere between the lower level of negative injunctions and the higher level of ethical perfection.[17] A great political struggle exists over the location of this pointer. Some want more ethical considerations explicitly stated in the law. We should improve human behavior via legal means, they contend, by mandating such items as decent worker pensions and clean air while at the same time outlawing such behaviors as exaggeration in sales and the marketing of Thunderbird to alcoholics. As positive examples of law's ability to alter behavior, they point to the Civil Rights Act, prohibiting racial discrimination, and to sexual harassment regulations now operating in the workplace.

Critics counter that if the legal pointer is moved too far up toward perfection, important values such as human freedom, creativity and spontaneity will be stifled. The marketplace buckles under a regulatory system that demands too much. The primary purpose of law, they contend, is not moral perfection but identification of behaviors that merit governmental punishment. As the old saying goes, "You can't legislate morality."

On the other hand, if the legal pointer is moved too low, individual freedom can easily lapse into license, resulting in harm to others. Truck drivers are permitted to haul toxic materials and milk, chemical companies to indiscriminately dump their waste, and multinational corporations to exploit overseas workers. It is imperative that the law provide a level playing field for such diverse groups as stockbrokers, bankers, creditors and computer engineers. Like soccer referees, the legal system also sanctions violators. Clearly, the legal pointer cannot be permitted to go too low. Figure 6.3 illustrates the tension.

Acts that are both ethical and legal

Ethics ————————————————————————————————————

Acts that are unethical but legal

Law ——————————————————————————————————————

Acts that are both illegal and unethical

Figure 6.3

In free societies, law is a moral floor, providing only minimal standards for acceptable behavior. It is anticipated that citizens will voluntarily live above its requirements. If they do not, the legal line will steadily creep upward, encroaching on human freedom as it rises. Hence companies that unjustly fire employees without due process should not be surprised when society responds by restricting such latitude in the future via legal reform. Likewise, large businesses that callously pull up stakes from small cities, leaving school systems, tax bases and social services in disarray, can anticipate increased governmental oversight of such closures. The legal pointer can also be expected to rise on advertisers who increase the use of violence in marketing children's toys.

The ideal society is one that has the least restrictive laws on the one hand and citizens committed to pursuit of the highest ethical ideals on the other. This formula maximizes individual freedom, restricts the size and influence of government and, at the same time, ensures a sense of community and ethical treatment of others. Eden was the last environment that effectively, albeit temporarily, implemented such a system.

Scripture underscores this important distinction between ethics and law. When a wealthy young man asked what he must do to be righteous, Jesus told him to obey the law—don't murder, commit adultery, steal, give false testimony in court or commit fraud—and to honor his parents. However, when pressed further, Jesus told him to donate all his wealth to the poor (Mk 10:17-22). While the floor set by the law was adequate from a human perspective, it could not make the young man holy, just and loving. Negative injunctions simply lack the capacity to do so.

In a similar vein, the accusers of a woman caught in adultery, while legally correct in pointing their collective finger at her, failed to recognize a higher moral calling of grace and nonjudgmentalism (Jn 8:1-11). Paul echoed this approach by exhorting his readers to observe the law—no stealing, murdering, committing adultery or leaving debts unpaid. In addition, he stressed that moral reasoning must not stop at the law but must move well beyond it. A higher standard beckons us: "Whatever other commandment[s] there may be, are summed up in this one rule: 'Love your neighbor as yourself.' Love does no harm to its neighbor. Therefore love is the fulfillment of the law" (Rom 13:8-10).

Questions for Discussion

I. Case for Discussion

Grimes Corporation (GC) is a large conglomerate that owns both FoodTime grocery store chain and Primo TV, a regional cable station. For several years product bar coding has enabled FoodTime to target mail advertisements to customers based on their purchases.

GC now wants to take technology a step further. It proposes to target FoodTime customers through Primo TV ads. These ads would be tailored to each household based on its FoodTime purchases and other information GC is able to obtain. Advertisers who want to sell their products or services would be charged for this service. For example, if a customer buys lots of diet food and GC discovers through

*other sources that the customer belongs to a weight-loss club, select companies would
be sold airtime to market their chocolate and pizza products directly into the home
between 8:00 and 10:00 p.m. Or if the customer belongs to Alcoholics Anonymous,
beer and wine manufacturers might want to purchase airtime to show their ads.
Customers are unaware of this marketing tactic. Presume that no law yet prevents
GC from pursuing this marketing strategy.*

1. How would positivism analyze this case?

2. How would an integrated Christian approach analyze this case?

3. What are your personal feelings about this marketing practice?

II. Workplace Application

1. Describe conduct you have observed at work that, though legal, seemed to be
less than ethical.

2. How did you and/or the other person(s) involved handle the situation?

3. What were the long-term consequences of this behavior?

III. Concepts to Understand

How might each passage be applied to a business context?

1. Law Is Necessary

Romans 13:1-7: According to Paul, what is the purpose of government? What
role(s) should law play in society?

John 18:31—19:6: How does Governor Pilate violate Roman law in this situation?
What function should law play in establishing a minimal standard of behavior?

2. Two Standards—Ethics and the Law

Jeremiah 31:31-34: What is the basic difference between the old and new
covenants? Which applies a higher ethical standard? How so? Does it have any
relevance to the discussion of law and ethics?

Matthew 5:17-20: What is the relationship between law and ethics?

Matthew 5:38-42: What does the law permit when one person intentionally injures
another? What does Jesus expect us to do in such situations? How do we square this
apparent tension between law and ethics?

Matthew 13:24-30: How does this parable argue for high ethical standards and at
the same time place limitations on the government's ability to coerce its citizens via
the law?

Luke 14:1-6: If Jesus were a positivist, what would he do?

Romans 1:18-32; 2:12-16: What arguments does Paul make to support a universal
ethic? On what basis can Gentiles (non-Jews), who do not have the Old Testament
law, be expected to behave in an ethical manner?

3. Mere Compliance with the Law Is Not Enough

Nenemiah 5:1-13: On what basis—legal or moral—does Nehemiah confront the
affluent and powerful of his society? Is he a positivist? Or does he adhere to an
integrated approach?

Matthew 5:21-22: How do the ethical demands of Jesus exceed those required by
the law? Is he suggesting that anger/hatred should be declared illegal and punished

by the government?

Mark 7:9-13: How do the Pharisees technically comply with the law but at the same time violate God's ethical standards?

Mark 10:17-22: Why doesn't obedience of the law satisfy Jesus? How does this passage support the argument that ethics represents a standard higher than the law?

John 8:1-11: Does Jesus invalidate the law against adultery? Ideally, how should ethics and law interact?

Romans 13:8-10: Are law and ethics synonymous?

4. Breaking Unjust Laws/Civil Disobedience

Exodus 1:15-22: How would the midwives handle this situation if they were positivists? On what theoretical basis do they disobey the law?

Acts 5:27-29: What is Peter's view of human law? When is it to be obeyed or disobeyed?

Revelation 13:1-10: How does this image of government compare with Romans 13:1-7? Which is the more accurate view?

7

AGENCY

Dogs owe no loyalty because they are not moral agents.
They lack the distinctly human faculty of rational choice.
Choose, they do; reason, they do not.
RAYMOND PFEIFFER

For while subordinates have many obligations towards their
superiors, this one, that they are bound to obey their
commands, stands out as special among the rest. Obedience
is a special virtue.
THOMAS AQUINAS

The term *free agent* is an oxymoron. One must choose
between being free or being an agent. One cannot be both
simultaneously.
ANONYMOUS

We must obey God rather than men!
THE APOSTLE PETER

T HE THIRD FALSE EXIT INVOLVES THE SO-CALLED AGENCY PROBLEM
that arises when the values of the employee diverge from those of the employer.[1] In such cases a tension exists between subordinates' desire to serve their
employers loyally on the one hand and to act in their own best self-interest (or
that of the community) on the other. This tension is particularly acute in the area
of ethics: what should employees do when given directives they consider
immoral? While the agency false exit overlaps with dual morality and positivism,
it presents a different angle to the problem. Expanding on Milton Friedman's
views in chapter five, the question is framed: are employees obligated to lay aside
their personal ethics when they go to work?

The potential for conflict is exacerbated for devout Christians working for secular companies. While acknowledging their fiduciary responsibilities to the employer, they also recognize two other "targets"[2] to whom duties are owed—God and the general public. These obligations are grounded in the New Testament's two great commands—to "love the Lord your God with all your heart, with all your soul and with all your mind" and to "love your neighbor as yourself" (Mt 22:37-40).

Thus Christian employees must simultaneously be cognizant of their responsibilities to several entities: God, employer and other neighbors. Vis-à-vis God, they view themselves as "servants" or "ambassadors" in a principal-agent relationship (2 Cor 5:20). And while acknowledging that their employers are neighbors to whom duties are owed, they include other stakeholders in this category as well—customers, creditors, suppliers, community and even competitors.

The potential for conflicting loyalties faced by Christian agents is roughly analogous to the situation of union members who have obligations to both their employer and the labor organization. Research indicates that if harmonious relations exist between company and union, employees experience little interrole conflict.[3] Similarly, if a business enforces high moral standards, Christian employees encounter minimal friction between their duties to God, neighbor and employer. However, if employers issue a mandate that impinges on the agents' love for God or neighbor, they are apt to suffer a great deal of ethical dissonance.

This chapter focuses on a narrower question: What should private-sector Christian employees do when ordered to commit an act which, *though legal,* violates their sense of obligation to God and community? In other words, how much moral "fudging," if any, is permissible on behalf of their employers? Consider the following five scenarios:

1. A clerk works for a video store that heretofore has not sold or rented X-rated movies. New owners have recently changed this policy. They anticipate that in the near future up to 25 percent of the videos will be pornographic.

2. A secretary is asked by his supervisor to look in another employee's desk after work hours. The supervisor suspects that illegal drugs may be found. Such a search is generally not an illegal act in a private company.

3. A computer programmer is asked to contribute to United Way. Since

one of the seventy agencies that receive these funds advocates (but does
not perform) abortion on demand, she declines to donate. Her manager,
insisting on "100 percent participation," pressures her to give a token
amount—even one dollar.

4. A supermarket clerk is asked for a pack of cigarettes by a customer.

5. On June 1 a sales representative for a clothing manufacturer makes a
verbal promise to a prospective buyer that a certain line of dresses will be
available for purchase until June 15. On June 10 the sales representative is
ordered by her boss to sell the dresses to another buyer for a higher price. If
she is able to communicate her revocation to the first buyer before he accepts,
no contract exists. The original offer was not in writing, and he gave nothing
of value to bind the sales representative to her promise.

Submissive Model

Two competing paradigms of employer-employee relations emerge from
Scripture by which such situations may be evaluated—the *submissive model*
and the *purist model.* In the former, employees place a strong emphasis on
loyalty and obedience to their employers, perhaps even utilizing the military
"chain of command" metaphor. Within the bounds of the law, superiors
should be accommodated; acquiescence to their directives is normative. In
accord with Milton Friedman's position discussed in chapter five, submissive
agents are amenable to venture beyond their own religious ethics so long as
their actions remain legal. In the situations described above, such employees
would be willing to compromise their own values to please those in authority
over them. Despite personal beliefs to the contrary, they would market
pornographic videos, look into a coworker's desk, donate to the United Way,
sell cigarettes and break promises to a customer.

Adherents of this model cite the writings of the apostles Peter and Paul.
Peter wrote: "Servants, be submissive to your masters with all respect, not
only to the kind and gentle but also to the overbearing. For one is approved
if, mindful of God, he endures pain while suffering unjustly" (1 Pet 2:18-19
RSV). Paul taught that slaves are to "obey in everything those who are your
earthly masters, not with eyeservice, as men-pleasers, but in singleness of
heart, fearing the Lord" (Col 3:22—4:1) and admonished Christian servants
to "be obedient to . . . your earthly masters . . . as servants of Christ, doing

the will of God from the heart" (Eph 6:5-9 RSV).

This paradigm minimizes the problem of conflicting loyalties. It envisions a harmony between the aspirations of the agent and those of the principal. Some theologians have construed Paul in a way that equates obedience to one's principal with obedience to God. Employers are thus given a mediating function between God and their employees. Deference is due because they serve as God's representative in the marketplace.[4] Such authority is implicitly necessary because of human sinfulness. Fallen employees, prone as they are to sinful self-will, need direction from earthly leaders. In this sense, employers play a role similar to that of governmental authorities who monitor citizens' behavior or of parents who shepherd their children.

Along these lines, Martin Luther instructed:

What your master or mistress commands, this God Himself has commanded you to do. It is not a command of men, even though it is given through men. . . . You serve as if Christ Himself were ordering you to do so. . . . For if the master takes the lead and steps into the mire, it stands to reason that the servant will follow.[5]

In an article dealing with legal ethics, a Christian attorney appealed to this model. He argued that in light of his oath to represent his clients "zealously within the bounds of the law," he would violate his "solemn oath" if he were to employ strictly personal religious standards. As a lawyer, he is obliged in certain situations to divorce professional and personal ethics. The law, not his religious beliefs, must define his conduct when representing another. To do otherwise would be to "lie to my client. I have accepted money under false pretenses."[6]

A secular corollary of the submissive agent was formulated by William Whyte Jr. a number of decades ago in his classic book *The Organization Man.* He observed that some employees "see an ultimate harmony between themselves and their companies."[7] Indeed, to some employers loyalty is *the* paramount employee virtue.[8] A business periodical recently published an article subtitled "An Agent Owes Unflagging—but Not Criminal—Loyalty to the Employing Firm."[9]

Purist Model

Unlike their submissive counterparts, purist agents refuse to compromise their ethics in order to accommodate their employers. Emphasizing holiness and ethical purity, they confront rather than yield to what they perceive to be immoral directives. They view their obligation to God and community as primary. Human managers are obeyed only so long as their dictates comport with Christian ethics.

This model finds its roots in both the Old and New Testaments. After the death of Christ, early church leaders were warned by civil authorities not to preach. Their response—"We must obey God rather than men!" (Acts 5:29)—established a strong precedent for challenging human authority.[10] The purist, in any conflict between divine and human imperatives, decides uncompromisingly in favor of the former.

Purists point to several Old Testament figures to support their position. Daniel, a faithful agent of a Babylonian king, received numerous promotions. However, when given a command contrary to his faith, he refused to comply even though the directive was within the bounds of civil law (Dan 6:10). A theologian has called this act "the great refusal." Like Daniel, Christians ought "not be bullied . . . into surrendering their commitment to God's will."[11]

Ancient Hebrew prophets such as Nathan, Micaiah and Balaam—though not technically agents of their kings—displayed a similar disposition. Nathan boldly confronted David for his crimes of adultery and murder (2 Sam 12:1-15). Micaiah, alone among four hundred prophets, resisted the pressure to give a favorable report to his king (1 Kings 22:1-37). Balaam repudiated an employment contract after God commissioned him to act in an opposite manner (Num 24:12-13). The prophets Isaiah, Jeremiah and Ezekiel also resolved their divine-human loyalty conflicts in favor of God.[12]

In the eighteenth century, Methodist founder John Wesley warned Christians against being "infected" by the lower ethical standards of secular society. He queried, "For who can touch pitch and not be defiled?"[13]

Purist agents are capable of only limited loyalty to their employers. One scholar describes this as "partial inclusion."[14] They may experience strong, but never total, identification with their employers. Such commitments are circumscribed by fealty to God and love of neighbor. In theological shorthand, covenant supersedes contract.

Analysis of the Submissive Model
Of the two paradigms presented, the submissive model is by far the more

deficient. Three flaws are preeminent. First, the model fails to properly identify Paul's and Peter's audience. Slaves, not freemen, were the apostles' intended recipients. This confusion springs in part from the King James Version of Scripture, which, penned in 1611, unfortunately translated the Greek words *doulos* (slave) and *oiketēs* (household slave) as "servant." Even the 1946 Revised Standard Version followed suit in its translation of *oiketēs*.[15]

This raises two questions. Why did the apostles counsel Christian slaves to submit to their masters? Second, what aspects of this teaching, if any, are applicable to today's employer-employee relationship?

Scholars speculate why the apostles took such a conservative position on slavery. They posit that a direct attack on the institution of slavery would have resulted in social revolt, severe punishment and/or massive unemployment,[16] along with increased persecution of the politically powerless church.[17] It is also likely that Paul's belief in Christ's imminent return to rule on earth led him to tolerate slavery as a temporary institution.[18]

None of these factors—human bondage, political impotence, feared unemployment for liberated slaves or eschatological expectation—has any bearing on discussions of modern employer-employee relations. Operating in democratic capitalistic systems, Western employees are free to accept or reject work on a contract basis. They may unilaterally terminate their employment at any time and for any reason to secure other work. As voters, they enjoy the right to reform the legal ground rules by which industrial relations are governed. Innovations such as worker's compensation, minimum wage, unemployment insurance and social security were unimaginable in the first century under Roman rule.

For these reasons, the submissive slave paradigm ought to be rejected as a basis for employer-employee relations today. With much of its supporting rationale no longer historically relevant, it has minimal modern application.

The second serious deficiency of the submissive model is its overemphasis on the agent's duty of loyalty. While fidelity is a Christian virtue, ringing true to the biblical sense of service and self-sacrifice, it can become a dangerous vice if taken to an extreme. One need only repeat the discussion in chapter six of the Nazi war criminals who based their defense on loyalty and compliance with German law. A more recent illustration is the Watergate conspirator who allegedly said he "would walk over his grandmother in order to reelect the President."[19]

At a certain point, loyalty lapses into servility. As discussed in chapter four, Christian love neither endorses doormat loyalty nor condones abuse. Servile agents become passive "cogs-in-the-machine,"[20] "amoral technicians"[21] who merely comply with directives. They view themselves as being without true moral choice, blithely downplaying their obligation to God and community for the sake of their employer. Further, they neglect their duty of self-love by forfeiting their inalienable God-given rights of dignity and self-respect.[22] Ironically, servility may even prove harmful to employers in the long run. Servile employees often lose creativity and the ability to make independent judgments.[23]

Thomas Aquinas grappled with this problem in his thirteenth-century work *Summa Theologica*.[24] He argued that the Christian faith restricts employer power to a finite "sphere of authority." God grants employers authority so long as their directives conform to divine law. However, this influence is defaulted when they require "indiscreet obedience" (that is, behavior contrary to Scripture or natural law) from their employees. Subordinates ought not obey such commands, but rather report directly to God. This concept is roughly akin to the modern legal notion of jurisdiction. Just as the California state legislature cannot raise the taxes of Virginians, so employers lack the authority to issue unethical commands.

But, one might object, what of the employment contract? Does not contractual justice commit employees to a higher degree of responsiveness to their employers' desires? The answer to this question is both yes and no. Yes, employees agree to exchange their skills for compensation and to apply themselves diligently to assigned tasks. But no, they do not assent to abandon their personal ethics to comply with immoral imperatives. Such acquiescence, unless clearly stated, should not be implied in personal service contracts. On the contrary, employees have every right to assume that they are not contractually obliged to act unethically.[25] It is certainly prudent for prospective employees to raise such issues during the interview process so as to avoid moral misunderstandings.

The final flaw of the submissive model is that it tolerates "altruistic sinning." Altruistic sinning is the laying aside of one's own ethics to please another. It misconstrues Peter's admonition that slaves should be submissive not only to the kind master but "also to the overbearing [crooked, cruel, perverse]. For one is approved if . . . he endures pain while suffering unjustly" (1 Pet 2:18-19 RSV).

Business examples of altruistic sinning include the General Electric employees who engaged in price fixing. One commentator described them as men who "surrendered their own individualities to the corporate gods they served."[26] Similarly, Gulf Oil managers who made illegal political contributions were grudgingly praised by the Securities and Exchange Commission as individuals who "did not personally profit . . . and who desired to act solely in what they considered to be the best interests of Gulf and its shareholders."[27]

While Scripture praises those who suffer sacrificially on behalf of others, it nowhere endorses altruistic sinning. Peter continues:

> But if when you do right and suffer for it you take it patiently, you have God's approval. For to this you have been called, because Christ also suffered for you, leaving you an example, that you should follow in his steps. He committed no sin; no guile was found on his lips. . . . when he suffered, he did not threaten; but he trusted to him who judges justly. (1 Pet 2:20-23 RSV)

One must ask why a principal would unjustly punish an agent who is doing the right thing. Scholars speculate that Peter foresaw that slave owners would command their subordinates to commit immoral acts.[28] A careful reading of the text indicates that Peter encouraged neither obedience nor rebellion in such cases, but rather an imitation of the faultless Christ.

Transposed to the twentieth century, Peter first taught that Christian agents, even slaves, ought not compromise their ethical standards to benefit their principals. Like Christ, they should attempt to love God and their neighbors. Second, for taking this stand they should anticipate harassment. This might range from harmless teasing to outright termination. Such treatment is normative: Peter taught that as Christ suffered unjustly, so will his followers. Third, as Christ prayed for his oppressors, Christian agents ought not retaliate for unfair treatment received. Rather, they should forgive and rely on God to judge those who mistreat them. This may seem rather hopeful, but as one theologian comments: "The extraordinary optimism of the New Testament as to the effects of non-resistance is a permanent legacy."[29]

Analysis of the Purist Model

The purist model possesses many strengths and is strongly preferable to the submissive model. Preserving the agent's dignity, it casts him or her as a moral agent responsible for making independent judgments. Determinism is rejected in favor of free will.[30]

Society benefits from such autonomy because its interests are more likely to be taken into account. By broadly defining "neighbor," purists include stakeholders—community, customers, suppliers, fellow employees, competitors—other than their employer in the calculus of their decision-making. This point is well illustrated by the behavior of a quality-control officer on the trans-Alaska pipeline. In the face of strong management pressure, he refused to write a favorable report. His integrity has been credited for not only protecting the environment but also watching out for the long-term interests of his company's shareholders.[31] Finally, as discussed in chapter six, viewing law as a moral minimum rather than as a ceiling, the purist model encourages companies and their employees to surpass regulatory standards and aim for an ethic of excellence.[32]

This is not to say, however, that the paradigm is without difficulties. Two modes of application of the purist model are possible—a legalistic approach and an accommodating approach.

The legalistic purist. Legalists apply the purist model in its strictest sense. If a requested action bothers their consciences, they do not comply. In the hypothetical situations given above, they would refuse to sell pornographic videos, break their promises to customers, make contributions to the United Way or even sell cigarettes to customers.

This application of the purist model misapplies the concept of holiness in several ways. First, it assumes that a facile answer exists for every ethical dilemma. Legalists are tempted to suggest simple solutions to complex problems. This ignores the fact that while Christianity does provide guiding principles, it does not for the most part provide detailed technical rules of conduct. Rather than utilizing a legalistic approach to ethics, Christianity focuses on the spirit of the law. It recognizes that gray areas exist in which there may be reasonable disagreement.[33]

Further, one must be wary when speaking of a homogeneous Christian ethic. Scripture has been interpreted differently by a variety of church traditions—Catholic, Calvinist, Orthodox, Thomistic, Anabaptist, Reformed, Quaker, Lutheran and others—which focus on a wide variety of issues and values. For example, whereas a pacifist Catholic might have little ethical difficulty working in a winery and a teetotaling Free Methodist might give scant thought to being employed in a munitions factory, each would experience moral trauma were they to switch jobs.

Second, legalistic purists display a tendency toward self-righteousness and judgmentalism. They run the risk of developing a holier-than-thou attitude toward their supervisors and fellow employees. Such smugness smacks of pharisaism and is roundly condemned in Scripture.[34]

Third, this approach underemphasizes grace and mercy. Legalists often become perfectionists, failing to acknowledge that life is ambiguous and that all human beings fall short of the ideal. The doctrines of grace and mercy emphasize human fallibility and divine forgiveness. God is not to be viewed as an accountant keeping track of our merits and demerits. Rather, like a spouse, he is primarily concerned about the sincerity, love and motivation of his human partners.

Finally, legalistic purists often lack creativity in seeking solutions to ethical dilemmas. Too often they resort to a single tactic when given what they perceive to be an immoral command—the ultimatum. By immediately threatening to quit or to report up the line, they may not be acting prudently.

The accommodating purist. On first glance, this second mode of applying the purist model appears to be an oxymoron. How can an employee be both a purist and an accommodator? This is a tension with which the apostle Paul struggled. On the one hand, he drafted a scathing purist letter to the Galatians. On the other, he was flexible in his dealings with the Romans. Likewise Jesus, though certainly a purist in his focus on personal holiness, displayed tolerance toward others who fell short of his ethical standards. Four scriptural principles distinguish accommodating purists.

1. *They accommodate their employers as neighbors.* Accommodating purists are not insensitive to their supervisor, nor do they seek confrontation. To the contrary, they acknowledge their employers as neighbors to whom love is owed. Such neighbor love may include the forfeiture of certain rights as well as flexibility in decision-making. By way of illustration, Paul's associate Timothy agreed to be circumcised in order to placate his fellow

Jews (Acts 16:3). Likewise, Paul advised members of the church at Rome to avoid eating meat offered to idols, not because it was wrong but because it might offend others (Rom 14:1-4).

Note, however, that this principle of accommodation has two major limitations in the employer-employee context. First, it does not encourage employees to engage in altruistic sinning. Neither Timothy's circumcision nor abstinence from meat was an immoral act. No "ethical fudging" was involved, but rather the sacrificing of morally neutral rights. Exercising such flexibility for a supervisor is by no means inappropriate.

Second, accommodation of employers is predicated not on their status as employer but on their status as neighbor. As with any other neighbor—family, coworkers, friends—agents may give employers the benefit of the doubt in morally unclear contexts. Just as they might attend R-rated movies with friends, so they might follow their supervisor's lead in a business decision. In either case, however, they should change their course of action when their conscience is violated.

The critical point here is that employees owe the same degree of ethical deference to their employers as they do to other neighbors—no more, no less. Employers have no special privilege in this regard.

2. They are tolerant in morally ambiguous situations. When Paul wrote, "Now we see but a poor reflection as in a mirror" (1 Cor 13:12), he might as well have been speaking of the ethical uncertainty often confronting employees. For example, in the desk search situation described above, more facts are needed to determine the ethics of such an invasion of privacy. What is the motive of the supervisor? What potential harms are there in *not* conducting the search? What is the background of the other worker? Since privacy is not a categorical right but prima facie at best, such additional factors may alter one's conclusion. In such complicated cases it is not surprising that sincere and rational Christians often disagree as to the proper course of conduct.

Likewise, answers may vary if facts are changed in the video store case. What if only 1 percent of the videos are X-rated and they are kept away from minors? What if the employee in question is not a clerk but a janitor or an outside auditor who visits the store only once a year? What degree of contact with pornographic material, if any, is tolerable?

Even the United Way situation is a bit muddied for the antiabortionist employee by the facts that her donation will (1) benefit sixty-nine agencies providing human services unrelated to abortion, (2) have a minimal impact on abortion rights and (3) fund an abortion advocacy group, not one that actually performs abortions. To further confuse matters, it should be noted that not all Christian traditions consider all abortions to be immoral per se (such as in cases of rape or incest).

These cases illustrate the difficulty of drawing arbitrary ethical lines to fit every situation. When confronted by a complex moral choice, Christian employees may be capable of only approximating the best answer. Unlike their orthodox Jewish counterparts, they have no "fence around the Torah" to give them the "right" answer to every question. In ambiguous situations they must seek God's guidance and derive solace from God's mercy. Likewise, they should display tolerance for their supervisors and coworkers when they face similar circumstances.

3. *They are not paternalistic.* Scripture portrays God as valuing free will so highly that sinful behavior is permitted. Ought not then Christians, to a certain degree at least, do likewise? Is it not presumptuous to take on a role of paternalism that God himself, at least at present, refuses to play? The sale of cigarettes by a purist store clerk is an apt illustration. If he refuses to sell the product, is he inappropriately limiting the free choice of the consumer?

Obviously there are limits to this argument. For a zealous antiabortionist to serve as a nurse in an abortion clinic in the name of patients' free choice is patently absurd. The continuum of acceptable and unacceptable employee actions must take into account such issues as causation (direct or indirect), the person harmed (consumer or a third person) and the degree of injury (serious or minor).

4. *They facilitate positive solutions to ethical dilemmas.* Like Joseph and Nehemiah of the Old Testament, accommodating purists avoid needless confrontation with their employers and are positive contributors to the work environment (Gen 39:1-23; Neh 2:1-8). Establishment of a quality supervisor-subordinate relationship is perhaps the key to avoiding major ethical clashes. Managers are more likely to oblige hardworking, loyal, personable employees than those who are aloof, cold, rigid and self-righteous. Ongoing dialogue discloses employee ethical comfort zones and limits managers' surprise when subordinates balk at carrying out man-

dates that violate their religious ethics.

If supervisors persist in issuing such directives, employees should request a one-on-one meeting. With maximum tact, they should state their apprehension and, if necessary, their intent to disobey. If managers rescind their orders, employees should brace themselves for a measure of ostracism and take every opportunity to repair any breach in the relationship. On the other hand, if managers insist on compliance, employees should weigh their options and pursue the matter with upper management and/or their union representatives. Should these alternatives fail, employees must be prepared to find work elsewhere. As one scholar has observed, "The theologically and socially responsible Christian in a business organization, lonely as he often feels, is to stand at times apart from the outside existing structures. . . . It is precisely this . . . solitude that often marks the life of one called to play a prophetic role in society."[35]

The employment relationship between King Saul and David provides an apt summary illustration. As Saul became more jealous of his agent David (and consequently more irrational in his dealings with him), David attempted to be an accommodating purist agent—both serving Saul and maintaining his own integrity. Only when the situation became intolerable did he leave Saul's employment. Reflecting Peter's counsel, David adhered to his own convictions, suffered unjustly, sought no vengeance on his former employer, but found his vindication in God instead (1 Sam 18:1—19:18).

Questions for Discussion

I. Case for Discussion

Sovanny, a college student majoring in biology, works part time as a waitress for the Eager Eagle Restaurant. One evening an eight-month pregnant customer orders a double whisky before her meal. The following conversation occurs.

SOVANNY: *Oh, I don't think you want to do that. I just studied the serious harm that alcohol can cause to babies. Fetal alcohol syndrome is a serious problem.*

CUSTOMER: *Hey, this is my baby, not yours. Besides, your job is to serve me. Now get me my drink.*

SOVANNY: *Just a minute, please.*

Sovanny finds her manager, Bob, and expresses her concerns. After Bob discusses the matter directly with the customer, he orders Sovanny to deliver the drink. She refuses and is fired.

1. Has Sovanny acted correctly? What, if anything, would you have done differently?
2. What moral guidance do the concepts of this chapter provide in this case?

II. Workplace Application

1. Identify moral dilemmas you have experienced (or witnessed) in your role as an agent in the workplace.
2. In hindsight, were these dilemmas resolved in an ethical manner?

III. Concepts to Understand

How might each passage be applied to a business context?

1. Loyalty and Disloyalty

1 Samuel 24:1-22: Why does David spare King Saul's life? Since Saul is attempting to injure him, isn't David justified in acting likewise? Why does David feel so loyal to Saul?

2 Kings 5:1-27: What duty does the servant Gehazi owe his employer? Is his punishment too harsh?

Matthew 24:45-51: What duties do servants owe their masters?

Luke 7:1-10: Why does Jesus praise the Roman soldier? What principles about loyalty and obedience does he understand?

2. Additional Duties

Matthew 22:37-40: What additional duties does Jesus place on subordinates? Identify potential conflicts between these duties and the duty of loyalty already owed their supervisors.

3. The Superior-Subordinate Employment Relationship

Ephesians 6:5-9: Does this passage support the submissive or purist model? What does it say about reciprocal superior-subordinate rights/responsibilities?

Colossians 3:22—4:1: How does this passage differ from Ephesians 6:5-9? What does it add? subtract? What is the significance of these differences?

1 Peter 2:18-25: How does this passage differ from Colossians 3:22-4:1 and Ephesians 6:5-9?

4. Purist Model

Daniel 6:1-28: In what way is Daniel a purist agent? Is he more legalist or accommodationist? What principles can be taken from this story and applied to today's marketplace?

2 Samuel 12:1-5: What risk does Nathan take by confronting King David? What risk would he have taken if he had not done so?

1 Kings 22:1-38: In what way(s) is Micaiah a purist? What price does he pay for defending his principles?

Numbers 24:10-14: Why is Balaam reluctant to prophesy even though he is ordered to do so? What lessons can we learn from this story?

Matthew 2:7-12, 16: Why do the wise men disobey King Herod? Could/should they have been more accommodating toward him?

Matthew 10:34-39: What encouragement and direction does Jesus give purist agents?

Acts 5:27-29: How broadly should Peter's statement be interpreted by modern employees?

5. Accommodating Purist

1 Corinthians 9:22: Are there any limits to Paul's apparently open-ended statement to "become all things to all men"?

Romans 14:1-23; 1 Corinthians 8:1-13: What relevance, if any, does this passage about meat offered to idols have for the modern workplace? What principles can be gleaned?

Acts 16:1-4: Why does Paul ask Timothy to be circumcised? Is he being too accommodating?

6. Positive Relationship with Supervisor

Nehemiah 2:1-8: Describe Nehemiah's relationship with his superior. How does this aid him when he is confronted by a moral dilemma?

PART 3

TOPICS

8

HONESTY &
DECEPTION *(Part 1)*

The secret of life is honesty and fair dealing: if you can
fake that, you've got it made.
GROUCHO MARX

I would not tell a willful lie to save the souls of the whole world.
JOHN WESLEY

No one trivial lie undermines the liar's integrity. But the
problem for liars is that they tend to see most of their lies in
this benevolent light and thus vastly underestimate
the risks they run.
SISSELA BOK

Food gained by fraud tastes sweet to a man, but he ends up with
a mouth full of gravel.
PROVERBS 20:17

M*EDICINE FOR WHAT AILS YOU. One of the earliest national advertising campaigns commenced in 1875 and ran for nearly half a century.
"Lydia Pinkham's Vegetable Compound" was promoted as the "positive
cure for all female complaints" (understood to include everything from
menstrual cramps to a prolapsed uterus). Both the bottle and the print
advertisement had a photograph of Mrs. Pinkham, the perfect image of a
gray-haired grandmother. Testimonials were given by women about the
product's curative powers.*

*There were three things, however, about which the public was unaware.
First, the product had an 18 percent alcohol content. Second, Lydia
Pinkham had died years before. And third, the company spent 75 percent
of its revenues on advertising.*[1]

The next three chapters explore the concepts of honesty, deception and disclosure. All three topics represent pervasive concerns in the marketplace. Consumers doubt claims made by advertisers, government officials investigate statements made by corporate officials, and labor negotiators question whether they should ever be anything but skeptical about claims made by their management counterparts. Even business professors have reason to wonder whether they should trust their students. Studies indicate that business majors are more likely to cheat on exams or plagiarize term papers than other college students.[2] As an accounting student at the University of Dayton rationalized, "When you get to college, you don't follow the same rules [on honesty] your parents laid down."[3] The temptation to accelerate such "moral adjustments" only increases after graduation: sales quotas must be met, hoped-for promotions obtained, and shipment deadlines met. Unfortunately, honesty is often the first casualty in such pressure-cooker situations.

Honesty, deception and disclosure are concepts that are often difficult to apply with precision in the business environment. For instance, were the Lydia Pinkham's Vegetable Compound ads deceitful or merely coy? What duty, if any, did the company have to disclose full information to the consuming public? Was its only ethical obligation negative in nature—not to communicate misinformation—or did it have affirmative duties to reveal relevant information as well? These questions underscore the point that rule-book ethics—a list of simple "dos and don'ts" to be applied to every situation—is woefully inadequate. Truth telling, dishonesty and concealment are complex subjects that require more sophisticated analysis.

Honesty

CHRISTIAN CON MAN. In six years John Bennett built his Philadelphia-based New Era Philanthropy Foundation into a powerhouse charity. Claiming to be a broker for several anonymous donors, Bennett first gave away modest sums of money to several nonprofit organizations. Later he asked these same organizations to "invest" so that his foundation could double their income within six months. For a few years the plan worked. However, when the Securities and Exchange Commission began to investigate, Bennett's house of cards collapsed.

After New Era declared bankruptcy, Bennett admitted to the SEC that

*the anonymous donors never existed. "Investors" then were owed over
$550 million, but New Era had assets of only $80 million. It was alleged
that Mr. Bennett had secretively taken over $4 million for personal use.
Included among those who were tricked: Young Life, the University of
Pennsylvania, World Vision, Wheaton College and the Academy of Natural Sciences of Philadelphia. "I had every reason to trust him," said the
president of the Seminary of the East. "He had a reputation for Christian
values and commitment to Christ."[4]*

Ethicist Lewis Smedes contends that honesty is crucial for three reasons: it
builds trust, establishes community and protects the dignity of the audience.[5]

Trust. Without honest communication, trust is impossible. While we may
sneer at the "suckers" who were tricked by John Bennett, all cooperative
ventures require some measure of trust. Indeed, well-placed trust translates
into profit. Accountants can even quantify the value of honesty on a company's balance sheet as part of its "goodwill."[6] Partners rely on each other to
fulfill promises, supervisors expect subordinates to fulfill their tasks, and
buyers depend on suppliers to ship quality goods in a timely manner.

Studies indicate that workers who believe that their employers are truthful
work harder. When trust is breached, however, employee productivity slack-
ens.[7] Norman Bowie contrasts Chrysler employees, whose quality of work
suffered as a result of their distrust of management at the bargaining table a
number of years ago, with General Motors's Saturn employees, whose high
level of trust in the corporation has translated into superior quality and
productivity.[8] Another observer compares trust to a bank account. "Reputa-
tional capital," built up through many instances of truth telling, can be
overdrawn by a single act of deception.[9] This is as true in business as it is in
marriage. And since few lies exist in isolation, the first untruth "must be
thatched with another or it will rain through."[10]

Community. The second value of honesty is that it fosters community.
When individuals trust each other, relational networks are built. As trust is
more highly prized, greater expectations for honesty are placed on an
expanding web of individuals—managers, marketers and accountants. This
produces communities of trust. As Sissela Bok wisely observes, "The veneer
of social trust is often thin. . . . Trust is a social good to be protected just as
much as the air we breathe or the water we drink. When it is damaged, the

community as a whole suffers; and when it is destroyed, societies falter and collapse."[11]

PLAY THE GAME. Rita is a new manager with Crane Construction Company. One of her first tasks is to formulate the annual budget for her division. Over lunch, a peer advises her to "be sure to inflate your estimated expenses by 15 percent and to ask for a few positions you don't really need. Upper management will chop them out anyway. Also, don't worry too much about overspending. The company gives no incentives for carrying over surplus at the end of the fiscal year and gives no rewards for underspending."

Communities that are deficient in honesty quickly become cultures of deception. Rita's company will no doubt pay several long-term consequences as new employees learn that fiscal honesty is regarded as being naive. The results are all too common in corporate life—waste, closed communications, empire building, slush funds, turf wars, excessive documentation and intrigue. Companies that operate in this manner are inherently unstable because fear of embarrassing discoveries looms in every corner. Cover-ups blossom. As one author observes: "Without trust, we change from a community to a pack, from a society to a gang."[12]

Dishonesty also "debases the currency of language, making business communication less efficient and more cumbersome."[13] Since we trust each other less, more attorneys are needed to review documents. Is it any coincidence that as the virtues of truthfulness and trust have decreased in American society, the number of attorneys has skyrocketed to over 850,000? Similarly, since 24 percent of all résumés contain substantial false information,[14] is it any wonder that more sophisticated human resource personnel are needed to ferret out the truth about applicants? College admissions officers now find it necessary to double-check the veracity of financial aid claims of incoming students. This "truth audit" function not only indicates an erosion of community but also imposes a huge cost—in essence, a tax—on doing business.

It is no exaggeration to conclude that capitalism itself is at risk when honesty and trust are disregarded. Witness certain nations in Africa, the former Soviet Union and Asia where corruption is endemic. Cheating, bribing and distrust erode the very foundation of their economic systems.[15] As English author Samuel Johnson once observed, even demons do not lie to one another, because the society of hell could not exist without truthfulness.[16]

Dignity. The third value of honesty is that it respects the dignity of those to whom communications are directed. As image-bearers of God, recipients are entitled to accurate information so that they are able to make free and intelligent choices. In the medical field, doctors are required to provide patients with full data to ensure that all consent is fully informed. The concept of "informed consent" also applies to the marketplace, where the dignity of decision-makers (for example, consumers, shareholders, employees, partners) must be protected by giving them sufficient information to preserve their autonomous choices.

FOOL'S GOLD. *"The precious metals market was rocked when the principal managers of International Nesmont Industrial Corporation, a Canadian gold-refining firm selling stock over the New York Stock Exchange, were charged with criminal fraud. For six months before being discovered they had stockpiled brass instead of gold bars."*[17]

One ethicist has gone so far as to compare dishonesty to physical assault: both rob recipients of their freedom and dignity.[18] No doubt investors in the Canadian gold-refining company felt so violated.

Adam Smith, the father of capitalism, prized the notion of informed consent. For transactions to be truly voluntary, both parties must have access to accurate information. Otherwise they cannot deal for mutual benefit. While it may seem ironic to those who view capitalism as an incubator for dishonest practices, Smith taught that the market operates properly only if honest dealings are the norm.

Deception

SLEEPING SICKNESS. *Oversleeping for the third time in a month, Trish is late to work. In a panic about what to tell her supervisor, she concocts a story about having to care for a deathly ill aunt.*

OVERCHARGE. *Under pressure by his law firm to make his quota of two hundred billable hours per month, Kevin inflates the hours he has worked for Acme Corporation this week from thirty-five to thirty-nine hours. I'll make it up next month, Kevin tells himself as he fills out the billing statement.*

TRUTH VERSUS COST-BENEFIT ANALYSIS. Jeung's company manufactures and sells computer keyboards. In his negotiations with Fruitcake Computers, he promises to deliver a thousand TRX keyboards by July 1. While he knows that his company will be unable to deliver the goods prior to August 15, he does not inform his new customer for fear of losing its business. He calculates that the late-delivery charges written into the contract can be easily absorbed by his company.

Deception may be defined as purposefully leading others to believe something we ourselves do not believe. This may be done through a wide variety of means, including written communications, verbal statements, body language, disguises and even silence. To say that deceivers are generally held in low esteem is an understatement. In the fourteenth century Dante placed them in the eighth circle of hell. Only traitors were at a lower level, and of course betrayal itself is generally a form of deception.[19]

Lying, a subset of deception, includes three primary components. First, it requires intentionality. Innocently misinforming someone about street directions does not constitute lying, whereas purposeful misdirection does. Second, it involves communication. Thus concealment, though often deceptive, does not constitute a lie. This subject will be discussed in greater detail in chapter ten. Third, the deceiver believes that the audience accepts the untruth as fact. See figure 8.1.

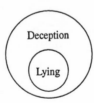

Figure 8.1

Scripture strongly condemns deception because it is diametrically opposed to God's holy-just-loving character. Indeed, "it is impossible for God to lie" (Heb 6:18), for he keeps all his promises (Num 23:19) and communicates nothing but the truth (Rom 3:3-4). Rather, deception is a primary attribute of Satan, who, Jesus warned, has "no truth in him. When he lies, he speaks his native language, for he is a liar and the father of lies" (Jn 8:44).

The ethical purity and moral separation required by holiness call for guileless behavior in the realm of truth telling. Of those who enter heaven, it is written that "no lie is found in their mouths; they are blameless" (Rev 14:5). Deceitful individuals, on the other hand, are held accountable to God, ultimately threatened with eternal judgment (see, for example, Rev 21:8, 27). Trish, Kevin and Jeung would be well advised to heed this warning.

Justice likewise condemns deception. Due process obliges Trish and Jeung to give honest information so that those to whom they are accountable (supervisor and customer, respectively) can make appropriate decisions. Kevin's lying also raises several justice concerns. By overbilling his corporate client, he infringes on its property rights and breaches his firm's contractual obligations. Further, by claiming to do more work than he has actually done, he undercuts the notion of merit within the firm. If pay, promotions and assignments are based in part on billable hours, he is acting unfairly vis-à-vis his fellow attorneys. Compensatory justice now requires him to admit his wrongdoing to the firm and to ensure that his overcharging is corrected.

Finally, love requires empathy, mercy and the sacrificing of rights for others. Certainly Trish, Kevin and Jeung have displayed none of these characteristics in their dissemblings. Love demands communication that is open, sincere and caring, not that which is secretive, manipulative and selfish.

Deception can lead to unforeseen, and often disastrous, consequences. As noted earlier, it attacks the very roots of honesty—trust, community and dignity. Scripture produces several relevant examples. When Jacob pretended to be his brother Esau in seeking a blessing from Isaac, their blind father, he destroyed the bond of trust between himself and his brother, splintered the family community, and violated Isaac's right to bestow his blessing on Esau and Esau's right to receive it (Gen 27:1-45). Long-term relationships were sacrificed for the sake of illicit short-term gain. Likewise, when Jacob's sons lied about the fate of their brother Joseph and Jacob later learned the truth, his confidence in them was undermined. Their lies nearly destroyed the family unit and certainly infringed on Jacob's dignity to make fully informed choices (Gen 37:19-36; 43:1—45:28).

Similarly, when Joseph was falsely accused by Potiphar's wife, his master's trust was destroyed and he was thrown into jail (Gen 39:1-23). Much more could certainly be said about Jeremiah's bemoaning a general lack of trustworthiness (Jer 9:4-8), Judas's betrayal of Jesus (Jn 13:18-30), and Paul's admonition to "put off falsehood and speak truthfully to [your] neighbor" (Eph 4:25).

Is Deception Ever Justified?

In an ideal world, our analysis would end here. Honesty, a virtue that reflects holiness-justice-love, is to be diligently pursued while the vice of deception is to be scorned. For while the former builds up trust, community and dignity, the latter—like a hungry termite in soft wood—devours credibility, cohesion and integrity. Unfortunately, our world is imperfect: sin has eroded both our ability to speak and hear the truth clearly. As a result, Norman Bowie writes of "ideal" versus "acceptable exchanges" in the marketplace, with the latter category providing some room for minor deceptions, ambiguities and selective concealments.[20]

Historically, the church has been divided as to whether exceptions to the general principle of truth telling exist. Several of the early church fathers— including Clement of Alexandria, Origen and Chrysostom—permitted untruths to be told if the cause was just and necessary.[21] Martin Luther went further, identifying "helpful lies" that are justified by the deceiver's altruistic motives.[22] Anglican priest Joseph Fletcher, discussed in chapter four, opened the floodgates by totally subordinating truth telling to his definition of love. Fletcher's analysis justifies any deception so long as it is motivated by love.

While orthodox Christianity rejects Fletcher's approach, many scholars do consider deception to be a viable alternative if certain conditions exist. These include the following: Have all other honest options been exhausted? Is the situation sufficiently dire? Is the deceiver's motive selfless? From this perspective, honesty is the general rule and deception the exception. Deception requires a reason: honesty does not. In other words, the deceiver must carry the burden of proof to justify his behavior.[23]

Other Christian thinkers have not been so sanguine about the idea of exceptions to truth telling. Augustine, for instance, compared the concept of "just lies" to "chaste adultery."[24] For him the debate about possible exceptions was resolved by the Scripture: "No lie comes from the truth" (1 Jn 2:21). Reformer John Calvin and Methodist founder John Wesley followed Augustine in adhering to this uncompromising position.[25]

While all lying was sinful to Augustine, he did fudge a bit in describing eight levels of the sin with decreasing levels of punishment.[26] Taking liberty to apply his teachings to the marketplace today, he would punish selfish liars more (for example, false advertisers and embezzlers) and altruistic liars less (for example, flatterers and protectors of fellow employees).

Following Augustine's lead, the ninth-century Irish church relied heavily on the penitent's motive to determine the appropriate sanction. Selfish liars were to receive either three days of silence or seven hundred lashes on the wrist, while altruistic liars were obligated to perform no penance whatsoever.[27] Critics quickly pointed to what they perceived to be a fatal flaw in this approach, however. If liars knew in advance that their "officious" (helpful, loving, altruistic) lies would be pardoned, what moral constraints would they feel about such lying? Further, did not such an approach cheapen the very notions of sin and repentance?

Others in the medieval church sought a way around the strictness of Augustine's position. Utilizing a doctrine called "mental reservation," speakers were not considered to be lying even if they intentionally stated untruths *so long as* they added information *in their minds* that would make their communications true.[28] For instance, if a supervisor were to say to a subordinate, "Your evaluation is average," while making the inaudible mental reservation that *it is average for the group of incompetents about to be fired,* she would not be lying. Or if a retailer were to respond negatively to the question "Do you think this lamp will sell well?" while silently adding mentally *at the Salvation Army thrift store,* no deceit is said to result.

Obviously such an approach is highly suspect and was quickly rejected by the church. It does, however, point out the extent to which some will go to identify exceptions to the principle of honesty. For while Augustine's absolutist position solves one problem—moral inconsistency—it creates another—a lack of flexibility in difficult situations. And as we shall see in the next chapter, the tension between these two has serious ramifications for the business practitioner.

Questions for Discussion

I. Case for Discussion

Two weeks after giving birth to her first child, a girl, Jan triumphantly visited the office to show off her daughter. She beamed as she asked her supervisor, Hue, "Isn't this the most beautiful child you've ever seen?"

Unfortunately, Hue thought she had never seen such an ugly combination of flab and wrinkles. Though inwardly comparing the baby to a prune, she wisely responded: "My, she is a healthy one."

These were not, however, the words Jan longed to hear. Pressing the issue, she asked: "You do think she is physically beautiful, don't you?"

1. How should Hue respond to Jan's second question?

2. Is lying ever justified? If so, when?

II. Workplace Application

1. Describe a workplace deception you have witnessed. Did it undercut trust, community and the dignity rights of others? What other impacts did it have?

2. Have you ever witnessed what you considered to be a "justified deception" in your work? Explain.

III. Concepts to Understand

How might each passage be applied to a business context?

1. Trust

Deuteronomy 27:17-18: How do these particular deceits affect trust? What are the long-term consequences of such behavior?

2 Kings 5:1-27: In what manner did Elisha's servant Gehazi violate his master's trust? What was the outcome of his dishonesty?

Romans 3:9-18: What impact does deceitfulness have on relationships?

2. Community

2 Kings 12:6-15: How does the honesty of the temple workers affect the Hebrew community?

Jeremiah 9:1-9: What eventually happens to a society built on deception?

Acts 5:1-11: How do Ananias and Sapphira's lies affect the early Christian community?

Ephesians 4:20-5:2; 1 Peter 3:8-17: How does honesty build up community? How does dishonesty destroy it?

3. Dignity

Leviticus 6:1-7: Whose rights are being protected? What sanctions are imposed on those who breach their duties?

1 Kings 21:1-26: What rights do Jezebel and Ahab violate? How does their behavior violate principles of holiness, justice, love, trust and community?

Micah 6:9-15: What punishments await those who deprive others through deception?

2 Corinthians 4:1-2; 11:13-15: How does Paul protect the dignity/free will rights of his audience? How do the false teachers violate these rights?

4. Deception as Contrary to God's Character

1 Samuel 15:27-29: According to the prophet Samuel, how is God different from King Saul?

John 14:6, 15-17; Titus 1:2: What is the association between each member of the Trinity and the concept of truth?

Romans 3:3-4: How does Paul contrast human nature with God's character?

Numbers 23:19; Hebrews 6:16-19: How are God's promises different from human promises? What does promise keeping have to do with lying?

5. Holiness and Honesty

Job 31:4-6: In what light does Job consider honesty to be an important virtue?

Psalm 15:1-5: What are David's criteria for the development of a close relationship with the Lord?

Colossians 3:5-10: What is the significance of Paul's placing lying and slander in this list of vices? Why should we avoid such behavior?

Revelation 14:5: What virtues do these 144,000 people possess?

6. Justice and Honesty

Exodus 23:1-8; Proverbs 14:5: In what ways does dishonesty undercut justice?

Psalm 5:1-12; 120:1-4: What does the psalmist pray regarding liars?

Luke 3:10-14: How does John the Baptist view honesty and justice?

Revelation 21:6-8: What ultimate outcome awaits liars? Why is dishonesty lumped together with this particular list of vices?

7. Love and Honesty

Leviticus 19:16-18: How do love and honesty intersect?

Proverbs 12:17-20; 24:26: In what ways does truthfulness foster love and peace?

Ephesians 4:14-16: What does it mean to "speak the truth in love"? Is there any tension between the two virtues of love and truth speaking?

9

HONESTY & DECEPTION *(Part 2)*

I try to be honest, but who can be honest *and live?*
NEW YORKER MAGAZINE

A lie is also a useful thing.
JAPANESE PROVERB

What is worse than doing evil is being evil. It is worse
for a liar to tell the truth than for a lover of truth to lie.
DIETRICH BONHOEFFER

Men are so simple that . . . one who deceives will always
find those who allow themselves to be deceived.
NICCOLÒ MACHIAVELLI

C HAPTER EIGHT CONCLUDED WITH A BRIEF DISCUSSION ABOUT EXCEP-
tions to honesty. Is deception ever justifiable? Augustine, Calvin and Wesley
thought not, but Luther, Bonhoeffer and others disagreed. This chapter will
explore the plausibility of five possible deviations from truth telling—conflicting duties, mutual deceits, no right to hear the truth, exaggeration and
ambiguity.

Conflicting Duties

*INFORMATION LEAK. Tom is the public relations officer for Universal
Chemical Company (UCC). A minor chemical leak has occurred at one
of UCC's plants, and Tom has been assured by UCC scientists that no
long-term risks have been created for the local community.*

Yesterday a former employee of UCC informed the media of the leak, presenting Tom with an unpleasant moral dilemma. If he admits that a problem exists, irrational panic among community members may force the plant to be temporarily closed. This would cost UCC shareholders a great deal of money and result in significant job loss for UCC employees. On the other hand, it would be untrue to deny the problem. Tom is torn by his loyalty to UCC, personal integrity concerns and the potential consequences of his actions. He is confident, however, that if he chooses to lie, UCC can cover up any traces of the leak.

What happens when the duty of truth telling conflicts with another moral duty? Two biblical stories cause particular difficulty for those who adhere to Augustine's strict prohibition against lying. In the first instance, Jewish midwives misled the Egyptian king after he had commanded that they put to death all Hebrew male infants. Rather than follow the king's mandate, the midwives delivered the babies and concocted a story about the ability of Israelite women to give birth without any medical assistance. In the second, the prostitute Rahab saved the lives of several Hebrew spies by lying to Jericho's soldiers about their whereabouts. In both situations the misrepresentations were intentional, communicated and believed by the hearers. Yet in neither instance does Scripture criticize the women for their actions. To the contrary, they are praised and rewarded (Ex 1:15-22; Josh 2:1-24; see also New Testament praise for Rahab in Heb 11:31 and Jas 2:25).

Rejecting Augustine's absolutist stance has its risks. If lying is ethically justifiable in those situations where truth telling conflicts with the obligation to protect life—as it appears to do with the midwives and Rahab—might not this rationale be extended to include other duties as well? For example, in the case above, could Tom argue that his obligations to protect the property rights of UCC shareholders and the job rights of employees supersede his responsibility to tell the truth?

The logical result of this approach is a hierarchical ranking of duties, with the preservation of life heading the list. When moral duties conflict, the lesser of two evils is the preferable selection. Those who accept this view are divided as to whether deception in such exceptional situations is morally permissible or morally wrong (albeit subject to a lesser punishment).

A second interpretation of the midwives and Rahab situations is to conclude that no lying occurred at all, since coercion was involved. By way of illustration, if a client were to put a gun to an attorney's head and demand that she lie, few would hold her ethically accountable. Such coercion removes the voluntary aspect of deception. If self-defense is an accepted exception to murder, some argue, lying should likewise be permitted in such high-stakes situations.

The problem with this approach in the marketplace, however, is that coercion rarely rises to life-and-death status. If Tom's superior were to force him to lie with the threat of dismissal if he refused, the measure of coercion would not be life-threatening. Since pressures to make moral compromises are often present, we must be extremely chary of extending the concept of coercion beyond the most extreme situations.

A third interpretation of the midwives and Rahab accounts is to conclude that while they were applauded for their fidelity to the Lord, Scripture nowhere honors their deception. It was, in essence, a forgivable sin, fitting eighth on Augustine's list of lies. One might argue that if Rahab, a brothel madam, had had more faith, the Lord would have provided her with a more ethically acceptable means of action. This more mystical approach posits that whenever two duties conflict, faith finds a noncompromising way out of the moral labyrinth (see 1 Cor 10:13). Following this view, Tom should pray and consult with a few close friends to come up with a creative alternative that would permit him both to tell the truth and to minimize collateral economic damage to innocent shareholders and employees. While this is the easiest and most satisfying answer, its plausibility in every situation is subject to debate.

Whether we utilize Augustine's view (all lying is sinful, but benevolent deception should receive a lighter punishment), coercion analysis (some lying is not sinful because it is not really voluntary) or a more mystical approach (God will always provide a means of escape so that no moral duty need be violated), tolerance of lying must be narrowly tailored to exceptional life-and-death situations involving the protection of innocent people. Stretching it to include situations comparable to the one in which Tom finds himself would appear to exceed biblical bounds.

Mutual Deceits

DO IT TO OTHERS BEFORE THEY DO IT TO YOU. A survey indicates that 46 percent of business practitioners approve of obtaining nonpublic infor-

mation from a competitor by having an employee pose as a graduate student working on a thesis. Eighty-six percent believe that their competitors would use this method against them.[1]

ALL'S FAIR IN LOVE, WAR AND BUSINESS. *A factory owner falsely claims that he would be forced into bankruptcy if his workers were to go on strike for higher wages. Fearful of losing their jobs, the employees agree to a lesser pay package.*

The second commonly cited exception to the duty of truth telling is when those receiving communications are on notice that what is being communicated is untrue, so-called mutual deceits. For example, when an actor claims to be Romeo, the audience understands that he is not who he is claiming to be. Nontruth telling is justified because everyone understands the fiction. If, with a wink and a smile, a mother informs her daughter that there is a dinosaur in the backyard, the child knows that some type of game is being played.

Likewise, when a basketball player fakes left and then dribbles right, the defender ought not be surprised or consider this to be unfair, because faking is understood to be an acceptable part of the sport. Extending the concept to the professional realm, when attorneys enter not-guilty pleas for their clients fully intending to later plea-bargain for a reduced charge, most of us would concur that no lying has occurred. Within the courtroom context, everyone understands that the initial plea is not the attorney's final word on the subject. Similarly, the intentionally misleading feints used by Joshua in his Canaan campaign (Josh 8:3-17) or by General Dwight Eisenhower before the invasion of France in 1944 are not generally regarded as deceptive, because the enemy did not expect the truth to be told.

Taking the concept to an extreme, envision a child's game called "Lying," where for ten minutes everyone agrees to tell nothing but lies. In this context, someone telling the truth would actually be the liar! Why? Because the audience has been put on notice that only lies will be communicated. Truth telling can itself become deceptive.

The last chapter noted that lying involves both the speaker's intentions and the audience's expectation to receive the truth. If, as in war, sports, theater or the game "Lying," the speaker knows that the audience does not expect the truth to be told and, in addition, the audience does not believe the communication to be true, arguably no lie has been told. Untruthfulness is not the total sum of lying: the speaker's motives, the hearer's expectations and the speaker's knowledge of those expectations are also essential factors. Thus if a car manufacturer's advertisement shows one of its vehicles climbing straight up a mountain, the audience is on notice that the message is not to be taken seriously. Likewise, if a diet soda company shows its customers floating among the clouds after drinking its product, consumers understand that the claim is not intended to be literally true.

It is important to note, however, that acceptance of the concept of mutual deceit is quite distinct from the doctrine of dual morality discussed in chapter five. According to the theory of mutual deceits, nontruths are permissible not because they occur in the rough-and-tumble of the marketplace rather than in one's personal life (as per dual morality), but because they do not constitute lies. If the speaker knows that the audience understands the communication to be untrue—as in teasing, acting and silly advertising—no deception has occurred. The primary issue with mutual deceits is not whether the communication has occurred in business or in private life, but whether the audience has been informed by the speaker that truthfulness cannot be expected.

Dual morality, on the other hand, stands for the proposition that dishonesty is tolerable in the business environment because of the intensity of competition. The intent of the speaker and the expectation of the hearer are irrelevant. Unilateral deceptions are justified in the name of "winning." Mutual deceits, on the other hand, involve an understanding on the part of both the speaker and audience that honesty cannot be expected.

In tolerating the concept of mutual deceits in limited situations, we must not underestimate its potential for involving serious moral dangers. The concept of justifiable nontruths is so volatile that it must be pigeonholed into a relatively small corner of ethical theory, to be applied only when all parties possess equal information and fully understand the "rules" of the communication.

The rarity of morally permissible mutual deceits should caution us against their use in the marketplace. When Volvo reinforced the ceiling of one of its vehicles for the sole purpose of withstanding the pressure created by a "bigfoot" truck driven over its roof in a hot-rod show, the audience could not have anticipated such a falsehood.[2] The deceit was unilateral, not mutual. Likewise, when an appliance store engages in "bait and switch" practices by luring customers with promises of special deals on certain items and then switching them to more expensive products, it alone possesses the relevant information. In doing so, these companies resemble the biblical rancher Laban, who baited his nephew Jacob with one unmarried daughter only to switch her with another at the last minute (Gen 29:15-30).

The problem of applying the concept of mutual deceits to the business environment is compounded by the fact that some groups lack the sophistication to effectively distinguish between true and untrue messages. Children, for example, are relatively incapable of separating fact from fiction. Not able to fully understand the tactics of adult marketers, they become easy prey. The apostle Paul would no doubt chide advertisers who hide behind the concept of mutual deceits vis-à-vis children (see Eph 4:14). Immigrants, before learning subtle cultural signals, are likewise often easy targets when they buy big-ticket items such as automobiles, appliances or real estate. Senior citizens, fearful for their personal and financial security, may be unaware of the manipulative sales tactics used by home security systems companies and financial advisers. People in emotional situations, such as at the death of a family member, are often incapable of rational analysis. Professionals who regularly deal in such situations—for example, funeral directors—have no legitimate justification for utilizing the doctrine of mutual deceits.

Even in situations where both parties have roughly the same level of moxie and business experience, mutual deceit rarely functions properly. In negotiations, both parties seldom possess equal information. Management negotiators generally have greater access to data than do their union representative counterparts. The relationship between realtors and prospective buyers is similar. When those who have access to inside information communicate, the listeners are at a serious disadvantage. If negotiators are to engage in morally acceptable mutual deception, they must make sure that the other party is aware of their intentions up front—for example, "Don't believe a word I say." Of course such a statement would be self-defeating, because a minimal level of trust is necessary to proceed in any negotiation.

Finally, business practitioners are ill-advised to engage in mutual deceit, because it often negatively affects innocent parties. Take the example of two competing companies, referred to in the case above, which have a well-known dog-eat-dog attitude toward each other. If in order to obtain nonpublic pricing information about the other, one company hires a college intern to pose as a legitimate researcher, what collateral damage might the student suffer? What impact would getting caught have on her career? on her views of professional honesty? The consequence of such behavior is quite different from the situation where a mother discusses the Easter Bunny with her child or an actress claims to be Shakespeare's Juliet.

In sum, the concept of mutual deceit is so ethically perilous because it has the tendency to chip away at ethical purity, erode due process and undercut love toward others. It should be utilized only in carefully prescribed situations where no deception is possible because everyone clearly understands the rules and innocent outsiders cannot be negatively affected. Since such sanitary procedures are nearly impossible to implement in the marketplace, it remains at best an isolated theoretical curiosity.

No Right to Hear the Truth

YOUR MONEY OR YOUR HONESTY. A robber insists that Regina, a clerk in a fast-food restaurant, put all of the available cash into a bag. After completing her task, the thief asks her, "Is that all of it?" She answers "yes" even though she knows another drawer of cash is nearby.

SINCE YOU ASKED... During a job interview, a supervisor asks Lisa what her husband's professional plans would be if she were offered the position and her family had to move. Recognizing this to be a question prohibited by law, she answers untruthfully: "If you hire me, he already has a fine job lined up here."

TO CATCH A THIEF. Gary suspects that someone is entering his office during the evenings. To catch the individual, he drafts a false memo and leaves it on his desk. When the information contained in the memo circulates back to him, he is able to track down the trespasser.

Regina, Lisa and Gary all justify their deceptive behavior by arguing that they have no duty to tell the truth in their respective situations. Why? Because, like the Nazis who asked Dutch citizens about the location of Jews hiding in their homes during World War II, the robber, supervisor and trespasser have all forfeited their right to the truth. This exception to truth telling differs from mutual deceit in that one party does not consent to the deception. While this position is not widely held among Christian ethicists, it does have a measure of appeal.

From this perspective the Hebrew midwives' deception was not unethical, because Pharaoh lacked the moral right to command them to commit genocide on innocent children. Rahab's untruthfulness to the soldiers of Jericho was permissible because they had no right to inquire about the spies she was hiding. Since no right existed, no corresponding duty to tell the truth came into play.[3] In a similar vein, King Solomon's artificial threat to cut a baby in half could be justified by the lies of one of the women claiming to be the child's mother (1 Kings 3:16-28). Likewise, advocates of this perspective argue that Joseph's tricking his deceptive brothers into risking their lives for their youngest brother Benjamin was a permissible deception because the brothers had forfeited the right to be told the truth by their earlier immoral act of selling Joseph into slavery (Gen 43:1—45:3).

As appealing as this exception to honesty may appear on the surface, it raises at least four serious concerns. First, it is difficult to accept the notion that an intentional misrepresentation can be justified by the other person's nonright to an honest answer. A lie is still a lie even if the hearer possesses low moral character. In the robbery case involving Regina, for example, it is much easier to justify her lie on other theories—for example, coercion or fearfulness induced by a life-and-death situation—rather than on the robber's lack of rights to expect the truth.

Second, this exception escalates the use of dishonesty by not reserving it as the final alternative. In the situations involving Lisa and Gary, for instance, other means could have been employed to deal with their unusual situations. Perhaps Lisa could have told her interviewer that his question was inappropriate and Gary could have set up a hidden camera. Acceptance of the notion that the other person has forfeited his or her right to be told the truth encourages dishonesty. Only when all other options have been exhausted should nontruthfulness even be considered. It is clearly a last-resort alternative.

Third, while lying to liars may appease some sense of compensatory justice (that is, an eye for an eye), it does not comport well with holiness and love. Ethical purity cautions us not to stoop to their lower ethical level lest we become like them. Higher moral ground, not the lowest common denominator, should be sought.[4] Further, Scripture encourages us to love our enemies and not to return evil for evil, but good for evil (Rom 12:14-20). Love's unconditionality argues against forfeiture of the right to be told the truth.

Fourth, deception often opens a Pandora's box of unforeseen negative consequences. Lying to liars may reinforce their sense that such behavior is normative. Further, serious mistakes may be made. What if a lie is communicated to a person whom the speaker wrongly presumes to be acting deceptively? Not only is that person wrongly harmed, but the scope and impact of lying are greatly increased as trust is broken. Further, dishonesty also has a way of backfiring on the speaker. What if, for example, in Lisa's situation, the interviewer was asking about her husband's employment situation in order to suggest possible job leads for him? In that case Lisa's deception would work against her own self-interest. Like boomerangs, lies often come back to the speaker at unexpected angles and velocities.

Exaggeration

REFERENCE INFLATION. Phil calls Joanna, his past supervisor, to ask for a reference for a promotion. When she consents, Joanna receives an evaluation form that asks her to rank Phil by percentile. Compared to other subordinates, Joanna would place Phil in about the sixty-fifth percentile. She realizes, however, that if she evaluates him at that level he will have little chance of being promoted. Rationalizing that other supervisors regularly inflate their ratings, she ranks him at the ninetieth percentile.

CLEAN STRETCH. Howard works for an advertising firm. A client asks him to develop an advertising campaign that says that its product will "clean in one application." While it is possible that it can perform this feat occasionally, Howard feels that such a claim would be stretching the truth.[5]

Many business practitioners feel that exaggeration is morally permissible in situations where no harm results. Such minor stretches of the truth permit pharmaceutical companies to claim that their pain relievers are "20 percent stronger than aspirin," 2 percent higher than reality; tire companies to boast that their tires drive as well in wet conditions as in dry when in fact there is a slight variance; and automobile manufacturers to claim that their electronic systems "never" need tuning. Exaggerated statements that cause no harm, they contend, should be permitted. Speech is not a precise science, it is argued, and a measure of truth-stretching is to be expected in human communication.

The claim that exaggeration is morally acceptable warrants several responses. First, exaggeration erodes communication and trust. When supervisors like Joanna artificially inflate their recommendations, honest managers are put in the awkward moral position of harming their former subordinates by telling the truth. Over time, human resource directors begin to discount the value of such recommendations because they represent watered-down reflections of reality. When patterns of deception become normative, a strong sense of cynicism arises. People simply stop believing each other, necessitating the creation of other fictions to compensate for the lack of honesty.

Second, what the exaggerator may perceive as being harmless embellishment may look and sound quite different to the audience. If, in the case above, Howard decides to follow his client's advice and claim that the product "will clean in one application," he may make a few more sales in the short term. However, he will also reinforce the jaundiced view that many consumers already have toward all advertisers' claims. Likewise, while a supervisor's comment to a subordinate that her work is "absolutely great" may be merely gratuitous chatter, the latter may interpret it as an indication of a possible pay raise or promotion.

Third, defenders of overstatement point to Jesus' exaggerated exhortations in encouraging his followers to gouge out their eyes if they lead to sinful behavior (Mk 9:43-48), to "hate" family members (Lk 14:26) and to renounce wealth because it is "easier for a camel to go through the eye of a needle than for a rich man to enter the kingdom of heaven" (Mt 19:24). On the surface this argument has a measure of appeal. On deeper reflection, however, it becomes apparent that there is a vast moral difference between Jesus' use of hyperbole—a form of speech the audience understood as being used for emphasis—and exaggeration, which alters the truth itself. While the former is used to punch home a point, the latter is employed to stretch the truth. As noted above, speaking the precise truth is only part of the picture. How the audience interprets the communication is equally critical.

Even purely "altruistic lies" are fraught with moral difficulties. Though intended for the highest purposes—for example, to aid a student, protect a colleague, assist a client or safeguard a community—such fabrications demean the people deceived (by presuming that they are incapable of dealing with the truth), erode the character of the liar (by undercutting his or her trustworthiness in the future) and often result in only short-term good (by ignoring long-term consequences).[6] Acceptance of the concept of altruistic lies quickly slides into a form of Fletcherism in which nearly any deceptive practice can be justified.

Ambiguity

PRETICKET TO RIDE. Carolina Textile Corporation (CTC) manufactures children's clothing. Heeding the request of many of its retail store customers, CTC has begun to "preticket" many of its product lines. This practice includes placing tags on items at inflated "suggested retail prices." In this manner consumers are led to believe that retailers are selling at cut-rate prices when in fact they are not.

A CLUB WITHOUT WALLS. Burger King advertises its "Kid's Club" as "fun, non-stop" with images of bouncing, happy children in a play area. In many locations, however, the real club offers only a membership card and some stickers.[7]

CHOCOLATE POTATOES ON A SUGAR CONE PLEASE. Hawks Ice Cream Company has great difficulty shooting a television ad because its ice cream keeps melting under the hot camera lights. Finally the marketing director comes up with what she thinks is a brilliant idea—replacing the ice cream with mashed potatoes.

Ambiguity comes in two forms—intentional and unintentional. Since the latter is present to some degree in every communication and is not motivated by the desire to mislead, our focus will be on the former. A rather humorous example of intentional ambiguity involved the early church father Athanasius. When asked by government persecutors sent to arrest him, "Where is the traitor Athanasius?" he responded, "Not far away."[8] This is not a lie—no untruth was communicated. Was he, however, deceptive via ambiguity?

Today ambiguities are often created by visual images. Grocers turn the "pull dates" on milk hoping that buyers will purchase the older milk first. Employees leave telltale signs that they are still at the office—planting coats and briefcases in appropriate locations and leaving computer screens on and doors open—while they are out running personal errands.

Ambiguities are also produced by "weasel words." Products claim to give relief for "up to" ten hours, provide "as much" relief "as the more expensive brand," "help" reduce cold symptoms and "virtually" eliminate any lingering aftereffects. All of these words are open to interpretation. What exactly does the toothpaste claimed to "help prevent cavities" do? Is Oil of Olay really able to keep its advertised promise to "help keep skin looking young"?

Some ambiguities are necessary and/or relatively harmless. Using mashed potatoes as a prop for an ice cream advertisement may be the only choice available and, so long as the ad does not deal with such matters as ice cream texture, will not deceive anyone.[9] To be completely aboveboard, of course, the company might briefly explain that props are being used. From an ethical perspective, the more the audience understands the better.

Other ambiguities are less benign. Carolina Textile Corporation's preticketing of its products, for example, is a calculated means by which to deceive customers into believing that they are getting a better deal from retail stores than they really are. Burger King's marketing strategy is also difficult to excuse. Although the company never directly states that its Kid's Clubs are similar to the playrooms provided by its prime competitor, McDonald's, its advertisements clearly give that impression. Likewise, banks that promise short-term high-yield return on individual retirement accounts (IRAs) but bury the declining long-term rate in fine print create deceptive impressions.[10]

Ambiguity is also present in Scripture. When Abraham told two different kings that Sarah was his sister, he was not lying, since she was in fact his half-sister. Nevertheless, he misled them by creating the impression that she was not his wife (Gen 12:10-20; 20:1-18). As one scholar notes, "Language is a soul-thing, not just a tongue-thing. It is a spiritual transaction."[11] Misleading impressions can be every bit as misleading as spoken or written lies.

Another form of ambiguity is the marketing of products and services by falsely associating them with ease and gratification. Cigarette companies lure younger customers by presenting images of hipness (Joe Camel) and physical attractiveness (Virginia Slims). Such images have nothing to do with the actual insidious affects of these products. Likewise, beer companies promise fun, friendship and sex appeal. The more common effects of heavy beer consumption—obesity, irrational behavior and addiction—are not portrayed. Automobile manufacturers often take a similar tack, implying that their vehicles provide self-esteem and power.[12] While there is nothing unethical per se about the concept of ambiguity by association—for example, placing toilet paper near a waterfall or a bicycle in front of a sunset—companies must be careful not to lead less sophisticated viewers to false conclusions about their products.

Concluding Thoughts

Honesty in commercial dealings builds trust, fosters community and respects the dignity of others. Deception is therefore to be accommodated, if at all, in very limited circumstances. The five possible exceptions to the duty of truth telling discussed in this chapter give very little wiggle room for marketplace deception.

First, deception might be permitted in life-and-death situations, but even this slight exception is disputed by many who would take a more mystical ethical approach.

Second, mutual deceits, when properly applied, are not really deceptions at all. Since both parties understand that the communications are untrue, neither expects the truth to be told. However, as we have noted, this theory is rarely applied in a balanced and open manner. Erroneous assumptions are made that the other party understands the altered moral rules. All too often the result is some form of unilateral deceit. The moral slope is slippery indeed, and it is advisable to avoid mutual deceits as much as possible.

Third, the notion that deceivers lose their right to be told the truth lacks direct scriptural support. Rather, we are told to love our enemies and to do good to those who do us evil.

Fourth, exaggerations alter the truth, generally to service selfish motives. Even in those situations where the deception is altruistic, trust is eroded and the people who are misled are demeaned.

Finally, intentional ambiguities rely on unequal access to information and prey on less sophisticated audiences.

For all of these reasons, while honesty is not always easy or profitable—at least in the short term—it is the surest path to a life of holiness, justice and love. Deception, if ever justifiable, should be restricted to the most narrow confines possible.

Questions for Discussion

I. Case for Discussion

Jensen's Nursery is a small seventy-year-old family company. Currently it is facing an extremely difficult economic situation. To meet payroll, CEO Elmer Jensen decides to advertise Easter lilies a full two weeks before they are expected to bloom. Hoping that this will draw in sufficient numbers of customers who will end up purchasing other garden items, Jensen's advertisement comments on the company's "renowned greenhouses that make plants grow better" and has a picture of a bumper crop of lilies from a decade earlier.

When Elmer's father was alive, the company established a loyal customer base. As competing nurseries have entered the area, however, this loyalty has waned. Elmer justifies his ad in three ways. First, the customers no longer deserve (or expect) complete truthfulness in advertising. Second, if the business fails, his aging mother would have to be moved from a private to a state nursing home. An excellent spring sale is essential. Finally, he is prepared to pay the government for any fines he might have to pay for false advertising, calculating that they will be less than the money he might make in sales.

1. Do any of the five possible exceptions to truth telling discussed in this chapter justify Elmer's strategy? Discuss each.

2. What do you think Elmer should do?

II. Workplace Application

1. Describe a situation at work in which two moral duties conflicted. How did you resolve the predicament?

2. Have you ever engaged in a mutual deceit with another person? Evaluate the experience.

3. Have you ever told someone a nontruth because you felt that he or she had no right to the information? What was the outcome?

4. Describe a work situation in which you or someone else exaggerated. Were the consequences positive or negative?

5. Describe a work-related intentional ambiguity. In your opinion, was the ambiguity morally permissible?

III. Concepts to Understand

How might each passage be applied to a business context?

1. Conflicting Duties

Exodus 1:15-22: Do the midwives lie to Pharaoh? How does the author of Exodus evaluate their moral behavior?

Joshua 2:1-24; Hebrews 11:31; James 2:25: Do these authors condemn Rahab's lie? praise it?

1 Samuel 19:11-17: Michal, David's wife, lies twice. Is either lie (or both) morally permissible?

1 Samuel 21:10-15: Is it ethically acceptable for David to pretend insanity in this context? See also the introduction to Psalm 34 and verses 12-13.

1 Corinthians 10:13: How does this passage resolve the problem of conflicting moral duties? Is it possible to build an entire ethical system on this verse? See also the story of Abraham's sacrifice of Isaac in Genesis 22:1-19.

2. Mutual Deceits

Joshua 8:3-23: How does Joshua trick his enemy? Are his military tactics analyzed as being unethical?

2 Kings 6:8-23: Does Elisha lie to the enemy army in verse 19 when he says that "this is not the city"? Does the military context of the story justify his comments? Or is he simply using ambiguous language?

3. No Right to the Truth

Genesis 43:1—45:3: Have Joseph's brothers forfeited their right to be told the truth by the way they treated him years earlier?

2 Samuel 12:1-10: Nathan misleads David with his story about the lambs. Is this ethical?

1 Kings 3:16-28: Is Solomon deceptive in threatening to split the infant?

2 Kings 10:18-30: Why is Jehu rewarded for his apparent dishonesty? Does this story have limited applicability?

Matthew 5:43-48; Romans 12:14-20: How are we to treat our enemies? Are we justified in telling nontruths to them?

4. Exaggeration

Isaiah 5:18-20: How careful should we be in our use of words?

Matthew 10:37-39; 19:23-26; Mark 9:43-48: When is the use of hyperbole ethical? When not?

5. Ambiguity

Genesis 12:10-20; 20:1-18: Does Abraham engage in lying? deceit?

1 Samuel 16:1-3: Does Samuel create ambiguity here? Is it morally acceptable?

1 Samuel 20:16-42: Is Jonathan's statement that David "asked for permission to go to Bethlehem" (v. 28) a lie? an ambiguity?

10

CONCEALMENT & DISCLOSURE

Three may keep a secret if two of them are dead.
BENJAMIN FRANKLIN

Corruption thrives in secret places, and avoids public
places, and we believe it a fair presumption that
secrecy means impropriety.
WOODROW WILSON

At stake is fidelity, keeping faith with those who have
confided their secrets on condition that they not be revealed.
SISSELA BOK

Everything secret degenerates. . . . Nothing is safe
that does not show how it can bear discussion and publicity.
LORD ACTON

T O A CERTAIN EXTENT, LYING AND CONCEALMENT (SECRECY) ARE INTER-
related. When a seller intentionally masks a product defect, for instance,
concealment can be every bit as deceptive as a spoken lie. Unfairness results
when insiders use secret knowledge to the disadvantage of those outside the
information loop.

This is not to say, however, that lying and concealment are synonymous. To
the contrary, there are times—such as when one protects the confidences of a
close friend—when secrecy is the only acceptable moral choice. The major
difference between the two concepts rests in the presumption that while lying is
wrong, secrecy need not bear the same presumption. Secrecy is a more neutral
concept, being neither negative nor positive per se. As the writer of Ecclesiastes

observes: "There is . . . a time to be silent and a time to speak" (3:1, 7).

The Latin word *secretum* connotes something hidden or separated, a line dividing those who have access to secret information and those who do not.[1] For insiders—whether a group of first-grade school friends or members of a corporate executive team—shared knowledge creates special bonds of trust and intimacy. For outsiders, however—such as ostracized schoolmates or midlevel managers—exclusion from the inner circle elicits feelings of powerlessness, suspicion and rejection.

The key question then becomes, When is it holy, just and loving to keep another's secret? When is it not? Since concealment is a morally neutral concept, criteria for its proper use must be established. Clarification is particularly critical for business professionals such as accountants, lawyers, bankers and counselors who regularly confront situations involving disclosure and nondisclosure concerns.

Secrecy Rights and the Duty to Conceal

Secret sharers possess three rights that should be respected. First, their dignity and sense of privacy ought to be protected. Second, any secrets that entail property rights should be handled with care. Third, those they confide in should display a degree of loyalty, particularly if a close relationship or contractual agreement is involved.

Dignity rights. Each of us possesses a God-given right to express our inner thoughts and feelings to others in confidence. It is our choice to select who enters and who is excluded from this zone of privacy. If, for example, a wife shares deep self-doubts with her husband, she understandably expects him to conceal the information from others. Once she has given him inside knowledge about her true sentiments, a special bond of trust has been created. Relational intimacy is impossible without such secrets. If he abuses this vulnerability by broadcasting her confidences to others without permission, she may feel a sense of betrayal.

CURIOUS GEORGE. Doug, the director of human resources for HRC Corporation, is surprised one day when George, a midlevel manager, confronts him in the hallway. Suspecting that one of his subordinates is depressed, George wants Doug to permit him to see the employee's complete personnel file. Doug hesitates because even though HRC pro-

vides such counseling free of charge to employees, it has a policy against disclosing the content of the sessions.

Doug refuses George's request, explaining that the purpose of the policy is not only to protect employee privacy but to encourage workers to seek outside help. Giving out such information would be counterproductive, Doug explains.

Judas, an insider in Jesus' closest circle of friends, was such a betrayer. He used his special knowledge as a means of destruction (Jn 18:1-9). Likewise, in Mao Tse-tung's China, spouses and children were expected to repudiate traditional family privacy by betraying relatives who expressed doubts about the political system. Like the "Thought Police" in George Orwell's dystopian novel *1984,*[2] the Chinese government attempted to eradicate all unacceptable ideas.[3]

Such experimentation in information control underscores the vital importance of protecting the right of selective concealment. In the HRC Corporation case, the company recognized this right by instituting a policy prohibiting disclosure of information gleaned in counseling sessions. The policy not only encourages self-disclosure but fosters a climate where professional assistance can be freely sought without fear that employees' confidential communications will be made available to their snoopy supervisors.

Property rights. Sharing confidences with others often involves property rights. Consider the following scenarios: a musician plays a newly composed tune for an intimate friend, an author runs a first draft of a book past his editor, and an inventor discloses a new product idea to a close associate. These incidents have two things in common. First, they involve the selective disclosure of something intimate—in this case personal creativity. Second, they include property rights that should be respected by the confidant.

HEARTBEAT OF AMERICA. Physio-Control Corporation (PCC) manufactures devices that use electrical shock to revive heart-attack victims. The potential market for its product is huge. Experts estimate that the device could save many of the 300,000 Americans who suffer cardiac arrests each year. PCC does nearly $200 million of business annually.

Three years ago five of PCC's key engineers and scientists left to start a rival company named Heartstream Inc., which now manufactures a similar electric shock device. PCC is suing Heartstream's founders, claiming theft of trade secrets and violation of noncompetition agreements.[4]

Property rights are also found in the form of trade secrets. Research intensive companies such as Physio-Controls, Microsoft and Johnson & Johnson live and die on their ability to protect their trade secrets. Employees who have access to manufacturing processes, blueprints, formulas, pricing data and customer lists are morally and legally obliged to conceal such information from competitors. To disclose such data—or, even worse, to use it for personal financial gain as is alleged of Heartstream founders—both betrays and violates their companies' property rights.

Loyalty rights. Loyalty creates special obligations between people. Predicated on either an existing relationship (for example, family member or friend) or on a contractual commitment (for example, employer-employee), secret sharers expect their confidential information to be protected. Fidelity in such situations is so universally valued that every young child understands what it means to carry the secret of another. Indeed, sharing such confidences represents one of our deepest emotional and social bonds.[5] Thus it should come as no surprise that when partners leave to start up a competing company, they are viewed with a jaundiced eye. Why? Because inside information and property rights have commingled with relationships based on loyalty to create heightened expectations of confidentiality.

Loyalty not only creates the possibility of betrayal of the secret sharer but also can place burdens on the secret keeper's freedom.[6] Confidants must be careful whom they talk with lest they divulge concealed information. Likewise, employees entrusted with corporate secrets are less mobile in their careers. This is particularly true for those who are required to sign nondisclosure documents that typically prohibit them from working in their fields for two to three years after leaving their current place of employment. While such restrictions pale in comparison with those imposed on ancient Egyptian temple workers, who were sealed alive in the tombs of the pharaohs to ensure complete secrecy, they restrict employee mobility nonetheless. Loyalty has its price.

Limitations on Secrecy Rights

PROMISE KEEPER? Henry and Sam are coworkers. One day Sam asks Henry, "Do you want in on a secret? Promise not to tell anyone?" Henry

promises, and Sam shows him some photographs of himself engaging in
sex acts with minors. Disgusted, Henry wonders what he should do.
Secrecy must never be considered an absolute right. Taken to an extreme, it
blocks the cleansing light of other moral considerations and produces harmful results. In Henry's case, for example, strict adherence to his promise
would result in abetting a sexual predator. In hindsight Henry realizes that
he would have been better off had he not issued a blank-check promise to
Sam in the first place. Having done so, however, he is faced with an
unfortunate moral choice. One possible way out is to contend that an "implied
condition" exists—that his promise to keep the secret is premised on Sam's
action being ethical—and that since it is not, he is justified in contacting the
police. A second and more direct way of dealing with his dilemma is to assert
that his duty to conceal the information is superseded by a higher obligation
to protect adolescents from exploitation.

All three of the rights on which secrecy is based—dignity, property and
loyalty—are limited in nature. One's own sense of personal autonomy, for
example, must never be used to take advantage of others. Likewise, property
rights are not unqualified and must be balanced with other ethical considerations. Loyalty is also a conditional right that if taken to excess can be
transformed from a virtue into a vice. Executives with inordinate group
allegiances ignore basic moral concepts, choosing rather to focus on what
actions best benefit the group. In doing so they imitate members of the Mafia
or secret societies. Extreme group fidelity, while providing cherished cama-
raderie, opens the door to ganglike behavior in which any act is acceptable.

Such unchecked loyalty was expected of executives of the food conglomerate Archer-Daniels-Midland (ADM). As one vice president recalls with
regret, he was slowly introduced to "how ADM does business"[7] and later
engaged in illegal price fixing with two primary Japanese competitors.
Secrecy and loyalty conspire to produce a form of "groupthink" in which all
other moral considerations are disregarded. As Voltaire warned, "Those who
can make you believe absurdities can make you commit atrocities."[8]

In this light it is best for agents to inform their superiors and clients up
front about the moral limits they place on the duty of confidentiality. It should
be made clear that they will never keep secrets that cover illegal acts or could
result in serious harm to others. For example, accountants should tell man-

agement that they will not maintain secrets about doctored books, engineers that they will not participate in covering up toxic spills, bankers that they will not turn a blind eye to drug money, and attorneys that they will not remain silent when informed of a potential homicide. To do otherwise is to overvalue the concept of secrecy and to undervalue both personal integrity and the rights of others.

The Duty to Disclose

Our analysis now turns to the flip side of the concealment/disclosure coin. If, as we have seen, there are circumstances in which secrecy rights should be respected, are there situations in which concealed information should be revealed? At least three criteria can be derived from the biblical principles of holiness, justice and love: a right to know, application of the Golden Rule and prevention of significant harm.

Right to know. Disclosure is required when others have a right to the concealed information. Patients, for example, have the right of "informed consent." This obligates not only doctors to gain permission prior to embarking on a medical procedure but also to fully educate their patients as to the pros and cons of each option. As insiders to specialized information, physicians possess an obligation to reveal.

> EDUCATED DISCLOSURE. *Recruiting pressures are so intense at some universities that the average Scholastic Assessment Test (SAT) score of incoming freshmen is manipulated. Northeastern University of Boston, for example, admitted to excluding foreign and remedial students from its composite SAT score in order to improve its image with high-school seniors. When public disclosure forced the university to include these two groups, its average dropped by fifty points. Neighbor Boston University engaged in a similar practice with its foreign students, including only their math, but not verbal, scores.[9]*

Based on the bedrock justice notions of personal dignity and free will, informed consent protects decision-makers by requiring others to disclose all relevant data. It obliges, for example, home sellers and their real estate agents to make known any liens or other encumbrances that have been placed on their property. Likewise, it requires employers to apprise their workers of any known workplace dangers, car dealers to disclose any latent (nonobvious) defects and universities to provide accurate SAT scores for inquiring high-school seniors.

The right to informed consent was violated in one layoff situation in New York. After dismissing several workers, the company hired an outside placement firm to aid them in securing new jobs elsewhere. The company did not inform its ex-workers, however, that it had instructed the search firm not to place any of them with competing companies. Lacking this information, many of the former employees took lesser-paying jobs outside their areas of expertise. Had this hidden conflict of interest been disclosed, it would have become apparent that the aid was, at least in part, a strategy of economic self-protection, and the ex-employees could have better protected themselves.[10]

Contract rights may also trigger the duty to disclose. Intelligent Electronics (IE), the nation's largest computer reseller, contracted with major suppliers such as IBM, Apple and Hewlett-Packard to market their unsold products. These contracts included a clause that required the manufacturers to pay for IE's advertising costs. When several years later it became known that fully half of IE's annual income came from unspent advertising funds, the manufacturers threatened to file suit for fraudulent concealment, claiming that they had the right to be informed of IE's practice of charging for unprovided services.[11]

It is important to note, however, that when another party lacks the right to know, disclosure is not required. A bank teller, for example, is under no obligation to volunteer information to a thief regarding the location of money. Unmarked police cars and timer lights on home security systems are likewise morally acceptable options, since lawbreakers do not have the right to full information. Note that this is not a justification for lying to liars but rather a limitation on the duty to reveal. As discussed above, concealment is a morally neutral concept whereas lying is not.

Scripture justifies nondisclosure in several contexts. God instructed Samuel, for instance, not to divulge to King Saul the primary reason for his trip to Bethlehem (to anoint David as the new king), but rather to refer to his secondary purpose (to offer a sacrifice; 1 Sam 16:1-3). Likewise, the magi who visited the infant Jesus refused to reveal their findings to King Herod. Why? Because they realized that he had evil intentions toward the child and hence had no right to the information (Mt 2:11-12). Shortly prior to his death, Jesus practiced intentional nondisclosure with the nefarious king, refusing even to speak with him (Lk 23:7-12).

In the case involving "curious George" (above, under "Dignity Rights"), HRC's human resource director is under no obligation to release confidential information to a nosy manager, because the latter lacks a sufficient right to know. While it would be wrong to lie to George—for example, "no counseling has occurred"—it is highly appropriate to inform him that "the company has labeled such information confidential and you are not permitted access to it." Secrecy is justified in this context; deception is not.

Golden Rule. The Golden Rule—"Do to others what you would have them do to you" (Mt 7:12)—adds a second dimension to our discussion about concealment and disclosure. This perspective asks what a reasonable person would want to know if he or she were in the other person's position. Considerations of holiness, justice and love are all elements of the Golden Rule—holiness in its call for purity of communication, justice in its demand to respect others' rights, and love in its concern about how concealment and disclosure will impact others.

NIGHTMARE NEIGHBOR. John, a licensed realtor, has been hired by the Fernandez family to sell their home. During the course of several conversations, John discovers that the next-door neighbor is rude, gruff, potentially dangerous and particularly hostile to environmentalists. Thus John is presented with a dilemma when he realizes that the first qualified buyers to show serious interest are lifetime members of the Sierra Club and Greenpeace. John ponders whether he should tell them about the neighbor.

Several executives at Greyhound Bus Lines provide an example of how the Golden Rule can be abused. A few years ago Greyhound offered a ninety-million-dollar stock offering to the public. The company failed to disclose, however, that its much-touted computerized "Trips" reservation system was not performing as promised. After the stock sale, but before the "Trips" problems became widely known, a handful of executives exercised stock options and traded their shares. Shortly thereafter, the defects became common knowledge and Greyhound's stock fell precipitously. The corporate insiders violated the Golden Rule in that had they been in the other shareholders' shoes, they would have desired more information about problems with "Trips" prior to purchase.[12]

The Golden Rule likewise obliges the Brown and Williamson Tobacco Corporation, America's third-largest cigarette manufacturer, to reveal that it has added ammonia to its cigarettes to make the addictive nicotine more potent. This is particularly egregious in light of the company's claim that its tar levels have been decreasing over the past twenty years. Any reasonable person would object to such concealment and demand fuller disclosure.[13]

A slightly tougher case is presented in the following scenario. What duty does a retirement home recruiter have to an applicant who erroneously believes that the home is affiliated with a particular church denomination?[14] Does the Golden Rule require the recruiter to correct the applicant's faulty assumption? While he might rationalize that he has not lied to her, failure to disclose would be to knowingly permit the retiree to base her decision on a false supposition. None of us would want to be treated in such a manner. An obligation to reveal exists in such situations, particularly considering the vulnerable state of the senior citizen.

This is not to say, however, that the Golden Rule always mandates full disclosure. Take a compact-disk player salesman who knows that the same product can be bought for fifty dollars less at another retail store.[15] Is he obliged to reveal this information? Arguably not. If the information is readily ascertainable through other means, the duty to disclose is reduced. Why? Because the Golden Rule does not require sellers to act paternalistically—to act as parents on the buyer's behalf—but to be fair and honest. Consumers also have a reasonable level of responsibility to educate themselves.

The tension between full disclosure on the one hand and paternalism on the other makes the case involving the potentially violent neighbor more problematic. In this situation there would appear to be little opportunity for the buyers to discover the neighbor's mindset without the realtor's disclosure. Unless such a duty of self-education is found to exist, disclosure is preferable. If the sellers and realtor were in the buyers' position, they would no doubt want such information to be revealed.

Prevention of significant harm. A third rationale for the duty to disclose is to prevent significant harm. For example, when manufacturers market foods that contain high levels of salt or caffeine, they have a moral duty to so inform consumers. To do otherwise would be to expose those with blood-pressure problems and heart conditions to serious health risks.[17] Likewise, employees have a basic right to know of potentially hazardous work situations. Legislation in these areas—for example, the Food and Drug Act (FDA) and the Occupational Safety and Health Act (OSHA)—build on the strong moral sense that when grave risks are involved, information should be revealed.

GREEN ACRES? Over a decade has passed since a reactor at the Chernobyl nuclear plant in Ukraine exploded and burned for ten days. Eighty-five percent of the families who once lived in the small town of Rudakov, just a few miles from Chernobyl, have left the area. The exodus began to reverse itself, however, when the director of a collective farm advertised in papers across the former Soviet Union to fill the ranks of those who have left. Refugees from war-torn Tajikistan, Georgia, Azerbaijan and Chechnya are the most significant in number. Nothing in the ads, however, mentions the fact that the fields are laden with deadly plutonium isotopes.[16]

The obligation to prevent harm often overlaps with the two other disclosure principles—the right to know and the Golden Rule. In the Chernobyl case, for example, the farmers should have been fully apprised of the dangers, not only because of the potential health hazards but because both their informed consent rights and the Golden Rule were violated as well. The farm director's concealment is clearly inexcusable.

In a medical setting, what duty does a nurse have to inform patients that their heart surgeon has a drinking problem that has seriously impaired her recent operating-room performance? Plenty. Even though such a disclosure may conflict with the nurse's sense of loyalty, a higher obligation takes precedence. Not only do the patients have a right to bodily safety, but the Golden Rule presumes that reasonable people would desire such knowledge, and great harm might result if the information is concealed. Granted, such a revelation may cause retaliation against the nurse, but morally correct choices are often costly.

Conflict Between Duties to Disclose and Not to Disclose: Whistle-Blowing

SCRAMBLED EGG. Norbert Giltner worked as a nurse at the Center for Reproductive Health (CRH) at the University of California at Irvine

(UCI). CRH is an internationally recognized fertility clinic. For more than two years he warned UCI management that in at least ten cases, human eggs and embryos were being taken from one patient and given to another without either's consent. When informed, UCI's auditor responded, "I'm an accountant. I have no idea what to do with that." Frustrated by the lack of internal response, Giltner eventually testified before a California Senate committee.[18]

Whistle blowers like Giltner are confronted with extremely uncomfortable options. On the one hand, if they disclose inside information to outsiders (for example, to the government, the media or special-interest groups), they are often perceived as traitors by their colleagues. James Roche, former president of General Motors, accused whistle blowers of "eroding . . . the loyalty of a management team . . . creating suspicion and disharmony . . . and spreading disunity and creating conflict."[19] On the other hand, if they conceal secrets that ought to be revealed, they violate the three principles of disclosure—the right to know, the Golden Rule and the prevention of serious harm. Their ethical challenge is to delineate the point on the moral spectrum at which the noble concept of confidentiality transforms itself into the immoral withholding of information.

Principles of holiness, justice and love require potential whistle blowers to answer four questions prior to going public with confidential information. First, what is the agent's motive? Some reasons—such as protecting the public—are legitimate. Others—such as self-promotion and the desire for revenge—are not. Ethical purity requires employees to engage in careful soul-searching prior to making any accusations.

Second, is the allegation based on accurate information? Adequate evidence, a fundamental element of procedural due process, is a critical prerequisite to any public disclosure. Guesswork prematurely revealed may needlessly ruin careers. For example, if Norbert Giltner had misinterpreted incomplete data, he could have slandered his colleagues and caused great consternation to many patients, parents and children.

Third, has the employee confronted his or her supervisor with the perceived wrong? Moral duties of loyalty, honesty and due process require agents to follow Jesus' pattern of approaching alleged wrongdoers prior to seeking outside assistance (Mt 18:15-17). Of course, this may be counterproductive if the supervisor is engaged in illegal activities such as embezzlement, industrial espionage or sexual harassment. In such cases it seems appropriate to bypass the immediate superior and take the matter up the management ladder, even to the board of directors if necessary. This approach has limited utility if the "higher-ups" are either tolerant of or participants in the unethical behavior.

Going outside the company with confidential information can be justified only if all viable internal remedies have been exhausted. External whistleblowing is a remedy of last resort. "Leaking" information anonymously is even less desirable because it affords those charged with wrongdoing little opportunity to defend themselves, thus undercutting due-process norms.

Fourth, what is the appropriate level of disclosure? Some information—such as a supervisor's political views or recent divorce—are strictly private in nature and ought not to be revealed by the subordinate to anyone.[20] Other data—such as an arbitrary management style or a poorly conceived marketing plan—may be relevant for discussion within the company. Often this form of internal whistle-blowing possesses a high element of risk. The most controversial level of disclosure—external whistle-blowing—involves going outside the confines of the company with sensitive information. This should be done only when an imminent public interest is involved.

This three-level approach was utilized by several engineers working for San Francisco's Bay Area Rapid Transit system (BART) while it was under construction. Suspecting that a control system was being improperly installed and could result in serious injury to passengers, they first discussed whether the matter was a major corporate concern. They next took their apprehensions to their supervisors, but when no response was forthcoming, they engaged in internal whistle-blowing by alerting BART executives. However, since the project was already over budget, the executives ignored their safety concerns. Only after the engineers were fired for insubordination did they take their concerns to the California Society of Professional Engineers and the state legislature.[21] Public pressure forced BART to take corrective safety action but, unfortunately, failed to resecure the engineers' jobs.

In a similar case, a private detective named Thomas Applegate was hired by the Cincinnati Gas and Electric Company to examine alleged timecard fraud on a nuclear power plant construction site. During the course of his investigation, he discovered that the plant was being assembled in such a poor manner that when completed it would constitute a serious health hazard to the local residents. After company officials waved off his concerns, he contacted a nonprofit organization, which called for public hearings. As new information surfaced, the government revoked the plant's license to operate, and it was never completed.[22]

Those who reveal inside secrets to outsiders often pay a high personal price. Studies indicate that up to two-thirds of such "ethical resisters" suffer job loss, demotions, personal harassment, punitive transfers and/or negative reviews that affect their employability at other companies.[23] For example, after Roger Boisjoly of Morton Thiokol Corporation testified before Congress about the reasons for the space shuttle *Challenger* disaster—faulty sealing rings and a poor decision-making process—company executives increased his discomfort level to the point where his health failed and he eventually left the company. An even more extreme case involved Mark Whitacre, a senior vice president at Archer-Daniels-Midland, who attempted to commit suicide after it was revealed that he had been an FBI "mole" within the company for two years.[24]

Prudent corporations, wishing to spare themselves the public embarrassment and potential legal action caused by such revelations, are setting up mechanisms for internal whistle blowers. The number of ombudsmen—high-level executives charged with handling such complaints—is increasing. This approach addresses the problem created by the traditional chain-of-command structure in which employees are frustrated by lack of access to upper management. If Norbert Giltner had had a right of entry to a university ombudsman, for instance, the issue might have been resolved internally.

Limited external disclosure is another option. Certified public accountants (CPAs) provide an interesting model in this regard. While the CPA Code of Professional Conduct generally forbids disclosure of confidential client information (even resulting in the forfeiture of license), it does permit CPAs to file ethics complaints against clients with state boards after exhausting all other mitigating steps. This moderate position provides limited protection for both the auditor and the client. Since the information is initially disclosed only to the state board, the client's information remains confidential (albeit to a wider group) and the CPA is able to get outside help to determine whether any ethical violations have occurred.[25] Other professions would be well advised to follow this model of selective disclosure. Organizational structures that encourage a midlevel step between complete silence at one extreme and full disclosure on the other should be encouraged.

Questions for Discussion

I. Cases for Discussion
DIVIDED LOYALTIES. *Gail works as an auditor for a national accounting firm. One of her clients, Alias Manufacturing Corporation (AMC), has performed well on the stock market for almost five years. During her audit, however, Gail discovers that AMC has unintentionally underreported some of its liabilities over the past year and is about to be hit with a major class-action lawsuit. She projects that AMC stock values may fall by as much as 35 percent within the next six months.*

One weekend Gail drives home to visit her aging parents. As their only child, she feels particularly responsible for their well-being. Stuck in the lower middle class on a fixed income, they are very excited to inform their daughter that they have recently invested half of their retirement funds in AMC. Stunned, Gail ponders what to do next.[26]

1. What information should Gail conceal? disclose? To whom?

2. Are there any creative solutions for Gail's ethical dilemma?

THE KEY TO SUCCESS. *In 1920 total sales of Listerine mouthwash were only $100,000. Two Chicago advertisers then attached an outdated medical term for bad breath—halitosis—to the product. They also created ads in which a man or woman with impeccable looks, wealth and social status nevertheless lost romance because of halitosis. The cure? Listerine, of course. Within seven years, annual sales skyrocketed to over $4 million.*[27]

1. In light of the last three chapters on honesty, lying and disclosure, did the two advertisers act ethically in their marketing of Listerine?

II. Workplace Application
1. Have you ever felt uncomfortable concealing information? What did you do to resolve the tension?

2. Describe a situation in which you improperly disclosed information.

3. Have you ever "blown the whistle"? What was your justification? What were the results?

III. Concepts to Understand
How might each passage be applied to a business context?

1. Duty to Not Disclose

Ecclesiastes 3:1, 7; Proverbs 17:28: When is the "time to be silent"? the "time to speak"?

1 Kings 18:1-4: Did Obadiah act ethically in hiding information from his employer?

Matthew 2:1-12: Why didn't the magi return to tell Herod about the birth in Bethlehem as he had requested?

2. Duty to Disclose

a. Right to Know

Leviticus 5:1: Why must potential witnesses volunteer to testify in court?

Luke 12:1-3: Why must this information be disclosed? Who has a right to know it?

b. Golden Rule

1 Samuel 19:1-3: How does Jonathan live by the Golden Rule in disclosing this information to David?

Matthew 7:12: Is this the "bottom-line" standard for Christian behavior? See also Matthew 5:43-48.

Ephesians 4:15: What does it mean to "speak the truth in love" in the marketplace?

c. Causes Significant Harm

1 Samuel 16:1-3: Does Samuel have a duty to disclose this information to Saul? If not, why?

1 Samuel 25:1-44: Is Abigail justified in not disclosing to her husband the gifts of his property to David (v. 19)?

3. Conflict Between Duties to Disclose and Not Disclose

Matthew 18:15-17: Is this model of dispute resolution applicable in the work environment? What applicability does it have to whistle blowers?

4. Optional Situations

Luke 23:7-12: Does Jesus have any moral obligation to respond to Herod's questions?

11

EMPLOYER-EMPLOYEE RELATIONS

The average worker wants a job in which he doesn't have to think.
HENRY FORD

To punish (an employee) atrociously, to crush him in such a manner that
the most hardened criminal would tremble before such punishment—
it would be necessary only to give his work the character of complete
uselessness. . . . Let him be constrained in his work as to pour water from
one vessel to another and back again, then I am sure that at the end
of a short period he would strangle himself or commit a thousand crimes
punishable with death rather than live in such an abject
condition or endure such treatment.
FEODOR DOSTOYEVSKY

Frederick Taylor warned American workers against the old-fashioned
virtue of "initiative." The workman who was required to do his job in the
one "right" way, he said, was no more being inhibited than was the
surgeon who was instructed in the one best way to perform an
appendectomy.
DANIEL BOORSTIN

If the whole structure and organization of an economic system is such as
to compromise human dignity, to lessen a man's sense of responsibility
or rob him of any opportunity for exercising personal initiative, then
such a system . . . is altogether unjust—no matter how much wealth it
produces.
POPE JOHN XXIII

BIT PLAYERS. *TriCon Corporation manufactures ball bearings for
airplanes. Company engineers recommend that significant changes be
made in the manufacturing process. Line workers, whose daily work*

| *would be directly affected by these alterations, have not been solicited for*
| *input. Some are very upset, charging management with gross insensitivity*
| *to their role.*

Perspectives differ as to the nature of the employer-employee relationship. To some it is a purely economic matter—pay for work—with contracts spelling out the respective rights and duties. For others a strong social element also comes into play. Employers and employees, they contend, are not abstract financial interests but human beings whose relationships are far more complex than just an exchange of money for task performance.

Two related employer-employee subjects—agency and confidentiality—have already been analyzed in earlier chapters. In this chapter we will focus on the reciprocal nature of the employer-employee relationship, and in the next two on three additional topics: termination, privacy and discrimination.

Scientific Management

Eighty years ago a mechanical engineer named Frederick Taylor coined the phrase "scientific management." With the zeal of an evangelist he preached the gospel of efficiency. Deriving inspiration from Adam Smith, the eighteenth-century economist who promoted the division of labor as a means of increasing worker productivity, Taylor conducted time and motion studies in a wide variety of industries. Smith's classic work on the various functions in a pin factory challenged Taylor to identify ever-greater efficiencies.[1] Taylor even risked the derision of his contemporaries by taking three years to reduce the number of shovelers at a local steel plant. Skeptics chuckled at the notion that such a simple job could be "better engineered." However, after redesigning both the tool and the manner in which the task was performed, Taylor was able to reduce the work force necessary from 600 men down to 140.[2]

Taylor's principles have been applied across business sectors. At General Motors, for instance, the work hour was divided into six-minute periods. Tasks were then so carefully defined that workers were evaluated by their every tenth-of-an-hour performance. Taylor even utilized these engineering standards in his personal life by counting the number of steps it took him to get to work and by refusing to wear the high-top button shoes popular in his time because it took too long to put them on and take them off.[3]

TriCon's move to reengineer its manufacturing process would no doubt receive Taylor's support. So long as the most efficient process results, employee concerns about being left out of the decision-making loop are irrelevant. "The man had been first [in the past]. In the future the system must be first," Taylor observed. Production workers are "more or less the type of the ox, heavy both mentally and physically." Expert engineers and sophisticated executives ("managerial heads"), not laborers ("hired hands"), understand the most efficient method of production. Taylor expected line workers to follow orders, not to think independently. "Scientific management made the worker into an interchangeable part," one historian concludes. Taylor put it even more succinctly: "The worker must be trimmed to fit the job."[4]

Barbara Garson, author of *The Electronic Sweatshop*, sees a renaissance of scientific management in some industries today. "Modern tools are being used to bring 19th-century working conditions into the white-collar world." Instead of Taylor's stopwatch, we now have surveillance cameras and computers to monitor workers far more effectively than he ever could have imagined possible. Companies that utilize such instruments tend to concur with Taylor's basic philosophy that leaders and engineers should make all of the decisions, leaving little, if any, opportunity for group interaction.

Electronic Banking Systems (EBS) is a Maryland company that processes donations for nonprofit organizations. It adheres to the principles of scientific management by having its engineers carefully prescribe workers' tasks—for example, keyboard operators must make eighty-five hundred strokes per hour and letter openers must process three parcels per minute. "We don't ask these people to think—the machines think for them," observes CEO Ron Edens. "They don't have to make any decisions." To ensure full performance, employees are not permitted to talk except during breaks, coffee mugs and pictures are prohibited on their desks, and all windows are covered to prevent distraction. Employee dissatisfaction is growing: to date two attempts have been made to form a union.[5]

Human Resource Management

Taylor's theory of scientific management has attracted many critics over the years. As early as the 1920s skeptics noted that when Worthington Pump Company implemented his techniques, the result was not higher efficiency but skyrocketing absenteeism due to low employee morale and high stress levels.[6]

A decade later Elton Mayo conducted an experiment by observing six Chicago phone assemblers over a three-month period. In an effort to create optimal working conditions, a variety of changes were made, such as increased lighting and decreased lighting. He discovered that whatever process changes engineers made—whether helpful or detrimental—worker productivity increased. Objective conditions seemed almost irrelevant.

From this data Mayo came to a conclusion exactly opposite that drawn by Taylor. Whenever human beings are shown concern and encouraged to work in teams, he contended, efficiency is increased. In other words, in determining worker productivity, the human factor is more significant than expertly designed processes.[7] Psychologist Frederick Herzberg took this logic a step further in the 1950s when he concluded that recognition, responsibility and the opportunity to fulfill one's potential are the primary employee motivators. Inversely, concerns such as pay, security and work conditions—while significant in reducing negative sentiments—are less capable of energizing workers to higher levels of performance.[8]

Theory X and Theory Y

In the 1960s Douglas McGregor coined the terms *Theory X* and *Theory Y* to describe two views about human nature. Theory X, which subsumes Taylor's scientific management, assumes that people generally are lazy, dislike work, avoid responsibility, and require external stimulus (usually compensation) to perform tasks adequately.[9] Theory Y, on the other hand, incorporates the Mayo/Herzberg human resource viewpoint and presumes that humans are creative, seek responsibility and can be self-directed.[10] It welcomes innovations such as quality circles and participatory management. Table 11.1 (on p. 152) captures the differences.

Ford Motor Company based much of its early success on the principles of Theory X. Its assembly line, a logical application of Taylor's principles, produced low-priced, high-value goods for mass consumption. By the 1970s, however, Ford was nearly bankrupt. Why? Not only had its products become bland, but its employee relations had degenerated into adversarial bickering. The company seemed to focus as much on matters of employer-employee

Theory X	Theory Y
Employees inherently dislike work and will attempt to avoid it, whenever possible.	Employees view work as being as natural as rest or play.
Employees must be coerced, controlled or threatened with punishment to achieve desired goals.	Employees will exercise self-direction and self-control if they are committed to the objectives.
Employees will shirk responsibilities and seek formal direction whenever possible.	The average person can learn to accept, and seek, responsibility.
Most workers place security above all other factors associated with work and will display little ambition.	The ability to make good decisions is widely dispersed through the population and isn't necessarily the sole ability of managers.[11]

Table 11.1

conflict as it did on customer satisfaction. Theory X had initiated this downward spiral by treating workers as interchangeable parts. They responded by joining unions. When management broke down each function into its smallest tasks, union leaders reciprocated by demanding specific work rules and job classifications.[12]

Without trust and a sense of dignity, the employer-employee relationship devolves into a rule-based legalistic relationship. The result: little creativity, low productivity and a gutted concern for quality. Things began to turn around for Ford only when its executives began to implement sound human-resource principles. Quality circles were introduced, employee suggestions were solicited, and union-management cooperation was fostered.

Productivity increased for the first time in many years.[13] Interestingly, many Ford advertisements now focus on line workers, not the vehicles produced. Its motto—"Quality is Job 1"—indicates this shift in perspective.

A similar story is told by Wayne Anderson, CEO of Pittron Steel. After a debilitating eighty-four-day strike, he began to change his attitude toward his employees. Rather than continue to separate himself from them per Theory X, he initiated a daily walk through the plant, learning their names and personal stories. A turning point in his relationship with them occurred when, in front of several workers, he picked up a thirty-pound hammer and could swing it for only a few minutes. Putting the tool down, he stated his respect for those who performed the task, thereby dignifying one of the lowest jobs in the company.[14]

Recent research indicates that employer respect is more critical to workers than was once commonly thought. Corroborating Herzberg's earlier work, one study indicates that income ranks only seventh in employee motivation, behind such factors as achievement, recognition, challenging work, opportunity for advancement, possibility of job growth and responsibility.[15] As Debbie Fields, owner of the highly successful Mrs. Fields' Cookies, notes: "I believe people will do their very best. I really do. . . . You say that people come to work for the money, and I disagree with that. . . . People come to work because they need to be productive. They need to feel like they are successful in whatever they do. . . . Money is not the issue."[16]

Which of these two theories—Taylor's scientific management or the Mayo/Herzberg human-resource view—is more consonant with Scripture? Does Christian thought lean more toward Theory X or Theory Y?

While possessing some strengths, Theory X has three serious deficiencies. First, it denigrates the value of human beings. Workers are not "oxen" who must be "trimmed to fit the job" by expert engineers.[17] Rather, each of us is a human being created in the image of God. Employees are not replicable commodities but unique examples of God's handiwork. To use Karl Marx's phrase, workers must not be transformed into "appendages of machines."[18]

Taylor's view of line employees continues in some industries today. In several poultry processing plants, for example, engineers have determined that "hangers" can hitch twenty-five live birds per minute to hooks at the front end of the "disassembly line." "Eviserators," in turn, can pull out the innards or cut off various body parts at a rate of up to ninety birds a minute. Surveillance cameras monitor every move. Unexcused bathroom trips merit a three-day suspension. Few, if any, transferable skills are developed for these near-minimum-wage jobs. Further, since the same motions are repeated over an eight-hour shift, poultry workers experience the third highest incidence of carpal-tunnel syndrome of any group (after meat packers and car-body assemblers). Greater work speed also increases product contamination, placing consumers at greater risk.[19]

Second, application of Theory X can result in extreme polarization between management and labor. Electronic Banking Service's Ron Eden, for example, sits in an upstairs office where he watches a television screen sending images from the eight cameras posted throughout the facility. His other primary management tool—poring over computer spreadsheets that quantify employee performance levels and error rates—combines to virtually eliminate any contact he might have with the line workers.[20]

While Theory X may be tolerated more by unskilled workers due to their weak bargaining positions, employers like Eden should beware. When workers are treated without respect, they find ways to respond in kind. If managers narrowly define every aspect of a job, leaving out any room for employee input or creativity, workers may quietly choose to do only the minimum work required, reserving their energies for outside interests such as family and personal hobbies. In highly regulated industries, workers have resorted to slowing down processes by "working-to-rule"—that is, meticulously following every company and governmental regulation. Often the best and brightest simply opt to work elsewhere, leaving the company with mediocre, poorly motivated employees. Such a talent drain can be ill-afforded in today's competitive environment. Or they may take collective action through unions that severely limit management's ability to take unilateral action. Witness the decline of the steel, railroad and automotive industries in the 1970s.

Third, Theory X limits the scope of ethical inquiry to two justice concerns—property rights and contractual obligations. While important, these do not provide an adequate moral basis for the broad scope of human relationships. Other ethical concerns—such as holiness, due process rights, love and respect for human dignity—must also be factored into the relationship.

A case involving Sears Corporation sadly illustrates this point. Some years ago Sears management attempted to increase auto parts sales by imposing quotas on its mechanics. Sensing pressure to increase corporate wealth (property rights) and please their supervisors (contractual obligations), many mechanics sold unnecessary parts and services—from brake jobs to alignments—to unsuspecting customers. Theory X produced submissive workers whose ethical portfolios were narrowly circumscribed. As a result, issues of holiness (purity in communication), substantive justice (customers' right to be told the truth) and love (concern for how the practice might affect others) were ignored. When the public discovered the fraud, Sears was forced to pay more than sixty million dollars in settlement awards.[21]

In sum, Theory X's philosophy of employer-employee relations is deficient. Workers should not be treated as chattel. The wide gulf between supervisors and subordinates is demeaning, and Theory X's ethical base is unbalanced.

Having said all this, however, there is at least one element of Theory X that rings true—the need for accountability. As imperfect beings, workers are apt to act selfishly and/or not concentrate on their tasks. A certain measure of structure is needed to focus their energies. While Theory X accomplishes this through traditional hierarchical management, many companies are experimenting with the notion of peer accountability. Whichever form of management structure is utilized, vertical or horizontal, having clearly articulated lines of responsibility is vital.

Accountability is necessary even in the church, God's primary model of community life. Paul, for example, did not hesitate to use the title "apostle," a position superior to that of several subordinates.[22] When necessary, he used his authority to hold others accountable and legitimated structure in other spheres as well—government, family life and the workplace (see Eph 5:22—6:9). He regarded responsible human authority as a gift from God—a common grace for all—that provides necessary order (Rom 13:1-7).

Such authority must not be regarded as unilateral, however. Scripture holds those with greater power—such as employers, government and parents—accountable too. Taylor was wrong in this regard. By making only line employees accountable, he placed too much confidence in company executives and engineers. They too are fallible, imperfect beings, capable of making poor economic and moral choices. By arrogantly ignoring employee input, many companies have gone awry.

The trajectory of biblical thought endorses such mutual accountability. While the Old Testament places priests over laity, the New Testament transforms the relationship into a more egalitarian priesthood of all believers (1 Pet 2:4-10). Paul likewise, while not explicitly calling for an end to slavery, undercut its rationale by demanding mutual accountability. Masters, like slaves, will be evaluated by their conduct (Col 4:1). To a Greek world that treated slaves as "living tools," this was a radical concept.[23]

Of course egalitarian thinking can be taken too far. Just as Theory X has its flaws, so Theory Y may also be challenged for some of its basic assumptions about human nature. Are all workers really capable of self-management? Might not some take advantage of employers who place blind trust in them? Sin's impact on human character must not be underestimated. Without a measure of control, some workers will misuse the latitude given them. After all, employers do have legitimate property rights interests to protect.

A Christian Perspective: "Covenantal Management"

INVESTING IN PEOPLE. Herman Miller, a Fortune 500 furniture manufacturer, has an admirable record of employer-employee relationships. It has the most productive work force in its industry, and a recent Fortune magazine poll found it to be one of the nation's ten most admired companies. For more than forty years employees have been offered stock options and have been given monthly reports on corporate profits and their productivity. Employee input is so valued that their suggestions save the company twelve million dollars a year.

Max De Pree, retired CEO and outspoken Christian, credits the company's success to "liberating people" and a "spirit of self-management." He describes work as "one of our greatest privileges" and comments that it "can even be poetic." Calling companies to move beyond contractual justice, he aims toward "covenantal relationships" between owners and workers.[24]

It seems evident that the Christian view of employer-employee relations has more in common with Theory Y than Theory X. Based on the notion of "covenantal management," the Christian perspective focuses on the broader relationship of managers and subordinates, not solely on the legal and economic aspects. Covenantal management has a much broader base, calling on employers to demonstrate *holiness* through purity, mutual accountability and humility; *justice* through rewarding merit, compensating for harm done, recognizing substantive rights and honoring procedural rights; and *love* through empathy, mercy and sacrifice.

Four components particularly characterize covenantal management, "Theory C": dignity, reciprocity, servant leadership and gift recognition.

Dignity

Dignity is a fundamental human right. The duty it creates weighs especially on employers due to their greater degree of power. They must not treat their workers as inanimate objects or variable costs, but as unique bearers of God's image who have the right to be treated honorably and fairly. Frederick Taylor, despite his Quaker upbringing, clearly missed the mark on this point. Author Vernon Grounds observes: "Human beings must not be treated as cogs in a machine, mere hands in a production process, faceless non-entities, replaceable employees whose feelings, needs and relationships can be ignored."[25]

Failure to imbue employees with dignity not only is morally wrong according to covenantal management but can be costly as well, particularly if skilled employees are involved. Take the case of InSpeech Inc., a company that provides rehabilitation services to nursing homes. Several years ago InSpeech rapidly expanded through the acquisition of a number of smaller health-care companies. The zealous focus on profit alone, however, led to a 57 percent annual employee turnover rate and, consequently, flat profit margins. After investigating the situation, executives concluded that there was a "huge disconnect" between the values of the therapists (high quality care) and those of InSpeech's leadership (financial success). As a result, workers felt disenfranchised and underappreciated. Senior management began to listen more carefully via focus groups and redrafted the company's central purposes and core values. Even the company's name was changed to reflect the transformation. Within five years the turnover rate at "NovaCare" was halved and the number of clinicians willing to work for the company jumped tenfold. NovaCare is now one of the largest providers in its industry.[26]

Reciprocity

Reciprocity is a relationship that acknowledges mutual duties and accepts mutual accountability. As a concept it flows logically from the notion of dignity. In exchange for employee diligence, honesty and cooperation, employers are expected to respect workers' intrinsic value, provide due process and behave with integrity. While these obligations may differ, reciprocity insists that both parties have rights and duties. Put another way, all relationships are two-way, rather than one-way, avenues.

EXECUTIVE SALARIES. While CEO at Herman Miller, Max De Pree capped his annual income to 20 times the amount earned by his average factory employees. Contrast this with other Fortune 500 CEOs whose salaries average 117 times more than their workers'.[27]

De Pree's self-imposed compensation cap is an example of reciprocity.

Recognizing that all Herman Miller workers contribute to the company's success, he created a symbol of the joint nature of their venture. This is not to say that reciprocity demands equal distribution of benefits—observe De Pree's twentyfold salary enhancement. Rather, it creates a sense of commonality, "covenant relationships" as he puts it.[28] Stated another way, it is a form of "social contract" that holds both parties mutually responsible for their actions. This involves a sense not only of justice but of the Golden Rule as well.

Contrast De Pree's perspective with that of senior Boeing Company executives who cashed in significant stock options at the same time they were announcing proposed cuts in line workers' medical packages. While this was not the central issue in the lengthy strike that followed, it did exacerbate an "us versus them" feeling among rank-and-file workers.[29]

Scripture provides several positive examples of reciprocal employer-employee relationships. As second in command to the Egyptian king, Joseph worked hard to enhance his master's property interests. In return, the king listened to Joseph, regularly deferring to his judgment. Both prospered from the mutual respect generated (Gen 41:33-49). Daniel likewise so consistently won the praise of his superior that he was promoted to the highest ranks (Dan 2:48-49; 6:1-4).

Paul taught that even the master-slave relationship should reflect principles of mutual accountability. On the one hand, slaves were encouraged to respect their master's authority. Diligent effort, not token "eye service," was expected. On the flip side, masters were counseled to treat their subordinates with respect, honesty and fairness. To do otherwise, he counseled, was to risk God's judgment (Col 3:22—4:1).

The concept of reciprocity—mutual respect, shared obligations and joint accountability—not only is biblically rooted but is enjoying a revival in current management thought. Business ethicist Patricia Werhane comments: "The reciprocal nature of employer-employee relationship entails some important employee rights, in particular the rights to fair treatment and respect . . . fair pay . . . information . . . due process. In addition to working, employees are expected to respect and be fair to their employers."[30]

Servant Leadership

De Pree contends that "leadership is a concept of owing certain things" to others.[31] Authority is not an avenue for self-promotion but rather a platform from which to serve others. The concept of "servant leadership," advanced by Jesus, stands in sharp contrast with the standard view that leadership is based on power and self-interest. "Not so with you," Jesus taught. "Instead, whoever wants to become great among you must be your servant" (Mt 20:24-28). In this spirit, the Old Testament figure Nehemiah noted that while typical leaders "lorded it over the people. . . . out of reverence for God I did not act like that" (Neh 5:14-16).

One executive who exemplified this form of Theory C leadership, covenantal management, was George Cadbury, former CEO of Cadbury Schweppes, an English manufacturer of chocolate products and beverages. Emphasizing openness and fairness, his company's positive employer-employee relations stood out in the fractious English labor environment. Cadbury achieved this high measure of harmony by respecting his workers' dignity, acknowledging the reciprocal nature of their joint efforts and having the attitude of a servant leader. He even provided employees with full financial information on such sensitive matters as acquisitions and divestments. It is impossible to even imagine Frederick Taylor, Ron Eden of EBS or TriCon's executives making the following statement: "You should manage in an open way: tell people what is going on and listen to what they have to offer, particularly when it concerns matters which affect them very directly."[32]

Cadbury realized that service is a broad concept, extending far beyond the employer-employee relationship. Too often executives hypocritically preach the value of customer service while failing to practice it in their management styles. A mixed message is sent to employees, who are usually clever enough to understand when service is a mere slogan. Servant leaders, by contrast, subordinate their own interests to the good of the whole, listening carefully, equipping others to succeed, building trust and responsibly marshaling corporate resources.

Gift Recognition

DOING IT MY WAY. Joyce Schwein is the vice president of finance for a large privately held corporation. She rarely defers significant decisions to her subordinates and even less frequently involves them in high-level discus-

sions with the executive management team. She is perceived as aloof and isolated; Joyce's top people sense the erosion of their influence, and as a result turnover is high.

Theory C posits that generating profits is not the sole social function of business. It also serves to develop people. As communities of individuals, companies can either encourage or stymie personal and professional growth. Fundamental to the Christian notion of leadership is the manager's responsibility to identify subordinates' gifts and foster their development. Scripture teaches that many talents—including leadership, administration, service and oral communications—may have divine origins (Rom 12:6-8). An Old Testament craftsman is even described as being "filled with the Spirit of God," a phrase generally associated with prophets and priests, in regard to his creative abilities (Ex 35:30-35).

Affirming and utilizing others' talents is becoming a more critical management tool. With the current corporate trend toward flattening organizations, executives must find creative ways to expand their human resource base without adding new hires. Industrial psychologists, in particular, are expending great sums of money and time to identify giftedness in workers. Enterprises that depend heavily on employee creativity are especially in tune with this line of thinking. As Joyce Schwein is discovering, profits dwindle when subordinates' gifts are squandered. Max De Pree concludes:

> It is fundamental that leaders endorse a concept of persons. This begins with an understanding of the diversity of people's gifts and talents and skills. . . . Each of us contribute in a special way. . . . Trust and human dignity provide the opportunity for personal development. . . . Leaders owe people the sense of freedom of enabling gifts to be exercised.[33]

Recognizing employee giftedness is but one of the many ways that covenantal management transcends Theory X. When management focuses on relationships rather than mere bottom-line efficiencies, workers are treated with dignity, not as pieces of expendable machinery. As Japanese manufacturers and the total-quality movement have demonstrated, low-level employees can make significant contributions to improving products, processes and services. Theory X, on the other hand, runs the risk of relying solely on "experts" who do not even perform the daily tasks being reviewed. This disconnection not only can lead to misdiagnoses of problems but often generates employee absenteeism, low morale and labor unrest as well.

Theory Y, while more akin to Christian management principles in spirit, has the tendency to downplay the reality of human sinfulness and the need for accountability. Such realities cannot be ignored. Covenantal management calls for reciprocal accountability and, while it is flexible as to whether it is more hierarchical or peer-oriented in character, sees a need for management controls.

What covenantal management does best is create environments where employers and employees sense they are on the same team. As companies such as Herman Miller demonstrate, great things can happen when all energies are focused in a common direction. Work becomes a shared mission, a community to which individuals gladly and proudly commit themselves. It becomes a choir of many voices combining to create something special. In such contexts, to borrow a Max De Pree line, "leadership becomes an art"[34] and the business enterprise a grand adventure.

Questions for Discussion

I. Case for Discussion

Harry recently took over management of his family's textile company. For more than thirty years his father ran the company with an iron hand. Workers of different nationalities, mostly Asian immigrants, were hired to reduce the chance of unionization. Wages continue to be paid on a piecework basis—that is, for actual sewing completed. Overall, workers' earnings average $1.50 over the federal minimum wage.

Schooled in Theory Y, Harry is troubled by what he sees. The sewing jobs are repetitive and boring. Little interaction occurs between the small cadre of white male executives and the predominantly female Asian line workers. Midlevel management positions are few because employee output is so easily measured.

Reviewing the financial statements, Harry learns that the company has been modestly successful over the years. Return on investment is slightly above industry standards. Stiff international competition makes Harry hesitant to raise wages or alter "the system."

1. Should Harry change the company's management philosophy and structure? If so, how?

2. What risks does Harry run if he does *not* make any changes?

II. Workplace Application

1. Does your supervisor lean more toward Theory X or Theory Y? What impact does this have on your level of motivation and performance?

2. If "covenantal management" were fully implemented in your company, what changes would have to be made?

III. Concepts to Understand

How might each passage be applied to a business context?

1. Human Dignity

Genesis 1:26-28: What are the managerial implications of the concept that humans are made "in God's image"?

Exodus 5:4-21: Describe the king of Egypt's management philosophy.

Isaiah 58:3: Why doesn't God hear the prayers of these managers?

1 Peter 2:4-10; Revelation 1:6: What are the managerial implications of the "priesthood of believers"?

2. Reciprocity

Genesis 41:33-49: How does Joseph's work demonstrate the principle of reciprocity?

Daniel 2:48-49; 6:1-4: Why is Daniel promoted? What admirable characteristics does he display?

Proverbs 18:9: To whom is a lazy worker compared?

Matthew 24:45-51: What is Jesus' main point in contrasting the wise and wicked servants?

Ephesians 6:5-9; Colossians 3:22—4:1: What reciprocity does Paul call for in these master-slave passages?

3. Servant Leadership

Deuteronomy 17:14-20: What leadership characteristics does a good king possess?

Nehemiah 5:14-16: How does Nehemiah's approach to management differ from that practiced by the prior leaders?

Matthew 20:24-28: What are the primary characteristics of Jesus' view of leadership?

John 13:1-15: What point does Jesus make about leadership when he washes his followers' feet?

1 Peter 5:1-4: What instructions are given to church leaders? Why?

4. Gift Recognition

Genesis 39:1-6: How does Potiphar identify Joseph's abilities? In what way does he utilize them for his own benefit?

Exodus 31:1-6; 35:30-35: How does Moses recognize Bezalel's gifts?

Acts 6:1-6: Why are these seven men chosen to become early church leaders?

Romans 12:6-8: What gifts does Paul identify? Are they transferable from the context of the church to the marketplace?

12

EMPLOYEE RIGHTS IN TERMINATION & PRIVACY

Employers may discharge employees for good cause, no cause,
or even for a cause that is morally wrong.
TEXAN JUDGE

The right to be left alone is the most comprehensive of rights and
the most valued of civilized men.
LOUIS BRANDEIS

We think the government's need to conduct suspicionless (drug)
searches . . . outweighs the privacy of employees. We are concerned
about the physical safety of fellow employees and the public interest.
U.S. SUPREME COURT

We would be appalled at the specter of the police spying on employees
during their free time and then reporting their activities to their employers.
Drug testing is a form of surveillance, albeit a technological one.
Nonetheless, it reports on a person's off-duty activities just as surely as
someone had been present and watching. It is George Orwell's "Big
Brother" society come to life.
U.S. SECOND CIRCUIT COURT OF APPEALS

A s discussed in chapter eleven, covenantal management respects workers' dignity, endorses mutual accountability, practices servant leadership and celebrates giftedness in subordinates. This chapter explores how these concepts apply to two critical areas of employer-employee relations—termination and privacy.

Termination

MOON RIVER. During her four years of employment as a nurse at Scottsdale Memorial Hospital in Arizona, Catherine Wagenseller consistently received excellent evaluations from her supervisor, Kay Smith. After returning from an eight-day Colorado River rafting trip with Smith and several other nurses, however, her evaluations plummeted.

During the trip there was a great deal of drinking and group nudity in which Wagenseller refused to participate. One of her least favorite activities was a rendition of the song "Moon River," during which group members would drop their pants and "moon" each other. Back on the job Smith began to harass Wagenseller, even using abusive language. Six months later Wagenseller was fired.[1]

Term and at-will employees. All workers are hired on either a "term" or an "at-will" basis. The major difference between the two categories is that the final date of employment is established for term workers at the time of hire. College students who work as summer counselors, for example, are term employees; they know exactly when their jobs will end. School teachers and union members likewise fit into this classification. At-will contracts, on the other hand, have no up-front cessation dates. They constitute the predominant mode of hiring, with nearly two-thirds of all American workers being employed on this open-ended basis.[2]

Legally it is much more difficult to fire a term employee. To do so a company must demonstrate "just cause" and provide "due process" to the worker in question. This means that the burden of proof is on the employer to show that the worker has breached contractual expectations by misconduct, poor work performance or insubordination. In addition, the employer must provide a forum in which the dismissed employee can tell his or her side of the story.

Historically the law has not provided such protections for at-will employees. Employers have presumed the right to fire at-will workers at any time, for any reason and in any manner. Unfortunately, because Wagenseller fit into this category, her supervisor believed that it was unnecessary to provide a reason for the termination. The harshness of this approach has led lawmakers and judges to modify the "at-will doctrine." As the legal system has moved in this direction, the number of wrongful discharge suits has increased 2,000 percent in two decades.[3]

Justifications for the at-will doctrine. Supporters of the traditional at-will doctrine make three arguments in its defense. First, they contend, property rights give employers the right to determine who should be permitted on their premises. Workers, like other invitees, can have their license to enter company property revoked at any time. Once terminated, they become trespassers and as such may be kept from coming on site.

Second, the employer-employee relationship is premised on norms of contractual justice. If a contract is open-ended and no promise of due process is made, then immediate termination without explanation is deemed fair. Some economists even view this arrangement as advantageous for workers. Since just cause and due process cost companies money, the argument goes, workers may opt to receive higher wages in exchange for less job security. To prohibit such contractual freedom smacks of paternalism.[4]

Third, the at-will doctrine is said to be highly efficient. Employees given termination notices on Friday afternoon are gone immediately: no extensive hearings, no need for properly documented files and no compensation during lingering suspensions.

Criticisms of the at-will doctrine. Critics take umbrage with each of these points. First, they contend that property rights are not absolute but must be balanced by dignity concerns. With no obligation to treat workers with respect and fairness, the at-will doctrine severely limits any sense of mutual accountability and comes perilously close to "treating an employee as a piece of property."[5] Workers are not given the opportunity to explain the reasons for their actions, even legitimate reasons.

When the at-will doctrine was conceived centuries ago in England, small family business operations were the norm, with owners managing their own employees. This is much less true today. In publicly traded corporations, shareholders typically have no management responsibilities. Instead supervisors like Kay White, who generally have no ownership interests in the company, make all the termination decisions. Of course, since most of these midlevel managers are themselves at-will employees, they are likewise subject to termination without cause.

A second perceived weakness of the at-will doctrine is its near complete reliance on contractual justice. Obligations to others are minimized to include only those explicitly agreed upon. Since Catherine Wagenseller was hired as an at-will employee with no job security promised, she arguably has incurred no injustice.

As discussed earlier, however, this definition of justice is far too narrow. Scripture includes several other concerns that must be factored into the equation. Wagenseller's dismissal violates her biblical procedural rights to an impartial decision-maker, a full gathering of the evidence and the opportunity to give her version of the events. Likewise, her substantive rights of dignity, sexual privacy and reputation have been undermined. Further, the notion of merit has been ignored because her dismissal had nothing to do with prior work performance but solely with her supervisor's odd personal habits.

Standing alone, contractual justice is also flawed in its presumption that employers and employees possess relatively equal bargaining power. As demonstrated in the Wagenseller situation, however, this is often not the case. At her hiring she was probably given a "take it or leave it" offer. Had she insisted on term employee status, the next applicant would no doubt have been summoned. Even more significant is the inequality between companies and workers at termination. If Wagenseller had quit, the hospital would have sustained little, if any, harm to its reputation. Employees come and go all the time. On the other hand, by firing her, the hospital has seriously impaired her ability to find comparable employment elsewhere in her field. The stigma associated with an involuntary termination often lingers for years, greatly damaging the person's career.[6]

To counter the third argument, that of efficiency, critics contend that the at-will doctrine actually creates inefficiencies by permitting incompetent or corrupt supervisors to cover up their mistakes by dismissing conscientious employees. An Illinois worker, for instance, was fired after he supplied information to state police about an embezzling coworker.[7] Certainly his dismissal did not foster an efficient corporate operation. Likewise, a New Jersey bank president was terminated when he began to suspect that members of the bank's board of directors were laundering illegal drug money.[8] These cases illustrate that the short-term convenience of being able to dump employees quickly is often outweighed by long-term concerns. A great deal depends on how the concept of *efficiency* is defined. If efficiency is broadened to include considerations such as employee morale, trust and respect, supervisor accountability, and the cost of workers' lawsuits, then the at-will doctrine may not be so efficient after all.

Over the past few decades, U.S. federal and state laws have begun to reflect many of these ethical concerns. Employers are no longer free to dismiss employees solely on the basis of race, gender, age or handicap. Likewise, terminations that follow employee reports of illegal corporate activities to appropriate governmental authorities—such as unsafe working conditions, minimum wage violations or serious threats to public safety—are now suspect. Some states go even further by ensuring a zone of privacy, prohibiting employers from intruding into workers' personal lives. In the Wagenseller case, the Arizona Supreme Court reversed a lower court decision by citing "public policy" as an exception to the at-will doctrine. Holding for Wagenseller, it concluded: "We are compelled to conclude that termination of employment for refusal to participate in the public exposure of one's buttocks is a termination contrary to the policy of this state."[9]

Concluding thoughts on termination. Covenantal management seeks to balance employer property and contractual rights with worker concerns about dignity and due process. While finding acceptable common ground may be difficult at times, there is one thing on which both parties generally agree: bringing in union representatives or judges is not in the best interest of either group. Such processes are adversarial, time-consuming and costly.

A much better and simpler solution is for companies to ensure simple due process. Employees threatened by disciplinary action or outright dismissal should be treated fairly by an impartial decision-maker (whether an ombudsman, internal human relations professional or outside arbitrator), ensured that all relevant evidence and supportive documentation have been considered, and provided the opportunity to describe their interpretation of the events.

This approach is not only ethically sound but prudent from a legal perspective as well. An eminent corporate attorney advises companies to vest supervisors only with the authority to suspend subordinates but never to fire. Authority to dismiss should be reserved for an internal expert who fully reviews each case.[10] To do otherwise is to invite unlawful termination suits, intrusion by governmental regulators, and quite possibly unionization. Studies indicate that poorly handled dismissals are the primary reason that workers form collective bargaining units.[11]

Privacy

Rooted in the biblical notions of dignity and personal autonomy, the concept of privacy encompasses a wide variety of concerns, such as the ability to maintain secrets and, as in the Wagenseller case, personal modesty. A particularly egregious violation occurred some years ago at a hospital on the East Coast. Fearing employee theft of prescription drugs, the security department set up a secret camera in the women's dressing room. Not only was the security guard who monitored the camera male, but live images of the locker room were inadvertently broadcast throughout the hospital via a closed-circuit system.[12] Target Stores also overstepped its boundaries a few years ago by asking applicants true-false questions such as "Evil spirits possess me sometimes"; "I would like to be a florist"; "I am fascinated by fire"; "I have had no difficulty starting or holding my bowel movement." In an invasion of privacy class-action suit filed by twenty-five hundred applicants, Target was forced to pay out over $1.3 million.[13]

Particularly problematic are situations involving nonwork behavior. A Pennsylvania employer, for instance, recently refused to hire applicants who ride motorcycles off-work.[14] The reasons: a desire for a healthy work force and concerns about lifestyle issues often associated with motorcycle riders. Privacy advocates were outraged, contending that corporate influence ought not extend so far into workers' private lives. Other companies have taken a similar tack by refusing to hire any applicants who smoke. To counter such actions, the tobacco industry has launched a major lobbying effort in state legislatures. As a result, nearly thirty states, under the banner of privacy rights, now prohibit companies from engaging in "smoker discrimination." While most states permit employers to charge higher medical premiums for smokers, this legislation illustrates the weight afforded the concept of privacy in the American legal system.[15]

If the law has stretched the notion of privacy a bit far, Scripture always roots it within the context of relationships. For while it is important to preserve autonomy, self-dignity and freedom from unwanted external intrusion, privacy must never be used as an excuse for harming others (see Gal 5:13-15; Rom 14:1-23).

Drug Testing

It is in this broad context of biblical concerns that drug testing, perhaps the most controversial privacy issue of our day, must be analyzed. *WELCOME BACK. Wanda Creer was a lab technician at Pacific Refining Company in Hercules, California. Upon returning from a six-week sick leave, she was ordered into the women's room, where a drug-testing firm employee watched her lower her pants and urinate into a cup. Creer was very angry and worried that her medication would create a "false positive." The company's attorney defended the action as necessary: "We've got an entire town right across the fence from the refinery. . . . One mistake could be catastrophic."*[16]

Advocates of random mandatory testing contend that it is necessary to reduce the fifty billion dollars lost each year by corporations to drug-related problems—absenteeism, theft, high turnover, high medical costs, liability and low worker productivity. The fact that nearly half of the Fortune 500 companies administer mandatory drug tests illustrates the severity of the problem.[17] Privacy concerns, though not unimportant, must be viewed within this larger framework.

Privacy defenders counter with horror stories like that of Wanda Creer. For drug testing to be truly effective, employees are given minimal notice and watched carefully through every step of the process. Unless all workers are observed urinating into cups, the results are suspect because some, seeking to escape detection, may smuggle drug-free urine in plastic bags hidden in various body cavities. Such behavior is perhaps more common than we might generally think: a few enterprising companies nationally market mail-order drug-free urine with money-back guarantees.

Holiness, justice and love. In this complex context of countervailing interests, what guidance do holiness, justice and love provide? At first glance, holiness would appear to favor mandatory drug testing. Workers should seek physical purity, avoid the deceptive behavior generally associated with drug use, and be held accountable for their actions. It must be noted, however, that holiness also includes the virtue of humility. Humility should give employers some pause about being overzealous in their drug-testing programs. Judging and controlling others is a possible tendency of holiness that must be closely monitored.

It is also important to ask what role business should play in monitoring off-work employee conduct. What duty, if any, do firms have to catch weekend marijuana smokers who are not impaired when they come to work on Monday? Should their only concern be work performance, which can be monitored by supervisors, or should they also encourage holy living by serving as appendages of the criminal justice system? One state judge takes strong exception to such logic: "The employer's interest is not in the broader police function of discovering and controlling the use of illicit drugs in general society."[18]

Justice concerns are also important. To protect their property and to ensure that contractual obligations are fulfilled, employers have the right to be told the truth about drug use that impacts employees' work performance. Employers should be able to expect workers to be productive, absenteeism to be moderate, health care costs to be reasonable, and liability to third parties to be kept to a minimum. All these rights are seriously undermined by drug-impaired employees, making a strong justice argument for drug testing.

The general public also has legitimate justice concerns in not wanting to be harmed by drug-affected workers. This is particularly true for people such as pilots and surgeons who possess the potential to cause significant harm. It is no surprise that Wanda Creer's company justified its actions along these lines by pointing to the safety concerns of the nearby community.

Fellow workers may feel a degree of ambivalence about mandatory testing. On the one hand, they may be very concerned about the dangers drug-affected coworkers bring to the workplace. The U.S. Supreme Court has recognized the right to a safe work environment as justification for mandatory urinalysis.[19] On the other hand, they may object to being tested in the first place. For every employee caught by urinalysis, ninety-nine others are subjected to the indignity of the testing process. Critics contend that this is comparable to peering into others' windows or tapping their phones. All involve private functions that should be protected in a free society: "One who intentionally intrudes . . . upon [another's] private affairs . . . is subject to liability to the other for invasion of his privacy, *if the intrusion would be highly offensive to a reasonable person*" (italics added).[20] Urinalysis may qualify as such an invasion, because urinating involves a matter so personal that in some public contexts it constitutes a minor criminal offense.

While many employers contend that this expectation of privacy is voluntarily waived by most workers, the integrity of consent so given is suspect. In nonunion companies one only has to look at the repercussions faced by workers who refuse to submit to urinalysis. If any disciplinary action would result, then consent cannot be said to be completely voluntary.

Finally, the principle of biblical love encourages employers to consider giving employees a second chance. So-called employee assistance programs (EAPs) provide counseling assistance to help workers overcome drug problems. When successful, EAPs return healthy and appreciative workers to their jobs.

Guiding principles. The subject of drug testing brings many ethical principles into conflict. As we have seen, the topic is a tangle of holiness, justice and love concerns. Five guiding principles will bring a degree of structure to the discussion.

First, employers should attempt to make the testing process as unintrusive as possible. The personal modesty and dignity of each worker should be respected. As illustrated by the Wanda Creer situation, however, this objective is often difficult to achieve. To prevent employee dishonesty, urinalysis requires each step of the process to be closely monitored. Perhaps as other tests are developed, such as hair follicle analysis, the intrusiveness will decrease and employee dignity will be better protected.

Second, mandatory testing should focus on workers who have the potential of causing significant physical or property damage. Greater justification exists for testing school bus drivers and heavy machine operators, for example, than law firm receptionists and store clerks. In such situations, safety rights supersede privacy concerns. Privacy rights, while significant, must be subordinated to higher moral concerns.

Third, test results should be used only for the purpose of drug testing. If a company's lab uncovers a latent physical problem, such as leukemia, this information ought not be used in any way to adversely impact the worker's career. Several years ago the Du Pont Company aroused employee suspicions when it used annual physical exams as a means to check its African-American employees for sickle-cell anemia without their knowledge. Claiming that its motives were not improper, Du Pont nonetheless discontinued the practice.[21] Informed consent, a significant justice concern, requires employers to limit the scope of inquiry and to appropriately handle peripheral information.

Fourth, employers must ensure procedural justice by utilizing only qualified labs and by closely monitoring the chain of custody of urine samples. Sloppy lab work, such as mixing samples, can result in workers being wrongly accused and their careers ruined. This problem is compounded by the fact that certain foods and medications can produce erroneous results. Like Wanda Creer, many employees fear the possibility of "false positives." To ensure accuracy, workers whose urine tests positive should have a second analysis conducted before facing dismissal. A more expensive (and precise) test can be given to validate the first.

Finally, companies should consider implementing employee assistance programs to give errant workers another chance. It must be noted, however, that love must always be balanced with holiness and justice concerns. In this framework, empathy and mercy do not require endless corporate patience with drug abusers. Indeed, in some cases, terminating employees may be the tough love needed to turn a life around: "Christian realism maintains that the ethics of pure love needs to be united with the rational norm of justice in order to be relevant."[22] To do otherwise is to equate love with permissiveness. The biblical notion of love is much stronger than that.

Questions for Discussion

I. Case for Discussion

WHOLESOME HYNES. Hynes Custodial Services (HCS) is a family-owned business specializing in corporate custodial care. Since many of its clients are sensitive to security concerns, HCS makes it a point to only hire janitors who possess high moral character. Further, the Hynes family is very religious and its members feel most comfortable with those who share their values.

The HCS application form states the following:

Thank you for your interest in HCS. We want only the best to join "our family." We therefore regretfully exclude from consideration all applicants who:

A. are ex-felons

B. engage in sky-diving

C. fail to make child-support payments

D. smoke

E. eat over a pound of chocolate or two pounds of red meat per week

F. have sexual relations outside of marriage

G. have had three or more moving traffic violations in the past year.

In addition, HCS staff conduct extensive personal interviews of applicants, former employers, teachers, coaches and spouses (past and present). A visit to applicants' homes is also required prior to hiring.

1. Have any privacy principles been violated in this case?

2. How do you react to HCS's approach? Which criteria do you deem to be appropriate? inappropriate? Why?

II. Workplace Application

1. Have you ever witnessed an unfair disciplinary action or dismissal at work? How did you react?

2. Have you ever been tested for drugs? If so, how did you feel about it? If not, how do you think you would react?

III. Concepts for Understanding

How might each passage be applied to a business context?

1. Due Process in Termination

See chapter three for biblical passages dealing with

☐ impartial decision-makers

☐ gathering all evidence

☐ the right to tell one's version of events

Genesis 1:26-27: What rights does being created in God's image give employees?

Deuteronomy 15:12-14: Does the provision of severance pay for slaves have any relevance as a precedent today?

1 Peter 5:1-4: How should leaders treat their subordinates? What does it mean to "lord it over" someone in the context of employment dismissal?

2. Privacy

Daniel 6:1-16: Is Daniel's off-work privacy violated? If so, how?

Romans 14:1-23: How does Paul view privacy rights? When should they be exercised? When should they be waived?

1 Corinthians 8:1-13: What does this passage add to the discussion in Romans 14?

Galatians 5:13-15: What does it mean to be simultaneously free (private) and bound (to care for others)?

13

DISCRIMINATION & AFFIRMATIVE ACTION

A woman has to be twice as good as a man to go half as far.
FANNIE HURST

If you will glance over the catalogues of our colleges and legislatures,
the advertisements of merchants and mechanics, you will almost never
find an Irish name amongst them, which shows you at least that
they do not rise to any rank among us. At the same time, if you will
search the catalogues of alms-houses, and prisons, and potter
field, there you will find their names in thick order.
A PROTESTANT CLERGYMAN COMMENTING ON
IRISH-AMERICANS IN THE 1830S

Much of our social world is built on a foundation of discrimination.
Quotas are sometimes the only way to break down old patterns
of discrimination.
TOM BEAUCHAMP

God does not show favoritism.
THE APOSTLE PETER

M*ALES PREFERRED. Mary Hernandez worked for Wynn Oil Company for seven years prior to applying for the position of director of international marketing. When she failed to attain the promotion, her supervisor quietly informed her that she was never seriously considered for the job because of its close association with South American customers and suppliers. Pointing to the Latin cultural bias toward males, he confided: "You would have great difficulty conducting business from a hotel room."*[1]

It would be reassuring to assume that the plethora of civil rights laws passed during the past few decades have succeeded in eradicating employment discrimination in the United States. Unfortunately, such is not the case. Marketplace prejudice is alive and well. For instance, three women working for a Minnesota mine company were recently subjected to unwanted touching, sexual comments and pornographic photos. Apparently some of their male coworkers did not believe that mining was "women's work" and sought to drive them from their jobs.[2] In another case a female accountant was denied partnership in a Big Six firm after several of her male bosses observed that she "overcompensated for being a woman," "needs a course at charm school," needs to "act in a more feminine way" and should "walk more femininely, talk more femininely and dress more femininely."[3]

All is not well on the racial front either. A few years ago Shoney's Inc., America's third-largest family restaurant chain, was forced to set aside $105 million to compensate African-American applicants and employees for its discriminatory practices. In sworn statements, managers admitted penciling in the letter *O* in the Shoney's logo on application forms from black applicants, guaranteeing that "they would not be called for a follow-up interview." The few who were hired were kept out of public view. One manager recounts hiding two African-American waitresses in a bathroom when her supervisor unexpectedly paid a visit. Until recently no blacks were hired as secretaries, data processors or mail clerks at the national headquarters in Nashville. Not one of the ninety division director positions was filled by an African-American.[4]

Categorizing people by ethnic groups is a universal human foible. Bosnia, Belfast and Beirut have become metaphors for the international problem of racial stereotyping. In the United States racial tensions are complex and multitextured. At the Martin Luther King Jr. Hospital in the Watts neighborhood of Los Angeles, for instance, Hispanic workers recently complained about racial bias by African-American administrators. Though half of Watts's residents are Hispanic, they constitute only 11 percent of the hospital's work force. The federal government investigated, and the hospital nearly lost its accreditation. When queried about the dearth of Hispanics in the managerial ranks, the hospital's former CEO explained that most "don't aspire to do better."[5]

While ignorance and economics contribute to discriminatory attitudes—studies indicate that much prejudice is subconscious[6]—our sinful human tendencies also contribute. In Jesus' day even educated religious leaders taught that only fellow kinsmen, and not other ethnic groups, were owed respect. Jesus countered such reasoning by making a member of an outcast minority group a hero in one of his most famous stories—the Good Samaritan (Lk 10:25-37). Jesus regularly went out of his way to interact with diverse gender and racial audiences, including Romans, Greeks and Samaritans (see, for example, Mt 8:5-13; Jn 4:1-42). In this manner he "deliberately ignored the ethnic prejudices of his own people."[7] The apostle Paul put it this way: "There is neither Jew nor Greek [racial division], slave nor free [sociopolitical division], male nor female [gender division], for you are all one in Christ Jesus" (Gal 3:28).

Affirmative Action

OLD BOYS CLUB. Alcorn City Light (ACL), a branch of city government, is a male-dominated bastion. Females hold fewer than 5 percent of the engineering, road crew and management positions but constitute fully 90 percent of the clerical staff. A great deal of hiring for the "male" jobs is not done through traditional advertising but through word of mouth. Further, clerical workers are paid 22 percent less than their road crew counterparts even though both groups require roughly similar educational and experience background. Finally, 98 percent of all outside contracting is done with male-owned companies.

After intense lobbying of city government by women's groups, extensive public testimony is taken. As a result, the Alcorn City Council passes the following resolution:

In light of the serious imbalances and historical discriminatory practices of ACL, the following targets shall be met within five years:

☐ *15 percent of the engineers, 30 percent of the road crew staff and 20 percent of management shall be female.*

☐ *Female-owned businesses shall receive 25 percent of all ACL contracts.*

☐ *Clerical positions will be paid at the same rate as road crew staff.*

The concept of affirmative action may be divided into two categories. The first, "weak" affirmative action, encourages employers to enlarge the pool of applicants to include more members of previously omitted groups. The second, "strong" affirmative action, is much more controversial and emotionally charged. It grants preferences to groups of people in hiring and/or promotions. Critics decry strong affirmative action as "reverse discrimination," claiming that it breaches the justice ideal of equal treatment. They point to the irony of legitimating current discrimination in order to eradicate past discrimination. "Two wrongs don't make a right," they contend.

Advocates of strong affirmative action generally make three arguments in its defense. First, they maintain that distributory justice requires proportional representation in the work force. Since, as in the Alcorn City case, this rarely occurs on its own, an equalizing process is needed. Gender and racial imbalances are fundamentally wrong and must be corrected. Second, rigid societal class structures must not be permitted to set in. Without a means to give employment access to society's "have-nots," permanent socioeconomic stratification results. Strong affirmative action is viewed as an insurance policy that prevents turmoil and unrest. Third, compensatory justice insists on restitution for those who have experienced past discrimination. If Alcorn City Light, for instance, repeatedly discouraged female applicants, it should be required to pay them civil damages.

Proportional representation. The goal of proportional representation is to make the workplace mirror national averages in racial, gender and age composition—to "make America look like America." Companies have the responsibility to reflect this diversity. If, for example, Native Americans are statistically underrepresented in a particular factory, proportional representation calls for their numbers to be increased. Advocates of this position generally assume that weak affirmative action is incapable of producing such balance and that strong affirmative action is necessary.

One method used to achieve broader representation is known as "race-norming." This process compares job applicants only against members of their own race, not against the total population. Say, for example, a Japanese-American scores in the ninety-fifth percentile of all applicants on an employment test. Under race-norming this figure is ignored because what really matters is how she compares with other Asian-Americans. Since as a group Asian-Americans score higher on standardized exams than any other composite ethnic groups, her comparative score could easily drop to 88 percent. In this manner companies are able to identify the top 10 percent of each major ethnic category separately.[8]

Is this concept consonant with biblical principles? While it can certainly be said that Scripture ameliorates the harshness of disproportionate distribution of resources by encouraging individual charity and governmental action, it balks at calling for equal allocation. Equal opportunity, not equal results, is the underlying principle of justice. Advocates of proportional representation ignore the fact that each of us possesses different motivations, interests and abilities. Given this, perfectly balanced gender and racial outcomes are generally unrealistic. Does the fact that there are no National Basketball Association players of Laotian descent, for instance, mean that rampant discrimination is present? Probably not. Very few Laotians even played the game until the 1970s or 1980s, and many, especially the hill peoples, tend to be rather short in stature. Mere underrepresentation does not constitute discrimination per se.

Hence in the Alcorn City Light case the fundamental scriptural question is not whether men and women are equally represented in each job category but whether any of them have been discriminated against. While the numbers certainly indicate that something is amiss and that the company's hiring and promoting processes should also be thoroughly evaluated to determine whether any gender bias has been present, statistical disparities alone provide a shaky moral base for strong affirmative action. Proportional representation ought not become an end in itself.

Social insurance. Others view strong affirmative action as a means to lessen social unrest. Targeting specific ethnic groups with enhanced job opportunities, they argue, defuses tensions and limits social stratification. While this perspective has some merit—underresourced groups may indeed resort to lashing out at society—it skates on thin moral ice. By focusing exclusively on ethnicity, for instance, it ironically runs the risk of exacerbating the very tensions it seeks to relieve. If, for example, Chicano-Americans, Cajun-Americans and Portuguese-Americans are given hiring preferences, what prevents Thai-Americans, Polish-Americans and Jamaican-Americans from becoming upset? A veritable "pushing and shoving match between self-interested groups" erupts, with each hyphenated group bringing its own agenda to the political arena.[9]

Further, the social insurance model reposits great confidence in governmental sociologists to determine which groups are at risk. They will determine whether Hmong-Americans, Somali-Americans or Ukrainian-Americans are the most needy and therefore deserving of strong affirmative action. Not only does this smack of paternalism, but it erodes individual free will. One author warns that citizens should be cautious about ceding such powers to governmental bureaucrats: "Once licensed, it rebounds upon its perpetrators as well as others. In the long and bloody history of discrimination, one ought to be very chary of sanctioning it."[10]

Compensatory justice. Of the three proposed justifications for strong affirmative action, compensatory justice resonates most closely with Scripture. Premised on the two fundamental biblical principles of nondiscrimination and restitution, it requires damages to be paid for the breaching of others' rights. In workplace discrimination cases, these rights include equal opportunity and unbiased decision-makers. Restitution calls for relief to injured parties, whether the harm occurred intentionally or through negligent behavior. Though nowhere linked in Scripture to support strong affirmative action, the logic seems inescapable: discrimination that causes economic harm results in a viable claim for restitution.

In this light we should applaud the judge who held a New York City sheet-metal union liable to minority applicants who, over a twenty-two-year period, were denied jobs solely on the basis of race.[11] Strong affirmative action is warranted to open the doors for individuals who were wrongly denied entry. Compensatory justice is also due those females who can demonstrate that they have been discriminated against by Alcorn City Light and by the African-Americans who were excluded from meaningful employment by Shoney's Restaurants. Denial of equal opportunity necessitates restitution.

This is not to say, however, that the concept of strong affirmative action based on compensatory justice is without its difficulties. Several exist. First, Scripture typically deals with the concept in terms of individuals, not groups. While it is true that the prophet Amos condemned entire nations for violating human rights and the ancient Egyptians involuntarily distributed resources unjustly garnered from the departing Jewish slaves (Ex 12:35-36), Scripture typically limits restitution to situations where three elements are present: a specific victim, a specific injury and a specific wrongdoer. If, for example, property is stolen, a fire accidentally set or loaned property negligently misused, each element is easily identifiable (Ex 22:1-15).

The difficulty of most strong affirmative action cases is that entire groups are deemed harmed and worthy of restitution. While this has worked in some situations—witness the reparations paid to Japanese-Americans interned during World War II—it is generally much more difficult to identify each victim and each wrongdoer. More typically, when individuals are lumped together into easily identifiable groups, nonvictims are inadvertently made eligible for compensation. If, for example, a corporation deems African-Americans to be eligible for a hiring preference, nothing prevents a newly arrived Ethiopian immigrant from also benefiting. In this manner a program whose stated purpose is to benefit those whose ancestors were enslaved and abused is extended to include nonvictims.

Broad-based affirmative action programs also unintentionally require compensation from those who have caused no harm. Imagine two legal refugees—one Iranian Kurd and the other Bosnian—applying for the same job. Would it be just to make the Bosnian "pay" for her ethnicity by giving the Kurd a preference for the position? Such reasoning makes sense only under proportional representation or social insurance models. The Bosnian has not caused any harm to the other and can rightly complain with the psalmist: "I am forced to restore what I did not steal" (Ps 69:4).

The only possible compensatory justice argument is that the Bosnian benefits from society's discriminatory attitudes and practices. Even though not a wrongdoer in the sense of perpetrating racial discrimination, she is a beneficiary of the system and hence shares in the burden of making good on the debt.[12] This reasoning raises several unsettling questions, however. As an unintended recipient of positive racial bias, should she be required to compensate others? If so, how much? for how long? These queries illustrate the difficulties of grasping for perfect justice in an imperfect world.

Concluding thoughts on affirmative action. Of the three justifications for strong affirmative action, the theory of compensatory justice squares most directly with biblical principles. As noted, however, even it raises serious moral concerns. The more injustices it creates—by rewarding nonvictims and forcing nonwrongdoers to pay—the more suspect it becomes. While Scripture provides examples of group sanctions and rewards, its trajectory moves in the direction of individual responsibility. Hence the more precisely a model of restitution is able to identify culprits and victims, the truer it is to the ideal form of justice.

It is also important to explore other social remedies that are more effective than employment preferences. Increased governmental funding of impoverished school districts, for example, could greatly enhance the quality of education for the underprivileged, creating a greater sense of equal opportunity for all and establishing a more level playing field. Giving companies tax breaks for locating in low-income areas, so-called enterprise zones, is another illustration. Finally, increased emphasis on enforcement of antidiscrimination and employment laws would logically lead to a reduced need for strong affirmative action as a remedial device.

Questions for Discussion

I. Cases for Discussion

Johnson Controls, a Wisconsin corporation, manufactures batteries. After eight pregnant female employees showed dangerously high lead levels in their blood, the company issued a policy excluding all women capable of bearing children from jobs that involve direct exposure to lead. A small group of female employees sued to keep their positions, claiming gender discrimination. One had even chosen to be sterilized in order to not lose her job.

Three levels of courts, citing the need for fetal protection, held for the company. The U.S. Supreme Court, however, reversed. In part, the court reasoned:

The bias in Johnson Control's policy is obvious. Fertile men, but not fertile women, are given a choice. . . . Johnson Controls's fear of prenatal injury, no matter how sincere, does not begin to show that substantially all of its fertile women employees are incapable of doing their jobs.[13]

1. Do you agree with the Supreme Court's decision? Why?

2. Should employment discrimination ever be permitted?

Kaiser Aluminum Corporation operates a large plant in central Louisiana. Several years ago, even though 40 percent of the local community was African-American, under 2 percent of the skilled craft workers in the plant were black. In response to a threatened lawsuit, Kaiser agreed that at least half of its internal trainees would be black until they constituted roughly 40 percent of all the skilled workers. In the first group of trainees, seven were African-American and six white.

Brian Weber, a white Kaiser employee, applied to get into the training program but failed. After discovering that he would have been selected if all thirteen positions had been open, he sued. Both lower courts held in his favor on the basis of illegal discrimina-tion. The U.S. Supreme, however, ruled in Kaiser's favor. In part, the court held:

It would be ironic indeed if a law triggered by a nation's concern over centuries of racial injustice . . . constituted the first legislative prohibition of all voluntary, private, race-conscious efforts to abolish traditional patterns of racial segregation and hierarchy. . . . At the same time, the plan does not unnecessarily trammel the interests of the white employees. The plan is a temporary measure.[14]

1. Which strong affirmative action theory—proportional representation, social insurance or compensatory justice—did the court utilize?

2. Do you agree with the court's decision? Why?

II. Workplace Application

1. Describe incidents of workplace discrimination you have witnessed.

2. What are your views on affirmative action?

III. Concepts for Understanding

1. Racial Discrimination

Leviticus 19:34; Deuteronomy 10:17-22; 24:14-18; 27:19: What duties do we owe other ethnic groups?

Matthew 8:5-13: How does Jesus treat the Roman foreigner?

Luke 10:25-37: Who are our neighbors? What duties do we owe them?

Acts 6:1-7: What racial tensions existed in the early church? How are they resolved? Is a quota system used here to pacify the Grecian Jews? Is this a form of affirmative action?

2. Gender Discrimination

Genesis 1:27: What are the implications of this passage in terms of gender relations?

John 4:1-43: Why are Jesus' disciples so surprised that he has engaged in a lengthy conversation with this Samaritan woman?

Romans 16:1-16: Note all of the women in leadership positions in the early church.

Galatians 3:28: In practical terms, what does it mean that "there is neither male nor female"?

3. Economic Discrimination

Amos 5:11-12; 8:4-6: How are the poor mistreated? What is Amos's reaction?

1 Corinthians 11:17-21: How do the Corinthian Christians discriminate against the poor? What is Paul's advice?

James 2:1-9; 5:1: Why does James criticize his readers? How should the poor and rich be treated?

4. Age Discrimination

Leviticus 19:32; Psalm 92:12-15: How should older members of the community be treated?

5. Handicapped Discrimination

Ezekiel 34:15-16: How does the Lord use the image of physical disability to make a point in this passage?

Luke 14:7-14: What role do the physically disabled play in this parable?

6. Restitution

Exodus 22:1-15: In what situations is restitution owed? Does the principle apply to discrimination cases?

Psalm 69:4: What injustice does the speaker perceive?

Luke 19:1-10: Why does Zacchaeus make restitution?

14

THE ENVIRONMENT

If you've seen one redwood tree, then you've seen them all.
RONALD REAGAN

On spaceship earth there are no passengers . . . only crew.
BUCKMINSTER FULLER

We shall continue to have a worsening ecological crisis until
we reject the Christian axiom that nature has no reason for
existence save to serve man.
LYNN WHITE

Mexico City is an omen. That jammed city of toxic air and leafless
trees may be the first to know asphyxiation by progress. One of the
world's oldest civilization suffers mankind's newest affliction. Mexico
City warns the rest of the species of all that has gone wrong with
modernity's promised millennium of happiness.
CARLOS FUENTES

SEVERAL DECADES AGO A UCLA PROFESSOR NAMED LYNN WHITE PENNED
an environmental essay that reverberates to this day. Contending that "the
roots of our trouble are largely religious," he argued that Christianity "bears
a huge burden of guilt" for the modern ecological crisis. Due to its "arrogance
toward nature," he recommended that the Christian faith be discarded as a
basis for environmental ethics.[1]

Rather shocking for its time, Professor White's view has become conventional wisdom in many circles today. As stories about global warming, ozone
holes, deforestation and acid rain appear with more frequency in our news-
papers, White's accusations take on an even more ominous tone. Is Christianity really to blame for these and other environmental calamities?

White pointed to several particular aspects of Christianity that he found objectionable. The first aspect is that Christianity's view of history is linear. While religions such as Hinduism envision time's movement as circular, with no beginning or end, Christianity points to a specific beginning in its creation story and a specific termination at the final judgment. White perceived the cyclical view to be superior from an environmental perspective because it provides greater incentives for humans to protect nature. If we believe that we will reappear on earth in some other life form after death, we will be more motivated to care for it now. The linear view, White contended, does just the opposite. By envisioning a terminal point in history when God will purify the universe, Christianity reduces human responsibility. Further, he argued, a linear perspective encourages economic and technological growth that contributes to environmental degradation.

More pointedly, White charged that the biblical story of creation grants humans a license to use nature selfishly. Referring to the narrative account of Adam and Eve, he concluded: "It is God's will that man exploit nature. ... Christianity is the most anthropocentric religion the world has ever seen." He added that if humans "share God's transcendence of nature," they are not accountable for how they manage it. Such exaggerated notions of human worth, he argued, establish a hierarchical pecking order that not surprisingly places humans on top.[2]

Anthropocentric Ethic

BARKING UP THE WRONG TREE. An avid conservationist, Mary Davidge faces an ethical dilemma. On the one hand, as a member of the Sierra Club and the Audubon Society, she strongly supports the preservation of ancient forests and habitat of endangered species such as the northern spotted owl. On the other hand, she is suffering from ovarian cancer and wants to take a promising experimental drug, taxol, which is derived from the rare Pacific yew tree. To harvest a sufficient amount of taxol to cure Mrs. Davidge and the thirty thousand other American women who share her malady, tens of thousands of yew trees would need to be cut.

"I want to be treated," she says almost apologetically, "but I don't want to see the forests destroyed either." Observes an executive at the National Cancer Institute: "This is the ultimate confrontation between medicine and the environment. I love the spotted owl, but I love people more."[3]

White accused Christianity of being "homocentric" (today we use the term *anthropocentric*)—that is, human-focused. If nature's sole purpose is to gratify human pleasures, he contended, it has no intrinsic value in itself. Exploitation of the material world is permissible, so the argument goes, as long as other humans are not harmed in the process. From this perspective, it makes eminent sense to harvest yew trees for the benefit of cancer victims unless a greater long-term benefit for other humans can be identified.

Author Richard Routley poses the same question in a slightly different format. Suppose the last surviving human was about to die from nuclear poisoning. Would it be morally wrong for him or her to cut down the last living tree out of spite?[4] The anthropocentric ethic would answer negatively. Since the sole purpose of nature is to serve humans, the tree would no longer have justification for its existence. This human-centered model is pictured in figure 14.1. Men and women look to God, not nature, for their primary reference point.

God

Humans

Gap

Nature

Figure 14.1

The anthropocentric approach is defective in at least four ways. First, it is arrogant toward both God and nature. The "last living tree" example points out its presumptuousness and cavalier disregard for the divine handiwork. Since God has created the material realm, it has value in and of itself. To argue that "redwood trees are replaceable by plastic trees,"[5] as another author does, is to ignore God's creativity. Likewise, the clearcutting of forests and strip mining for minerals in many Western states have left unsightly and dangerous holes in the environment. One need only visit the huge open copper pit near Butte, Montana, to grasp the point.

Second, anthropocentrism easily lapses into egocentrism. With no accountability for how nature is treated, it is often used as a means to exploit and harm other humans as well. "What we call man's power over nature turns out to be a power exercised by some men over other men with nature as its instrument," C. S. Lewis wisely observed.[6] One example of such exploitation is in the dumping of toxic wastes in Third World nations. When African and Latin American countries banned such imports, multinational corporations turned to China instead. In a single year, Australian companies exported 580 metric tons of mercury waste and lead acid batteries to China. One province had to shut off its water supply eight times during the same time period because of "black tides" caused by waste seepage.[7] In Mexico City, thermal inversion caused by air pollution makes the air quality so bad in January that schools must shut down. Scientists estimate that half of the city's newborn infants suffer from toxic levels so high that nearly four million of the next generation, or 20 percent, will have IQs below 80.[8] Wanton disregard for nature goes hand in hand with disregard for human rights.

Third, the anthropocentric approach depletes resources, leading to scarcity. Times have changed since John Locke observed over two centuries ago that there are "plenty of natural provisions" and "few spenders."[9] With the planet's population set to double in the next fifty years, there are now "many spenders" and fewer natural resources. In Locke's day the use of common resources, such as land for herding animals, caused minimal problems because there was sufficient space. Today, however, we need only look at nations such as Haiti to underscore the point that resources such as air, water and land risk being overtaxed. One person's short-term utilization of any of these resources may lead to long-term harm to the whole; witness our polluted oceans and dirty air.[10] William Ruckelshaus, former CEO of Browning Ferris Industries and head of the U.S. Environmental Protection Agency, warns: "We need to face up to the fact that something enormous may be happening to our world. Our species may be pushing up against some immovable limits on the combustion fossil fuels and damage to ecosystems."[11]

Even a product as apparently harmless as disposable diapers can create serious resource problems. While these diapers may be a great convenience to parents of infants and provide high rates of return for manufacturers such as Procter & Gamble, they are compounding America's solid-waste difficulties. With eighteen billion ending up in American landfills annually, their cumulative effect is staggering. This is exacerbated by the fact that they may take up to five hundred years to biodegrade.[12]

Finally, the anthropocentric ethic tends to posit faith in technology as the savior for all environmental problems. If one technology creates an unwanted ecological byproduct, the argument goes, just invent a new one to remedy it. An extreme example of such confidence involves an innovative approach advocated by a special panel of scientists commissioned by Congress. To counter global warming created by the carbon dioxide from excessive burning of fossil fuels such as oil and coal, they propose dumping hundreds of thousands of tons of iron into the ocean to create a huge bloom of algae. In theory, the algae would then soak up enough carbon dioxide to end the threat of global warming. Critics quickly labeled the idea of enriching the oceans with iron the "Geritol Solution" and questioned its unknown effects on the food chain.[13]

While technology has brought many undeniable benefits in health care, transportation and product development, it has also created unwanted byproducts. In the United States alone, manufacturers annually generate one ton of toxic waste for every man, woman and child.[14] Twenty-three tons of sulfur dioxide are emitted into the air via smokestacks each year, costing society twenty-five billion dollars in health costs and environmental degradation.[15] As America attempts to deal with these problems, they multiply in emerging countries such as Brazil and Indonesia.

One author refers to this tradeoff of the "good life" for wasteful byproducts as a "Faustian bargain with technology." What looked like a good deal for Faust in the short term—extending his youth, knowledge and power—produced undesired results in the long run—losing his soul.[16] Technology brings a great deal of benefit but also presents a bill on which payment is due. Warns a technophobe: "Progress has lacked the capacity to amputate its errors as it discovers them in the bosom of success."[17]

This point is illustrated by a tragic occurrence in Puerto Rico. When a corporate farm introduced the steroid estrogen as a growth stimulant for poultry and cows, the chemical accidentally entered the human food chain. As a result, three thousand girls under the age of ten—some as young as two years old—experienced premature sexual development such as menstruation and fully developed breasts. Technology intended to improve the quality of life inadvertently resulted in serious and unforeseen side effects.[18]

Biocentric Ethic
"Biocentric ethics" shifts the focus away from humans and more broadly

targets all of nature. It argues that as just one of the planet's ten million species, *Homo sapiens* cannot be permitted to dominate the environmental scene. Since no one life form possesses a monopoly on moral rights, we must humbly take our place among all living entities.

This perspective encompasses a wide variety of ideologies, political groups and religious beliefs. As one author notes: "It is a pluralistic movement which contains many diverse strains."[19] What all these groups share is a rejection of the hierarchical notion inherent in the anthropocentric model and a call for a more egalitarian environmental approach. Some expand the group of stakeholders that should have a voice in all ecological decisions to include animals. Others include plants. Some go even further by granting moral standing to entities such as clouds, rocks and rivers.

When the environmental ethic is democratized, every entity, both human and nonhuman, is given a "vote" in ecological decisions. At the practical level, this approach has significant ramifications. For instance, in the debate over whether more northern Alaska lands should be opened for oil exploration, one writer comments: "The inherent value of the caribou cannot be cashed in terms of human economic benefit."[20] This sentiment is echoed by the founder of the radical group Earth First, known best for its tactic of placing hidden spikes into trees to prevent logging: "A grizzly bear has just as much right to life as any human and is far more important ecologically."[21]

This model also has many religious expressions. *Hinduism,* for example, teaches that nonhumans possess reincarnated spirits. While humans are regarded as the apex of life, all living beings are believed to be imbued with souls. For this reason it is not surprising to see sacred cows wandering the streets of rural India. Likewise, *animism*—the belief that each plant, stream and hill has its own spirit—leads to a strong respect for nature. One is reluctant to cut, plow or shovel if spirits must be placated. Lynn White lauded animism for its protection of the environment, regarding it as being vastly superior to Christianity.[22] *Pantheism* goes even further, making nature itself, in essence, "god." It views all life as being part of one fabric. The ecosystem combines all life forms into a single coherent unity. No external creator exists in this worldview and humans have no special right to govern nature. Listen to the pantheistic sentiments of an environmentalist working in South America: "I try to remember that it's not me, John Seed, trying to protect the rain forest. Rather I am part of the rain forest protecting myself; I am that part of the rain forest recently emerged into human thinking."[23]

A variation of this perspective is expressed by a relatively new movement that regards the earth itself as a living being. A group of scientists hypothesize that the earth is alive, capable of monitoring its own temperature, acidity and chemical balance. Some New Agers have transposed this scientific theory into the spiritual realm. If the earth is a being that unites all forms of life, they reason, it should be honored accordingly. They deify the planet, renaming it Gaia, after the female earth goddess of the ancient Greeks. For them "mother earth" is no metaphor but a spiritual truth. One scientist, though critical of the earth worship movement, nonetheless concedes: "Gaia is less harmful than standard religion. . . . At least it is not human-centered."[24]

Hence biocentric ethics may take on one of two forms. While both lump humans and nature together, they differ as to the role of God. In figure 14.2, biocentric view 1 acknowledges a transcendent God, whereas biocentric view 2 does not. Pantheism, spiritism and earth worship fit into the latter category.

The anthropocentric view	Biocentric view 1	Biocentric view 2
God	God	
Humans	———	
Gap	Gap	
Nature	Nature/Humans	Nature/Humans = "god"

Figure 14.2

While the biocentric approach successfully addresses many of the problems inherent in anthropocentric ethics, it possesses several difficulties of its own. As in figure 14.2, it has the tendency to make God so transcendent as to be irrelevant (view 1) or to depersonalize him entirely (view 2). In either case, the personal holy-just-loving God becomes irrelevant to environmental discussions. In God's place, divine power and character are vested in other forms of life or in the earth itself.

Such thinking is nothing new, but a rekindling of ancient beliefs. Nearly two thousand years ago the apostle Paul warned: "They exchanged the truth of God for a lie, and worshiped and served created things rather than the Creator" (Rom 1:25). A New Age proponent exemplifies the tendency in biocentric ethics to devalue the Creator and to overvalue the creation:

If we are addicted, confused and express disempowering tendencies, Gaia reacts with earthquakes, tornadoes, floods and extreme weather changes that force us to reassess our values, work together, and create a way of life anew. . . . Whenever some conscious living entity becomes enlightened, Gaia is happy and experiences intrinsic joy herself.[25]

Another practical outcome of this perspective is the devaluation of humans. Since yew trees have the same substantive and due process rights as Mary Davidge, for example, it is doubtful that their harvesting could be justified. Notes one biocentricist: "All things in the biosphere have an *equal right* to live and blossom and to reach their own individual forms of unfolding and self-realization."[26] Thus human and nonhuman needs are commingled; no priorities are self-evident. Humans are reduced to "nothing more than one mode in a cosmic web."[27] To even suggest that we have more inherent value than a bug or a puddle is to be guilty of a form of "bigotry,"[28] the very discrimination condemned in the previous chapter. One might even argue that nature deserves restitution for past harms incurred, a sort of environmental affirmative action. Rather than building more housing developments, factories and warehouses, perhaps more wetlands should be expanded, no-cut zones enlarged, pollution controls increased, and dams torn down. Having scarred nature like a "cancer," humans are currently in the debt column.[29]

Theocentric Ethic

Lynn White premised his case against Christianity on the assumption that Christianity is anthropocentric in character. A closer reading of Scripture, however, indicates that this presumption is erroneous. The Christian faith is "theocentric"—that is, God-centered—not human-focused. This is particularly true in regard to nature.

A theocentric view regards God as both Creator and Master of all life. Separate from and superior to the created universe, God is neither part of that creation, as in pantheism, nor transformed into a lesser god, as in Gaia worship. To the contrary, as sovereign Lord over every planet, river, animal, plant and human, he belongs at the center of every environmental discussion. Christianity rejects anthropocentric ethics because it usurps God's rightful role as originator and sustainer. It is important to note that Adam and Eve were not given title to land but were, in essence, sharecroppers charged with caring for the Lord's garden (Gen 2:15). Millennia later, when the Hebrew slaves returned to Israel, God made this principle abundantly clear to Moses: "The land is mine and you are but . . . my tenants" (Lev 25:23).

The Worth of Nature

As part of God's creative expression, the material world has intrinsic value. Before human beings even enter the biblical narrative, nature is affirmed as being "good" six times by its Creator (Gen 1:4-31). Since Scripture does not clearly state God's purpose in creating the universe, we must be careful not to presume that it was done solely for human benefit.[30]

In this regard, theocentric ethics concurs with biocentric ethics in rejecting the anthropocentric approach. Plastic trees do not have comparable value with redwoods, and the final person on earth would not be justified in cutting down the last tree for no good reason. Christianity teaches that if a tree falls in the forest and no human hears it, the tree has still fallen. Why? Because God hears it.

The value Christianity reposits in nature contrasts with the views of many Eastern religions. Many of these faiths, ironically praised by Lynn White for their environmental ethic, have strong gnostic tendencies that define spirituality as ridding oneself of any connectedness to the material realm. The physical order is scorned for the sake of spiritual truth. Christianity rejects such dualism as a false form of holiness, rejoicing in both the spiritual and material realms. It celebrates nature and encourages harmonious living with its nonhuman elements.[31]

Francis Schaeffer rightly points out that the incarnation, resurrection and ascension of Jesus all speak directly to the high value Christianity imputes to the material world. Preexistent in heaven, Jesus took on human flesh when he descended to earth (Jn 1:1-18). After death he ascended with his physical body into paradise. In many religions the idea of a "glorified" or "spiritual" body (1 Cor 15:42-44) would be a tasteless oxymoron, since the flesh is regarded as unclean. Not so in Christianity, which embraces the tangible as a gift from God.[32] Likewise, it is no coincidence that the sacraments of communion and baptism utilize bread, wine and water since the physical world is regarded as a means through which God sends grace and humans reciprocate in worship.

The Human Role

What role do human beings have in the created order?

> *SMELL OF DEATH. Cosmic Images Inc. develops its own line of cosmetics for women. Its researchers regularly utilize laboratory animals, typically rats and pigs, to test the toxicity of new products. The animals often develop severe internal health problems and occasionally die from chemical exposure.*

The human position in God's creation is twofold. First, we are part of it: "Dust you are and to dust you will return" (Gen 3:19). There is no room for false pride as in the anthropocentric ethic here. Made up of the same raw materials as pigeons and petunias, we are charter members of the natural order. In this sense we really are one with the mountains and ought not be surprised that our lung system is the same as that of other mammals.[33] St. Francis of Assisi captured this notion when he spoke of "Brother Ant" and "Sister Fire."[34] As finite beings, we must deal humbly with our fellow creatures.

Besides these shared characteristics, however, Scripture unambiguously states that we are also the crown jewel of God's handiwork. The creation story climaxes with the first male and female being brought into existence. Alone created in God's image (Gen 1:27), humans share divine characteristics of rationality, moral responsibility, inventiveness and capacity for spirituality.[35] Jesus underscored our special worth when he rhetorically asked, "Are you not much more valuable than they [birds]?" (Mt 6:26).

Figure 14.3 captures the tension between these two ideas. On the one hand, as finite beings we have much in common with nature. On the other hand, we bear the personal stamp of God on our character.

God (infinite Creator)	AND	God (personal, rational, eternal)
Gap		Humans (personal, rational, eternal)
Humans (finite creation)		Gap
Nature (finite creation)		Nature (impersonal, nonrational, temporal[36]

Figure 14.3

Under this paradigm humans possess a special role vis-à-vis nature. On the one hand, we are called to steward God's good creation, to exercise responsible authority. At the same time we exercise this "dominion," however, we are to be mindful of how we manage the Master's property. This entails responsibilities as well as privileges, since our control is only temporary and we must give account for our actions. Nature must be treated with respect, because we too are created beings. Like Adam, we are to be good earthkeepers and exude a "friendly paternalism"[37] toward other forms of life.

Thus while cutting down yew trees to save the lives of cancer patients is a legitimate enterprise, it seems objectionable to harm animals merely for the sake of making perfume. The first situation involves life and death, the latter the production of luxury goods. Theocentric ethics, undergirded by a strong sense of conservation, demands a more solid justification for using nature for human benefit. For example, among the land provisions in the Mosaic Code, farmers were prohibited from planting crops every seventh year so that the land might rest (Lev 25:1-5).

In many ways our role is similar to that of an artist's assistant. Just as the aide handles the master's canvases with great care, so must we treat nature with appropriate consideration. Wanton behavior toward animals, plants and inanimate objects not only violates the divine trust placed in us but displays a callous disregard for God's artistic sentiments. Caring for nature is a logical extension of our caring for God. Schaeffer summarizes this thought well: "Loving the Lover who has made it, I have respect for the thing he has made."[38]

Furniture maker Herman Miller illustrates one company's attempt to act as a responsible steward. For years the Eames chair was Herman Miller's "signature piece." Made of Honduran mahogany, it sold for well over two thousand dollars. When it became apparent to a company engineer that the wood had become endangered, he persuaded management to switch to walnut and cherry. The change, made out of respect for God's creation, resulted in a modest price increase and uncertainty about future sales.[39]

The Impact of Sin

Though the material world was created "good" and humans are made in God's image, it is apparent that all is not well on planet Earth. The advent of sin has had a great impact both on the way we make choices and on nature itself. Scripture paints a sobering picture. Sin has destroyed the initial harmony between humans and nonhumans: weeds make the land difficult to farm, and humans and animals are hostile toward each other (Gen 3:14-19). Human nature has changed too. Far from reflecting a proper "dominion" of God's creation, we have too often "dominated" nature, transforming a benevolent paternalism into harsh exploitation. Collectively, we callously dump chemicals down storm drains, pollute the air and neglect to care for the soil.

Unfortunately for nature, its fate is symbiotically linked to ours. When our first ancestors sinned, nature was directly affected by the resulting deterioration. Much as crack babies are affected by the misdeeds of their mothers, so the earth has been injured by human behavior. As the apostle Paul observed: "The creation was subjected to frustration, not by its own choice, but by the will of the one who subjected it, in hope that the creation itself will be liberated from its bondage to decay and brought into the glorious freedom of the children of God. We know that the whole creation has been groaning . . . up to the present time" (Rom 8:20-22). Earthquakes, volcanic eruptions and predatory animals were not part of the divine plan but resulted from human sin, which infected the natural realm.[40] The result: harmony has been replaced by a measure of ecological chaos. The blame for this tragedy rests squarely on our shoulders. Because of human sins, the prophet Hosea laments: "The beasts of the field and the birds of the air and the fish of the sea are dying" (Hos 4:3).

Restoration

Scripture points to a future date when nature will be restored to its original design. Animals will live in harmony with humans and with each other. Plants will flourish as they did in the Garden of Eden.

Isaiah envisioned this eschatological hope: "The wolf will live with the lamb . . . and the infant will play near the hole of the cobra" (Isa 11:6-8). In other words, all of nature—not just humans—will participate in this restoration. Rather than languishing, it will experience liberation and glorious freedom (see Rom 8:20-22).

The Role of Business

While this hope is grand, what of the present? What expectations are realistic in an age that reflects neither the harmony of the past nor the hope of the future? Scripture makes it clear that our task is to responsibly steward God's creation in the here and now. Hard choices may be necessary. It must be noted, however, that we are belatedly discovering that long-term economic viability and sensitivity to ecological needs are not necessarily opposing objectives, but necessary balances to each other. About the same time Herman Miller changed the lumber in its Eames chair, it took another action that made both environmental and economic sense. Estimating that its employees used over 800,000 disposable Styrofoam cups annually, management distributed a corporate coffee mug to each worker. Styrofoam usage was also reduced 70 percent in packaging, resulting in a savings of $1.4 million.[41]

Businesses must reject the anthropocentric ethic that encourages them to focus solely on return on investment for shareholders. Rather, they must view themselves as managing God's resources—both human and material—for the benefit of all stakeholders. That progress can be made in this direction is exemplified by cooperative efforts between corporations and environmental groups. At a National Wildlife Federation dinner at which Monsanto Chemical Company was honored for its antipollution efforts, its CEO observed, "Corporations like ours are experiencing what can only be called a revolution in environmental stewardship."[42]

Biblical stewardship honors such efforts. Being neither anthropocentric or biocentric, it leads us to care for nature as one aspect of our vocational calling to love God and neighbor. Companies ought not exploit nature for selfish short-term gain, but rather manage it carefully. As stewards of the Lord's property, they must be ever conscious that theirs is an "in-between" role. While unique among all created beings, possessing a special place in God's kingdom, humans are also part of that creation. As such, companies are obligated to be responsible managers of their material resources.

Questions for Discussion

I. Case for Discussion

Bluebird Smelter has operated for more than forty years in a small western Montana town. Employing eighty-five of the town's six thousand residents, its tall stack is visible for miles around. Though it has reduced its sulfur dioxide emissions by 75 percent over the past two decades, it still spews out a plume of harmful chemicals daily.

A state public health report indicates that sulfur dioxide causes emphysema, lung cancer and tuberculosis. Retirees and environmentalists have joined in an attempt to shut the smelter down. They have commissioned a study that indicates the following costs and benefits:

Benefits of keeping the smelter operating

Employee payroll and benefits	2,100,000
Economic impact on local businesses	4,600,000
Local taxes	125,000
Corporate charitable contributions	20,000
	$6,845,000

Costs of keeping the smelter operating

Five excess deaths per year	5,000,000
Other health problems created	450,000
Property damage	1,000,000
Reduction of aesthetic value and quality of life	500,000
Lost revenues and taxes from tourism	500,000
	$7,450,000[43]

1. How would the following environmental ethics evaluate this case? What recommendations would each make? Why?

    a. anthropocentric
    b. biocentric
    c. theocentric

2. What do you think should happen? Why?

II. Workplace Application

1. Describe any environmental moral dilemmas you have experienced either at work or elsewhere. How were they handled?

2. What is your environmental philosophy?

III. Concepts for Understanding

1. Intrinsic Value of the Physical Realm

Genesis 1:1—2:3: What is God's relationship with nature? Why is it created?

Leviticus 25:1-5: Why are the Hebrews instructed to let their land "rest" every seventh year?

John 1:1-5, 10-14: What role does "the Word" (Jesus) play in creation? From an ecological viewpoint, what is the significance of the statement that "the Word became flesh"?

Romans 1:19-20: How does God use nature to communicate with us?

1 Corinthians 15:3-28, 35-49: Why does Paul think Jesus' resurrection is so important? What does it add to an environmental ethic?

2. God as Owner

Leviticus 25:23: How is it possible for the Hebrews to simultaneously own their land and to be tenants?

1 Chronicles 29:10-13: According to David, what authority remains vested in the Lord?

Psalm 24:1-2: In practical terms, what does it mean for the Lord to own everything?

3. Human Role

Genesis 1:26-31; 2:4-25: How are Adam and Eve similar to other creatures? How are they different? What does it mean for them to "have dominion" over nature? In what ways do they exercise this role?

Psalm 8:1-9: How are humans both humbled and exalted in this psalm?

Matthew 6:25-30: Does Jesus recognize intrinsic worth in animals and plants? What does he mean by the statement that humans are of more value?

Mark 5:1-20: Do the pigs and the demented man possess equal moral rights?

4. Impact of Sin

Genesis 3:17-24: What impact does human sin have on plant life? on animals? on human relationships with nature?

Leviticus 18:28: How does God protect his land?

Isaiah 24:1-6: What is the relationship between human sin and ecological calamity?

Hosea 4:1-3: Why does "the land mourn," and why do the animals die?

Matthew 27:45, 51: Why does the earth quake and the sky darken when Jesus is crucified? What is the relationship between evil and ecological discord?

5. Restoration

2 Chronicles 7:11-15: How does God use nature to get our attention?

Isaiah 11:1-9: What is the relationship between the coming of the Messiah and the restoration of nature?

Romans 8:19-22: In what ways does Paul personify nature? Why does he employ this literary device?

15

PROPERTY

This American system of ours gives to each of us a great
opportunity if we only seize it with both hands and then make
the most of it.
AL CAPONE

There are three conversions necessary: the conversion of the heart,
mind and the purse.
MARTIN LUTHER

Gain all you can, save all you can, give all you can.
JOHN WESLEY

Bread for myself is a material problem: bread for other people
is a spiritual problem.
NIKOLAI BERDYAEV

T HE TOPIC OF PROPERTY LOGICALLY FOLLOWS THE PRECEDING CHAP-
ter's discussion about nature. Personal property involves the appropriating,
development and ownership of natural resources. Scripture has a great deal
to say about it; two of the Ten Commandments—prohibitions against stealing
and coveting—focus directly on property issues, and Jesus spoke more on
the subject than on any other except the kingdom of God.[1]

In biblical times personal property was tangible and easy to identify—
for example, land, livestock, coins and tools. Today it is a much more
complex matter. A great many of our possessions are intangible, abstract
and divisible; stocks, patents, mutual funds, derivatives and copyrights
could not even have been envisioned two millennia ago. One scholar
labels such goods "evaporated property," lamenting that "with liquidity,
morality becomes expendable."[2] While his conclusion—that the more

abstract property becomes, the more difficult it becomes to deal with morally—is debatable, there can be little doubt that ethical issues involving ownership have become increasingly intricate.

A second complicating factor in understanding the appropriate role of property is the wide range of perspectives presented in Scripture, so wide that Frenchman Jacques Ellul concludes that they are "contradictory."[3] American author Richard Foster takes a more moderate approach, identifying two streams of thought as the "light" and "dark" sides of property.[4] This chapter will follow his lead in discussing how to utilize property in ways that are holy, just and loving.

The Light Side of Property

CRUISING. Kathleen and Cora are partners in K & C Catering. After several years of financial struggle, the business is finally operating in the black. When Kathleen mentions that she plans to take a portion of her share of the profits to enjoy a Caribbean cruise with her husband, Cora's body language is less than affirming. Pressing the point, Kathleen asks, "So what's wrong with enjoying the fruit of our labor? We've slaved hard to earn this."

Cora responds, "It's your money, so I don't want to sound critical. But I couldn't justify a cruise when there are so many needs in our community. You know what its like at the homeless shelter when we deliver our leftovers on the weekends."

With a degree of sarcasm and hurt, Kathleen replies, "Thanks a lot, friend, for raining on my parade."

The conversation between Kathleen and Cora illustrates four positive and four negative aspects of property.

1. Property as God's gift. As noted in chapter fourteen, Christianity celebrates the material world, viewing it as a gift from a benevolent deity. Scripture affirms the right to possess physical goods as private property if they are acquired properly and used responsibly.[5] A generational account of Abraham's family illustrates the point. The patriarch, his son, grandson and great-grandson all credited God's benevolence for their personal and collective wealth (see Gen 13, 26, 31, 41, 45). Later descendants, while suffering as slaves in Egypt, were promised both a portion of Egypt's wealth and a land of their own "flowing with milk and honey" (Ex 3:7-8). After entering their land of promise, they were assured of a trade surplus with border nations and, over time, silver and gold became as common as stones (2 Chron 1:15).[6] In wisdom literature, the writers of Psalms and Proverbs assured the righteous that they would prosper. Even Job doubled his property at the conclusion of his trials (Job 42:10-16).

Likewise, several New Testament events view property in a positive light. Prosperous women supported Jesus' ministry out of their abundance (Lk 8:2-3), and a wealthy man provided an expensive tomb for Jesus' burial (Jn 19:38-42). Affluent benefactors also contributed to the early church (Acts 2:45; 4:32-37). Images used to describe heaven in the book of Revelation are replete with gold, silver and precious stones (Rev 21:18-21).

Of course not every use of property is blessed by God. Dealers of addictive drugs and deadly nerve gas abuse God-given material substances. However, when property is used in a holy, just and loving manner, it is to be appreciated as an expression of divine kindness. In this context, Kathleen and Cora can be confident that their business enterprise, if operated honestly and fairly, has God's approval. Those who imitate God by creating new products and services should be applauded; profit is not a dirty word.

2. Property as sacramental in character.[7] Sacraments are tangible God-ordained avenues through which divine grace is conferred and human worship elicited. The most common sacraments—baptism and Communion —illustrate how ordinary material goods such as water and wine can be transformed into vehicles of divine-human interaction. While many Christian traditions confine the concept of sacrament to specific church rituals, utilization of property for sacramental purposes is a broader theme that transcends such limitations. Few would disagree with the notion that God desires our property to be commissioned as special channels of worship and wholeness.

Several biblical examples illustrate this point. After fleeing from Egypt as slaves, Abraham's descendants donated so much property to build a tabernacle that the construction workers had to refuse any more gifts (Ex 35:20—36:7). Similarly, both the magi who brought expensive gifts to Jesus' parents at his birth (Mt 2:11) and the prostitute who poured perfume on his feet just prior to his death (Lk 7:36-50) utilized their property in a sacramental manner. This is particularly significant in the case of the prostitute whose perfume had quite possibly been acquired with fees paid for her services. Jesus also took special note of a widow who, in contributing all of her meager resources to the temple, exchanged her property for spiritual treasure (Mk 12:41-44).

Kathleen and Cora likewise have the option of using a portion of their profits creatively for sacramental purposes. As it was for the medieval peasants who voluntarily contributed to the construction of glorious cathedrals, the primary focus of such giving is to glorify God.

3. Property as reward. As discussed in chapter three, meritorious justice operates under the principle of cause and effect. It posits that those who sow the seeds of hard work and wise business decisions should reap a harvest of economic rewards. Prosperity is viewed as a natural outcome of due diligence.

Meritorious justice applauds people like the Nordstrom family, who over a period of some forty years parlayed a small Seattle shoe store into a national clothing chain with a reputation for excellence in service. The fact that the four former members of the company's executive team are now quite wealthy ought not strike anyone as unjust. To the contrary, this is eminently fair. They are reaping what they have sown. Like Kathleen, they have earned the right to "enjoy the fruit" of their labor.

The book of Proverbs systematizes this logic into a rather straightforward formula: self-disciplined people who maximize their efforts prosper, whereas people who are lazy and self-indulgent do not (Prov 20:13; 24:30-34). While later biblical writers question the universality of this hypothesis—the psalmist asks why the wicked prosper, the writer of Ecclesiastes sees little justice in the matter of income distribution, and Jesus does not lay blame on the disadvantaged (Lk 13:1-4)—the general principle of property as a reward is not eradicated. Jesus, for example, considers it only fair that hard work receives compensation and poor effort is sanctioned (Mt 25:14-30).

4. Property as a means to aid others. One of the most significant aspects of property is the ability it provides to help others. Generosity is a matter of the heart, property but a means of expression. The case of Oseola McCarty, an eighty-seven-year-old Mississippi washerwoman, exemplifies this principle.

Unable to attend school past the age of twelve, she gave her life's savings—$150,000 collected from cleaning laundry over seventy-five years—to a local university for student scholarships. When asked why she had lived so frugally, patching the holes in her shoes and owning only a one-channel black-and-white television set, she responded, "I wanted to share my wealth with the children. . . . Maybe I can make it so the children don't have to work like I did." People in her hometown simply refer to her donation as "The Gift."[8]

Scripture lauds those who so utilize their property to benefit others. The good Samaritan in Jesus' parable comes to mind as one who made his assets available for a stranger (Lk 10:25-37). Barnabas, an early church leader, sold a piece of real estate to benefit the fledgling Christian community (Acts 4:36-37). Paul went so far as to recognize generosity as a spiritual gift, heaping particular honor on a Greek church for sharing its financial resources with impoverished Christians in Jerusalem (Rom 12:6-8).

The Dark Side of Property

Unfortunately, the concept of private property does not receive uniformly positive reviews in Scripture. To the contrary, it is portrayed negatively in at least four ways.

1. Property as an idol. Thirteen executives of Honda America were arrested for participating in a fourteen-year kickback scheme.[9] In exchange for ten million dollars worth of clandestine payments to a senior vice president, six regional directors were given various favors. During the investigation it became evident that the pursuit of property and power had replaced integrity as their primary ethical reference point.

Jesus recognized the power of property to cloud our spiritual vision. When he labeled love of wealth as "Mammon"—what we might call materialism today—he went so far as to personify it as a rival god, an idol (Lk 16:13). Like the one true God, Mammon claims to provide security, freedom and power.[10] Indeed, it "can be a master the same way God is."[11] While the very first principle of holiness—zeal for God—demands that we choose the proper master, property's ability to wrest our loyalties ought not be underestimated.

The power of Mammon is sadly illustrated by the plight of a managing partner of a prestigious Chicago law firm. Submitting false vouchers to clients over six years, he raked off more than $784,000 to buy furniture, jewelry and Chicago Bulls basketball tickets, and even to pay his children's dental bills.[12] Like his Honda counterparts, he made Mammon his primary focus.

2. Property as false security. When John D. Rockefeller was asked how much money is enough, he replied, "Just a little bit more than you have."[13] This surprising remark from the richest man of his era demonstrates the illusionary nature of the belief that an abundance of property guarantees personal satisfaction. Even though the pursuit of wealth as a means of achieving security, independence and status is a predominant value in American culture, Scripture warns us that wealth is transitory in character, disappearing like a mist, wilting like a flower and rotting like a dead log (Prov 23:5; Jas 1:9-11; 5:1-3). And even if we are able to maintain an abundance of goods throughout our lifetime, as Job noted, "naked we came from our mother's womb, and naked we will depart" (Job 1:21).

Materialism is a poor substitute for reliance on God. While both promise a sense of identity, purpose and protection, Mammon is simply incapable of delivering on its promise. Business executives who make acquisition their god unwittingly imitate the central character in one of Jesus' stories. A rich farmer, flush with cash, tore down his barns to build bigger ones and then indulged in self-congratulations: "You have plenty of good things laid up for many years. Take life easy; eat, drink and be merry." Unfortunately he died that very evening and was labeled a "fool" for placing his security and priorities in things rather than in God (Lk 12:19-21).

Christians are by no means exempt from such false reliance. John Wesley observed a four-step process. First, holy living promotes the virtue of self-discipline. Second, self-discipline generates hard work. Third, hard work produces a measure of prosperity. Finally, prosperity decreases dependence on God. Thus, ironically, while applied faith often results in greater affluence, affluence does not return the favor.[14] Stated another way by Moses: "When you have eaten and are satisfied . . . be careful that you do not forget the LORD your God . . . then your heart will become proud . . . [saying], 'My power and the strength of my hands have produced this wealth for me.' But remember the LORD your God" (Deut 8:10-18).

3. Property as temptation. Robert Cowan, CEO of Kansas-based American Teleconferencing Services, permits each of his employees to take out an interest-free no-questions loan of up to one thousand dollars. Why? To reduce the temptation of employee theft.[15] Taking possession of others' property without permission is a great lure. Pity the single parent who handles company cash every day but can barely make financial ends meet at home.

While property itself is not morally negative, the desires it produces often are. Two such vices are covetousness, lusting after others' property, and greed, wanting more even after our basic needs have been met. Scripture unequivocally condemns both, noting that "envy rots the bones" (Prov 14:30) and that there ought "not be even a hint . . . of greed" among us (Eph 5:3). Judas's betrayal of Jesus for thirty pieces of silver (Mt 26:14-16) is a tragic example of Paul's well-known admonition that "people who want to get rich fall into temptation. . . . For the love of money is a root of all kinds of evil" (1 Tim 6:9-10).

4. Property as a threat to human relationships. The Dart Group, an international conglomerate controlled by the Herbert Haft family, holds significant stakes in several subsidiary corporations such as Crown Books, Trak Auto and Shoppers Food Warehouse. After turning the Dart Group over to his oldest son and moving toward retirement, Haft ignited a family civil war by returning to the helm and removing both his son and his wife from positions of authority. Sadly, the clan's property was used as a battleground rather than as a means of common enterprise.[16]

The Haft case illustrates that property, when combined with emotions such as anger, envy and betrayal, can be transformed into something divisive. Richard Foster notes, "People jockey to find out what other people earn because, in our society, money is a symbol of strength, influence and power."[17] Abraham and his nephew Lot—till then quite close—went their separate ways because their employees argued over land access. Lot's next residence, soon-to-be-destroyed Gomorrah, reflects the powerful influence that property can have on human relationships (Gen 13:5-12). Likewise, Jacob, Abraham's grandson, breached a twenty-year affiliation with his father-in-law in large measure over a series of property disputes (Gen 31:1-9). "A greedy man stirs up dissension," warns the writer of Proverbs (28:25).

Property also divides people along socioeconomic lines. The more afflu-ent tend to live, socialize and work with those in their "class." The urge to protect hard-earned property then serves to increase the gap. In doing so, "mammon . . . sucks the milk of human kindness out of our very being."[18]

This is illustrated by the practices recently ascribed to an American mining company doing business in Indonesia. Having invested nearly five billion dollars to develop gold and copper mines, the company is allegedly displacing native peoples, dumping toxic materials into local rivers and paying the Indonesian military to intimidate those who resist its desires.[19]

The prophet Amos bitterly opposed such bullying, accusing the wealthy and powerful of his day of prizing things over people (Amos 2:6-7). James likewise lamented the preferential treatment given to the wealthy (Jas 2:1-9), and Paul chided the more affluent Christians for separating themselves from their poorer colleagues at common meals (1 Cor 11:20-22). Ezekiel went even further, charging his contemporaries not only with acts of intentional harm to the less fortunate but with negligent omission as well. Sodom's primary sin, he charged, was not sexual immorality but affluent indifference to the poor (Ezek 16:49).

Stewardship of Property

As we have seen, there is a dynamic tension within the biblical concept of property. On the one hand, warnings are given not to pursue property lest it become our guiding star and master. This path leads to idolatry, greed, covetousness, false security and isolation from others. On the other hand, property should be appreciated as a divine benevolence, a means by which God can be honored, a reward for diligent effort and a vehicle through which others can be served.

On balance, it is best to regard property as a tool, something that can be used for either good or ill. Like a chain saw, it is a powerful device that can provide firewood for warmth, healing and comfort on the one hand, or can cause destruction, pain and isolation on the other. To use such a potent tool properly, we must first clearly understand that ownership is a complex responsibility.

God as Property Owner and Humans as Stewards

As analyzed in the previous chapter, the earth and everything in it belongs to the Lord (Ex 19:5-6). While we may have "present and historical title," God retains "transcendental title."[20] From this perspective, we are not unrestricted owners, but rather stewards who have been delegated the responsibility of exercising dominion over the physical world. Since God remains the ultimate owner, our duty is to manage the property with due care and to be held accountable for how we perform. This view flies in the face of most Western thought of the past three hundred years, which raises individual ownership to a nearly sacred level.

Property Rights

Most companies do not want to admit that they have a white-collar crime problem. . . . It's called the Judas Effect. . . . According to a recent Peat Marwick study, employees steal from their companies regularly. 76% of the companies surveyed have experienced fraud in their organizations within the last 12 months. The median cost to each company: $200,000. . . . The total cost to corporate America . . . is $100 billion annually. . . . We have a nation of thieves. . . . Between 2% and 5% of each sales dollar is a premium that companies must charge customers to make up for losses due to internal crime.[21]

The Eighth Commandment's negative injunction—"You shall not steal"— makes it abundantly clear that even though God is the supreme owner of all property, individual property rights are also to be respected (Ex 20:15). Like other substantive rights (for example, to be told the truth, to maintain one's reputation, to not be discriminated against), property rights create a protective zone that others ought not puncture. Property rights represent important justice concerns because they protect a sense of dignity, privacy and personal identity.

Examples of property rights violations abound. Among the more colorful abusers are the former president of Alaska's Better Business Bureau who was charged with writing over nineteen thousand dollars in checks to herself[22] and the hurricane-fence manager near Chicago who not only stole materials from his employer (gates and fencing) but also put in competing bids to prospective customers and did the work on the side himself.[23]

One company even hired a photographer to fly over a new plant being built by Du Pont Chemical Company to decipher a secret manufacturing process.[24] Also of note is the small software firm that hired an agent to acquire its competitor's source codes by claiming to be a representative of a governmental intelligence agency. The result—a lawsuit that alleged copyright infringement, fraud and unfair competition—was settled out of court.[25]

Marketplace theft includes a wide variety of offenses: padding expense accounts, using company cars for personal purposes, taking office supplies, using company trade secrets (for example, customer lists, formulas, pricing information) for personal benefit, buying confidential information about competitors, copying software without permission and being paid for work not done. One study indicates that employees who surf the Internet at work waste an average of one and a half hours daily by performing nonbusiness-related functions.[26]

Scripture obligates those who violate others' property rights to make restitution. Under the Mosaic law, thieves were required to reimburse their victims fourfold, and those who damaged others' property negligently had to make restitution (Ex 22:1-6). Property rights are meaningful only if reciprocal duties to respect them are enforced. Restitution remains a key remedy in both our civil law and criminal justice systems. The state of Utah, for example, collects over a million dollars annually from juvenile offenders alone.[27]

Property Duties

SHOE ON THE OTHER FOOT. Mencke Shoes is a closely held family corporation operating in southern California. Prior to the Los Angeles riots in the early 1990s, the Mencke family did not have a retail store in south-central Los Angeles. Afterward, however, one family member argued, "We should do something to improve life in L.A." Prolonged debate ensued as to whether a new store should be opened near the riot area.

The traditional Western view on private property is a hybrid of three theories of justice. First, the substantive right of ownership creates a zone of privacy that others have a duty to respect. Second, owners are obligated not to harm others by using their property in inappropriate ways (for example, pollution, nuisance). If harm is caused, restitution is appropriate. Third, owners may take on additional duties (easements, construction liens, restrictive covenants) if they contract to do so. Contractual justice imposes only those obligations that are entered into voluntarily.

From this perspective, the Mencke family has no obligation to even consider opening a store in south-central Los Angeles. Their substantive ownership rights place duties on others to respect their property, no direct harm is being caused to others by their failure to open such an outlet, and they have no contractual obligations to the city or to its residents. Of course, if they determine that a profit is to be made in the venture, they may voluntarily choose to open the store. But under the traditional view of property rights, they have no duty to contemplate such a move.

Do these three justice concerns constitute the entirety of biblical ethics? By no means. While a more broad-based scriptural view might not require the Mencke family to open the store, it would take their discussion further. Given that they are stewards, what duties does the true owner of the company—God—place on them? What obligation does neighbor love impose?

In the early years of television, a show entitled *The Millionaire* was quite popular. The plot revolved around an agent of an unseen benefactor who sought out and delivered gifts of one million dollars to needy individuals. While the agent might expect to receive a reasonable salary, he would be considered a thief if he kept any of the intended pass-through funds for himself.

Likewise, as stewards of God's property, we steal from others when we fail to utilize resources in a compassionate and responsible manner. The twin duties of stewardship and neighbor love significantly alter the perspective of the Eighth Commandment. Since God is the true property owner and we are obliged to love our neighbors, we become thieves if we fail to pass through sufficient resources to others.

In this manner the Eighth Commandment is transformed from a negative injunction, the protection of our property rights, to an affirmative duty, our obligation to be generous toward others. John the Baptist appears to have approached property issues from this perspective when he challenged the more affluent in his audience to share extra coats and food with the needy (Lk 3:11). Lewis Smedes captures this sentiment well:

> Whatever rights a person has to possess property are rooted in the duty he has to use them for the good of his neighbor. . . . The person who refuses to accept his rights to property in terms of duty to fellow man has forfeited the moral right to possession and has by the same token sacrificed something of his genuine personhood.[28]

Scripture identifies five groups to whom we have particularly acute property obligations: widows, orphans, handicapped, foreign-born and the poor. Moses exhorted Abraham's descendants to "love the [foreign-born] as yourself" (Lev 19:34; cf. Ex 22:25-27), and Isaiah demanded feeding the hungry, clothing the naked and providing shelter for the homeless (Is 58:6-10). In the New Testament, Jesus instructed his disciples to be hospitable to the poor, the crippled, the lame and the blind (Lk 14:13) while James encouraged his readers to "look after orphans and widows in their distress" (Jas 1:27).

God imposed specific property duties on the society of Israel some two millennia ago. These included a mandatory 10 percent contribution from those with property for the benefit of orphans, widows and the foreign-born (Deut 14:28-29); a requirement that the land remain fallow every seventh year and that whatever the land yielded during the sabbath year would be food for the Israelites, their servants, their hired workers and the temporary residents who lived among them (Lev 25:1-7); a requirement that debts be canceled every seventh year (Deut 15:1-11); a command that farmers not pick their crops bare at harvest so that the poor could follow after the workers and gather food from the unpicked plants (Lev 19:9-10); and a requirement that the land be returned to its original owners every fifty years (Lev 25:8-17). It is important to note that relieving poverty, not distributing all goods equally, was the primary focus.[29]

While these Old Testament precedents do not provide crystal-clear guidance to businesses like the Mencke Shoe Company, they do illustrate that property ownership is a complicated moral concern. That businesses have property duties as well as property rights is evident. South-central Los Angeles has many widows, children without parents, handicapped, foreign-born and poor. Complete passivity in the face of need is sinful. While there may be other means for the Menckes to give aid (for example, charity or internships for inner-city youth at their other stores) and any sense of compassion must be balanced against economic realities (no company can operate without profits), they must also acknowledge that as God's stewards they are duty-bound to aid others in some manner. "From everyone who has been given much, much will be demanded" (Lk 12:48). Whether investing in Los Angeles would be the best use of these resources is a difficult question, but the principle of property duty remains.

Scripture promises that generosity is good not only for the recipient but for the giver as well. When money is used as a tool for good, we destroy its ability to control and seduce us. We "profane it, taking away its sacred character."[30] Giving also restores our souls: "He who refreshes others will himself be refreshed" (Prov 11:25).

One final question about property duties remains: what obligations do corporations and individuals have to pay taxes and comply with governmental regulations? Should laws that affect land usage (for example, zoning or wetlands protection) be obeyed? While Scripture realistically assesses the potential dangers of an overreaching government (see Rev 13), it generally supports its right to demand the payment of taxes and to enforce its laws. As an instrument of God's "common grace," it is a divinely appointed institution whose purpose is to promote social order. As such, government is also God's steward and has the authority to limit property rights for the common good (Rom 13:1-7).

Striving for Balance

Finding a balance amid such countervailing principles is no small task. Focusing solely on property's light side leads to materialism and hedonistic hoarding. The so-called health and wealth gospel, popular with many televangelists, follows this errant path. At the other extreme are those who concentrate on the dark side of property and call for complete divestiture. Religious asceticism is usually associated with this perspective, and monks— be they Hindu, Buddhist or Catholic—best exemplify its pursuit of abstinence. However, neither extreme represents the total biblical witness. A more balanced perspective entails five elements.

1. Accept the responsibility of being stewards. First, we should embrace the privilege of being stewards. Total divestiture can represent an abdication of responsibility, an avoidance of divine delegation. True holiness does not confuse physical and moral separation, but attempts to redeem worldly obligations rather than shunning them. Further, complete dispossession may bring only modest relief to the needy. The ability of monks to serve others, for instance, is severely limited by their lack of material resources. Isn't it better to create wealth, manage it wisely and then distribute it judiciously? After all, the marketplace is not a stagnant set of fixed goods but an ever-changing pool of opportunities and assets. It should be utilized as a vehicle through which humanity can be served and glory is brought to God.

Jesus illustrated the virtue of wise property management in one of his parables. Three agents were given various amounts of their employer's money to administer. The two who increased the sum were praised whereas the one who did not was chastised (Mt 25:14-30). As stewards of divine assets, each was obliged to administer the entrusted resources prudently. Just so, it is our responsibility to manage effectively all that is in our possession—money, abilities, relationships, and opportunities. In this regard, we would do well to imitate the ants who work hard storing up provisions now so that the community will have adequate resources later (Prov 6:6-8).

2. Be zealous for God in the marketplace. The first attribute of holiness is zeal for God. In the context of managing property, this means having correct priorities. Loving God, not acquiring property, must always be our highest aspiration. For while possessions are blessed by God, they must never become idols. As Foster notes, we must learn "to possess money without being possessed by it."[31]

Jesus achieved this balance while laboring at his trade as a carpenter. He did not flee from financial obligations, but rather maintained his zeal for God while crafting furniture, paying bills and meeting tax obligations (Mt 22:15-22). His life illustrates the point that holiness is not a call to isolation but to responsible living. Likewise Paul, in his dual role as church planter and tent maker, maintained a proper perspective on the use of property. While greatly valuing economic self-reliance, he never permitted property to become the center of his life (Phil 4:10-13). The concept of vocation encompasses who we are and all that we do. Property must find its niche within this context, not vice versa.

3. Resist property-related temptations. Property temptations are not limited to the wealthy but, as noted in Proverbs, extend to the poor as well: "Give me neither poverty nor riches. . . . Otherwise, I may have too much and disown you and say, 'Who is the LORD?' Or I may become poor and steal, and so dishonor the name of my God" (30:8-9). For while the wealthy tend to grow comfortable and self-reliant in their affluence, the poor are tempted to covet what others have, and at times to act on their impulses. Does this imply that being middle-class is optimal? Not necessarily. Middle-income people can be every bit as greedy and Mammon-focused as either the rich or the poor.

The key is to recognize the seductiveness of property. Like illicit sexual desire or the lure of wine to an alcoholic, the yearning for more property can become addictive. While the degree of this pull varies from person to person, the desire to possess ever-increasing amounts is a near-universal human experience. This underscores the importance of Paul's comment: "I have learned to be content whatever the circumstances. I know what it is to be in need, and I know what it is to have plenty" (Phil 4:11-12). Like Paul, we are not to be mastered by property, but to master it.

4. Value people over property. Too often the bottom line of profit becomes the sole criterion for making business decisions. An appropriate view of stewardship recognizes that all God-given resources—both property and human talents—are to be properly managed. Scripture makes it abundantly clear that human beings are to be valued more highly than property. Put another way, we are to love people and use things rather than use people and love things.

An extreme example of abusing people for the sake of property is the growing illegal international market in human body parts. Allegations that corneas have been ripped out of mentally ill patients in central Argentina, kidneys from street children in Honduras and livers from corpses in Moscow are almost too repulsive to mention.[32] Less sensational, but nonetheless problematic, are those nations that covet international trade but engage in serious human rights violations. Clothing giant Levi-Strauss refuses to do business in countries that utilize either child or prison labor. In addition, it requires overseas companies with which it does business to limit their workers' hours, pay fair wages and ensure reasonably safe working conditions.[33]

Sadly, not all American manufacturers adhere to such standards. A toy-factory fire in an overcrowded Bangkok sweatshop resulted in nearly two hundred deaths, the worst industrial fire in history. Several large American companies—including Toys "R" Us, J. C. Penney, Fisher-Price, Hasbro and Gund—had their toys fabricated at the Thai factory.[34]

Managers, whether international or domestic, should always take into account the human consequences of their decisions. They should be sensitive, for example, to subordinates going through divorce, lending a sympathetic ear and perhaps even lowering productivity expectations in the short term.

Similarly, advertising executives should reject lucrative cigarette accounts because of the health hazards associated with the product. The well-being of people, not just the pocketbook, must be factored into all decisions.

The Old Testament extends this principle to prohibit the charging of interest to the poor (Deut 23:29-20) and to require that debts be canceled every seven years (Deut 15:1-11). Why? Because concern for the less fortunate takes priority over individual property rights. In the New Testament, James admonishes employers for not paying their day laborers in a timely manner. While this enabled the owners to collect an extra day's interest on their accounts, it also meant that the workers' families had to forgo their evening meals (Jas 5:4). Such a practice not only violated the contractual agreement but also indicated their priority of property over people. Jesus warned such misers that it is possible to gain the whole world but lose one's soul (Mt 16:26).

5. Be slow to criticize others' use of property. As we have seen, there is no precise formula for balancing property rights and duties. Property fairly earned is a reward for hard work and is to be viewed as a gift from God. At the same time, however, when property is grasped too tightly and becomes a primary focus, it can become a barrier to our relationships with God and with others.

So while some people feel justified owning summer cabins and new cars, others do not. While some give away large sums of money, others donate less. While some are sorely tempted by greed and covetousness, others are not seriously affected. While Kathleen may feel comfortable cruising in the Caribbean, Cora does not. In such gray situations we would be wise to heed Paul's advice and let God have the final word: "Who are you to judge someone else's servant? To his own master [God] he stands or falls. . . . Each of us will give an account . . . to God" (Rom 14:4, 12).

Questions for Discussion

I. Case for Discussion
CABIN FEVER. Dave and Bonnie Wells are a middle-aged couple with two children, ages twelve and ten. Dave is an accountant and Bonnie is a school teacher. Both work hard and are involved in numerous church and charitable causes. Dave's uncle recently died, leaving him an acre of land near a resort lake and sufficient funds to build a modest cabin.

Bonnie and the kids think that building a cabin is a great idea, but Dave feels uncomfortable having a second residence when so many people do not even have one. Further, he is trouble by the two-hour one-way drive, particularly about the extra carbon-dioxide fumes his car will emit. Bonnie counters by pointing out that the kids are perfect ages to enjoy water sports. She argues further that they need more family time and that they could provide work for the old contractor who lives near the lake.[35]

1. What advice and guidance does this chapter provide the Wellses?

2. What would you do if you were in their situation? Explain.

II. Workplace Application

1. Describe a situation, at work or elsewhere, in which property was used in a positive way.

2. Describe a situation in which property was used negatively.

3. Which way do you tend to view property—more positively or negatively? Explain.

III. Concepts for Understanding

1. The Light Side of Property

a. Property as God's Gift

Genesis 13:2; 26;12-16: How is the wealth of Abraham and his son Isaac critiqued?

Deuteronomy 28:1-14: What material blessings await the righteous?

2 Chronicles 1:12-17; 32:27-29: How do Solomon and Hezekiah acquire their wealth?

Luke 6:38: What blessing accompanies generosity?

b. Property as Sacramental in Character

Exodus 35:20-29; 36:4-7: How do the Hebrew refugees use their property to honor God?

Mark 12:41-44: In what way does the widow's contribution take on a sacramental quality?

Luke 7:36-50: How does the woman use her property as a means to worship God?

c. Property as Reward

Proverbs 20:13, 21:5, 20; 24:30-34: What do these proverbs teach about the concept of merit?

Luke 19:11-27: Is it fair that one of the servants is rewarded more than the others? Why?

d. Property as a Means to Aid Others

Acts 4:36-37: In what way is Barnabas generous? How does it help others?

Romans 12:8; 15:26-27: In what way is contributing to others' needs a "spiritual" gift?

2 Corinthians 8:1-5, 9, 13-15: Why does Paul praise the Macedonian (Greek) churches?

2. The Dark Side of Property

a. Property as an Idol

Matthew 6:19-24: Why do each of these illustrations have only two options?

Matthew 19:16-30: Why does the rich man not follow Jesus? What does Jesus mean by an "eye of the needle" in verse 24?

Luke 16:13-15: What stark choices does Jesus give? How does his audience react?

Hebrews 13:5-6; 1 Timothy 3:3: What dangers does loving money present?

b. Property as False Security

Psalm 10:4-6: How does wealth blind this man?

Proverbs 22:1; 23:5; 27:23-24: In what contexts is the insecurity of prosperity discussed?

Ecclesiastes 5:10-14, 19: In what ways is the pursuit of wealth a trap?

Luke 12:16-21: What lesson is to be gleaned from this parable?

James 1:9-11; 5:1-3: How reliable is wealth?

c. Property as Temptation

Proverbs 14:30: In what ways does envy "rot the bones"?

Mark 7:21-22; Ephesians 5:3: With what other sins is greed associated?

1 Timothy 6:9-10: What are the dangers of materialism?

James 4:1-3: Why is this Christian community divided?

d. Property as a Threat to Human Relationships

Genesis 13:5-13: Why do Abraham and Lot go their separate ways? Could this have been avoided?

1 Kings 21:1-23: How does Ahab's covetousness lead to murder?

Ezekiel 16:49: What is Sodom's primary sin?

Jeremiah 17:11: What happens to ill-gotten gain?

James 2:1-9: How does wealth divide people?

3. Property Rights

Exodus 20:15: What is the content of the Eighth Commandment?

Exodus 22:1-15: What restitution is owed to those whose property rights are violated?

Proverbs 23:10: What property right is violated?

Ephesians 4:28: What restitution should a thief make?

James 5:4-6: How are these employers stealing from their workers?

4. Property Duties

Deuteronomy 14:28-29; James 1:27: To what groups are property duties owed?

Isaiah 58:6-10: What duties do the affluent have to the less fortunate?

Luke 3:11-14: What obligations does John the Baptist place on property owners?

EPILOGUE

A THEOCENTRIC APPROACH TO BUSINESS ETHICS

T his book is predicated on the notion that ethical ideals are grounded in the character of God. While not denigrating human-centered ethical systems (such as utilitarianism or duty-based reasoning), this theocentric approach moves beyond both consequences and moral rules, aspiring for nothing less than Godlike behavior.

The quest to imitate God focuses on three predominant divine traits: holiness, justice and love. Together they form an ethical paradigm through which all human actions may be evaluated. This has serious implications for how we should behave in the marketplace, including several issues discussed in the body of this book:

1. Purpose of business and overall perspective
   - ☐ Vocation: business as a source of meaning and service
   - ☐ Stakeholder perspective: taking into account the interests of owners, employees, suppliers, customers and community
2. Marketing
   - ☐ Honesty
   - ☐ Appropriate disclosure
   - ☐ Sensitivity to customers' strengths and weaknesses
3. Law
   - ☐ The duty to supersede the letter of the law
4. Employer-employee relations
   - ☐ Employee loyalty
   - ☐ Conflicts of interest
   - ☐ Participatory versus top-down management

☐ Labor negotiations

☐ Privacy rights: drug testing, applicant interviews, off-work behavior, impact of technology

☐ Whistle-blowing

☐ Sexual ethics: harassment, discrimination, inappropriate conduct

☐ Due process in layoffs, dismissal and discipline

☐ Discrimination

☐ Affirmative action

5. The environment

☐ Balancing jobs and environmental protection

☐ Environmental stewardship

6. Property

☐ Property rights

☐ Stewardship/property duties

☐ Compassionate use of wealth

☐ Financial disclosure

Imperfect Human Beings

Of course, living up to the holy-just-loving standard is easier said than done. As morally flawed individuals, we tend to ignore God's character and engage in self-delusion. Rather than serving God and others through our businesses, we are tempted to act egoistically. It is all too easy to gravitate toward the following moral errors:

☐ Idolize business success

☐ Set lower ethical standards in the marketplace (dual morality)

☐ Act as legal positivists, complying with only the minimal letter of the law

☐ Lie and conceal relevant information

☐ Benefit from conflict-of-interest situations

☐ Exploit employees

☐ Cheat employers

☐ Abuse the environment

☐ Hoard wealth

Grace

Christian ethics makes provision for the gap between the high moral aspirations of the theocentric approach and the way we really live. It is self-evident that we all fall far short of the holiness-justice-love standard. Rather than be overly discouraged by this ethical deficit, we should humbly accept God's offer of grace. Through the death of his Son there is forgiveness; through his Holy Spirit there is hope of moral improvement.

This is why even our ethical failings can have a silver lining. Recognizing our imperfections, we are drawn to the grace of God, which in turn leads us to assess ourselves modestly and to treat others with tolerance.

Notes

Chapter 1: A Christian Ethic for Business

[1]Humanist philosopher P. H. Nowell-Smith, quoted in Richard Higginson, *Dilemmas* (Louisville, Ky.: John Knox, 1988), p. 55.

[2]R. Meiners, A. Ringleb and F. Edwards, *The Legal Environment of Business,* 5th ed. (Minneapolis: West, 1994), p. 191.

[3]Dietrich Bonhoeffer, *Ethics* (New York: Macmillan, 1979), pp. 232-33.

[4]William Barclay, *Christian Ethics for Today* (San Francisco: Harper & Row, 1971), p. 27.

[5]For a further discussion of the difference between ethics and morals see Meiners, Ringleb and Edwards, *Legal Environment,* p. 193.

[6]Donald Bloesch, *Freedom for Obedience: Evangelical Ethics in Contemporary Times* (San Francisco: Harper & Row, 1987), p. 32.

[7]Ibid., p. 32.

[8]For a more complete discussion, see chapter two.

[9]For a more complete discussion, see chapter three.

[10]See also chapter four.

[11]John McClenahen, "Good Enough," *Industry Week,* February 20, 1995, p. 59.

[12]"Kidder-Peabody's Takes a Ride," *Fortune,* August 1994, p. 24.

[13]J. I. Packer, *Rediscovering Holiness* (Ann Arbor, Mich.: Servant, 1992), p. 107.

[14]Oliver Williams and John Houck, *Full Value: Cases in Christian Ethics* (San Francisco: Harper & Row, 1978), p. 61.

[15]Laurel Touby, "In the Company of Thieves," *Journal of Business Strategy,* November 1993, p. 27.

[16]Joe Maxwell, "President's Alleged Misdeeds Cost Christian School Millions," *Christianity Today,* April 3, 1995, p. 98.

[17]Lewis Smedes, *Mere Morality* (Grand Rapids: Eerdmans, 1983), p. 18.

[18]Robert Tomsho, "How Greyhound Lines Re-engineered Itself Right into a Deep Hole," *Wall Street Journal,* October 20, 1994, p. A1.

[19]Williams and Houck, *Full Value,* p. 28.

[20]Carol Ostrom, "CEO Plunges into Unknown," *Seattle Times,* May 25, 1991, p. C9.

[21]Tim Ferguson, "Inspired from Above, ServiceMaster Dignifies Those Below," *Wall Street Journal,* May 8, 1990, p. A25.

Chapter 2: Holiness

[1]Stanley Ayling, *John Wesley* (Nashville: Abingdon, 1979), p. 95.

[2]From a case developed by Douglas Downer, Seattle Pacific University graduate student, 1994. See also Robert Almeder and Milton Snoeyenbos, "Churning: Ethical and Legal Issues," *Business and Professional Ethics Journal* 6, no. 1 (1987): 22.

[3]J. I. Packer, *Rediscovering Holiness* (Ann Arbor, Mich.: Servant, 1992), pp. 68-69.

[4]William Lawrence, *Beyond the Bottom Line: Where Faith and Business Meet* (Chicago: Praxis Books, 1995), p. 15.

[5]John Stott, *Christian Counter-Culture: The Message of the Sermon on the Mount* (Downers Grove, Ill.: InterVarsity Press, 1978), p. 17.

[6]Ibid., p. 49.

[7]George Stevens, "Business and Law Respondents: What Is Ethical Behavior?" *Journal of Education for Business* 68, no. 6 (1993): 348.

[8]Raju Narisetti, "Intelligent Electronics Made Much of Its Profit at Suppliers' Expense," *Wall Street Journal,* December 6, 1994, p. A1.

[9]Dietrich Bonhoeffer, *The Cost of Discipleship* (New York: Macmillan, 1975), p. 45.

[10]Quoted in Robertson McQuilkin, *Biblical Ethics: An Introduction* (Wheaton, Ill.: Tyndale House, 1989), p. 90.

[11]Packer, *Rediscovering Holiness,* p. 120.

[12]Max De Pree, *Leadership Is an Art* (East Lansing: Michigan State University Press, 1987), pp. xix-xx, 12-13.

[13]Packer, *Rediscovering Holiness,* p. 163.

[14]Susan Gaines, "Handing Out Halos," *Business Ethics,* March/April 1994, pp. 21-22.

[15]McQuilkin, *Biblical Ethics,* p. 72.

[16]Will Durant, *The Story of Civilization, Part IV: The Age of Faith* (New York: Simon & Schuster, 1950), p. 60.

[17]Dana Milbank, "Being a Consumer Isn't Easy If You Are Boycotting Everything," *Wall Street Journal,* April 24, 1991, p. A1.

[18]Packer, *Rediscovering Holiness,* pp. 187-88.

[19]Simon Kistemaker, *The Parables of Jesus* (Grand Rapids: Baker, 1980).

Chapter 3: Justice

[1]Lewis Smedes, *Mere Morality* (Grand Rapids: Eerdmans, 1983), p. 23.

[2]Joan Rigdon, "Oracle CEO Is Accused of Using Firm's Resources to Benefit Company He Owns," *Wall Street Journal,* October 10, 1994, p. B10.

[3]Thomas McCarroll, "Who's Counting?" *HNH Journal,* April 13, 1993, p. 48.

[4]Richard Chewning, *Business Ethics in a Changing Culture* (Reston, Va.: Reston, 1984), p. 166.

[5]Thomas Donaldson and Patricia Werhane, *Ethical Issues in Business: A Philosophical Approach,* 4th ed. (Englewood Cliffs, N.J.: Prentice-Hall, 1993), p. 207.

[6]Thomas Burton, "Caremark Faces Heat for Paying Doctors Who Sent It Patients," *Wall Street Journal,* November 11, 1994, p. A1.

[7]Smedes, *Mere Morality,* p. 55.

Chapter 4: Love

[1]Donald Bloesch, *Freedom for Obedience: Evangelical Ethics in Contemporary Times* (San

Francisco: Harper & Row, 1987), p. 97.

[2] Lewis Smedes, *Choices: Making Right Decisions in a Complex World* (San Francisco: Harper & Row, 1991), p. 54.

[3] Mark Robichaux, "Dart and Ronald Haft Reach Pact Seeking End to Bitter Legal Feud," *Wall Street Journal,* October 9, 1995, p. B4.

[4] Charles Swindoll, *Improving Your Serve* (Waco, Tex.: Word Books, 1981), p. 53.

[5] Tom Peters, *The Pursuit of Wow!* (New York: Random House, 1994), p. 130. See also Tom Peters, *In Search of Excellence* (New York: Warner Books, 1982), p. 156.

[6] Quoted in Bloesch, *Freedom,* p. 33.

[7] Ibid., p. 33.

[8] Ibid., p. 93.

[9] John Stott, *Christian Counter-Culture: The Message of the Sermon on the Mount* (Downers Grove, Ill.: InterVarsity Press, 1978), p. 122.

[10] Will Durant, *The Story of Civilization, Part IV: The Age of Faith* (New York: Simon & Schuster, 1950), p. 796.

[11] Joseph Fletcher, *Situation Ethics* (New York: SCM, 1966), p. 98.

[12] Bloesch, *Freedom,* p. 35.

[13] Fletcher, *Situation Ethics,* p. 120.

[14] John Davis, *Evangelical Ethics* (Phillipsburg, N.J.: Presbyterian & Reformed, 1983), p. 12.

[15] Fletcher, *Situation Ethics,* p. 27.

[16] William Barclay, *Christian Ethics for Today* (San Francisco: Harper & Row, 1971), p. 81.

[17] A. Kotchian, "The Payoff: Lockheed's 70-Day Mission to Tokyo," *Saturday Review,* July 9, 1977, pp. 7-12.

[18] Smedes, *Choices,* p. 32.

Chapter 5: Dual Morality

[1] Oliver Williams and John Houck, *Full Value: Cases in Christian Business Ethics* (San Francisco: Harper & Row, 1978), pp. 141-46.

[2] Albert Carr, "Is Business Bluffing Ethical?" *Harvard Business Review,* January-February 1968, p. 143.

[3] J. Ladd, "Morality and the Ideal of Rationality in Formal Organizations," *The Monist,* LaSalle, Ill., 1970, p. 130.

[4] Milton Friedman, "The Social Responsibility of Business," in *Ethical Theory and Business,* ed. T. Beauchamp and N. Bowie, 2nd ed. (Englewood Cliffs, N.J.: Prentice-Hall, 1983), p. 81.

[5] George Steiner and John Steiner, *Business, Government and Society* (New York: Random House, 1985), p. 333.

[6] Ibid., p. 27.

[7] I. Tarbell, *The History of the Standard Oil Company* (1904; reprint Gloucester, Mass.: Peter Smith, 1963), 1:99.

[8] Steiner and Steiner, *Business,* p. 333.

[9] Carol Ostrom, "CEO Plunges into the Unknown," *Seattle Times,* May 25, 1991, p. C9.

[10] Abraham Kuyper, *Lectures on Calvinism* (Grand Rapids: Eerdmans, 1931), p. 78.

[11] Ostrom, "CEO Plunges," p. C9.

[12] D. Reeck, *Ethics for the Professions: A Christian Perspective* (Minneapolis: Augsburg, 1982), p. 34.

[13] Richard Chewning, *Business Ethics in a Changing Culture* (Reston, Va.: Reston, 1984), p. 31.

[14] Richard Chewning, *Biblical Principles and Business,* 3 vols. (Colorado Springs: NavPress, 1989), 1:259.

[15] Ibid., p. 127.

[16]Ibid., p. 128.

[17]T. Beauchamp and N. Bowie, *Ethical Theory and Business,* 4th ed. (Englewood Cliffs, N.J.: Prentice-Hall, 1993), p. 65.

Chapter 6: Law

[1]H. Kelsen, *Public Virtue* (New York: Macmillan, 1973), p. 202.

[2]J. Austin, *The Province of Jurisprudence Determined* (1832; reprint New York: Noonday, 1954), p. 184.

[3]W. J. McDonald, ed., *New Catholic Encyclopedia* (New York: McGraw-Hill, 1967), 10:258.

[4]Nita Geranios, "Food-Truck Whistle-Blowers Feel Threatened, Blackballed," *Seattle Times,* December 2, 1990, p. B6.

[5]Christopher Stone, *Where the Law Ends: The Social Control of Corporate Behavior* (Evanston, Ill.: Harper & Row, 1975), pp. 93-96.

[6]H. L. A. Hart, "Positivism and the Separation of Law and Morals," *Harvard Law Review* 71 (1958): 593.

[7]D. Welch, ed., *Law and Morality* (Philadelphia: Fortress, 1987), p. 94.

[8]Albert Carr, "Is Business Bluffing Ethical?" *Harvard Business Review,* January-February 1968.

[9]Welch, *Law and Morality,* pp. 153-54.

[10]Wolfgang Gaston Fridman, *Legal Theory* (London: Stevens & Sons, 1953), p. 457.

[11]C. Adams, ed., *The Encyclopedia of Religion* (New York: Macmillan, 1987), 10:320.

[12]Ibid., p. 321.

[13]Lewis Smedes, *Choices* (San Francisco: Harper & Row, 1991), p. 50.

[14]Charles McGuire, *The Legal Environment of Business* (Columbus, Ohio: Charles E. Merrill, 1986), p. 692.

[15]Ibid., p. 690.

[16]Thomas Mulligan, "The Moral Mission of Business," in *Ethical Theory and Business,* ed. T. Beauchamp and N. Bowie, 4th ed. (Englewood Cliffs, N.J.: Prentice-Hall, 1993), p. 67.

[17]Lon Fuller, *The Morality of Law* (New Haven, Conn.: Yale University Press, 1963), pp. 9-10, 27-28.

Chapter 7: Agency

[1]K. Eisenhardt, "Agency Theory: An Assessment and Review," *The Academy of Management Review* 14, no. 1 (1989): 57-74.

[2]L. Westra, "Whose Loyal Agent? Towards an Ethic of Accounting," *Journal of Business Ethics* 5, no. 2 (1986): 119-28.

[3]H. Angle and J. Perry, "Dual Commitment and Labor-Management Relationship Climates," *Academy of Management Journal* 29, no. 1 (1986): 35.

[4]J. R. Michaels, *1 Peter,* Word Biblical Commentary (Waco, Tex.: Word, 1988), pp. 137-42.

[5]J. Pelikan, ed., *Luther's Works: The Catholic Epistles* (St. Louis: Concordia, 1967), pp. 82-84.

[6]J. Van Duzer and A. Hill, "Personal Ethics and Professional Loyalties," *Christian Legal Society Quarterly,* Summer 1989, pp. 14-15.

[7]W. Whyte Jr., *The Organization Man* (New York: Simon & Schuster, 1956), p. 4.

[8]P. Lawrence, *The Changing of Organizational Behavior Patterns: A Case Study of Decentralization* (Boston: Harvard Business School, 1986), p. 208.

[9]R. Decker, "It's Your Duty to Be a Company Man or Woman," *Purchasing,* May 8, 1986, p. 63.

[10]D. Welch, ed., "Martin Luther King's Letter from Birmingham City Jail," in *Law and Morality* (Philadelphia: Fortress, 1987), pp. 147-64.

[11]J. Wharton, "Exposition of Daniel 3:16-18," *Interpretation* 39, no. 1 (1985): 170-76.

[12]S. DeVries, *1 Kings,* Word Biblical Commentary (Waco, Tex.: Word, 1985), pp. 259-72.

[13]John Wesley, *The Works of John Wesley* (Grand Rapids: Baker, 1979), 6:469.

[14]D. Randall, "Commitment and the Organization: The Organizational Man Revisited," *The Academy of Management Review* 12, no. 3 (1987): 461.

[15]K. Wuest, *Ephesians and Colossians in the Greek New Testament* (Grand Rapids: Eerdmans, 1974), p. 137.

[16]John Stott, *God's New Society* (Downers Grove, Ill.: InterVarsity Press, 1979), pp. 250-59.

[17]Bo Reicke, *The Epistles of James, Peter and Jude,* Anchor Bible (New York: Doubleday, 1964), p. 98.

[18]T. Ogletree, *The Use of the Bible in Christian Ethics* (Philadelphia: Fortress, 1983), p. 164.

[19]Randall, "Commitment," p. 466.

[20]A. Konrad, "Business Managers and Moral Sanctuaries," *Journal of Business Ethics* 1 (1982): 195-200.

[21]R. Wasserstrom, "Lawyers as Professionals: Some Moral Issues," in *Ethical Theory and Business,* ed. T. Beauchamp and N. Bowie, 4th ed. (Englewood Cliffs, N.J.: Prentice-Hall, 1993), pp. 325-27.

[22]J. Childress and J. Macquarrie, *The Westminster Dictionary of Christian Ethics* (Philadelphia: Westminister Press, 1986), pp. 429-33.

[23]Randall, "Commitment," p. 467.

[24]Thomas Aquinas, *Summa Theologica* (New York: Benziger Brothers, 1947), pp. 1644-46.

[25]J. Cederblom and C. Dougherty, *Ethics at Work* (Belmont, Calif.: Wadsworth, 1990), pp. 27-28.

[26]Randall, "Commitment," p. 466.

[27]T. Beauchamp and N. Bowie, eds., "A. Michalos—The Loyal Agent Argument," in *Ethical Theory and Business,* 2nd ed. (Englewood Cliffs, N.J.: Prentice Hall, 1983), pp. 247-54.

[28]Michaels, *1 Peter,* p. 138.

[29]Reicke, *James, Peter and Jude,* p. 100.

[30]I. Stewart, "Accounting and Accountability: Double Entry, Double Nature, Double Identity," *Crux* 36, no. 2 (1990): 13-20.

[31]A. Sullivan, "Alaska Pipeline Gets Sham Safety Checks," *Wall Street Journal,* August 4, 1992, p. A1.

[32]L. Fuller, *The Morality of Law* (New Haven, Conn.: Yale University Press, 1964), pp. 9-10, 27-28.

[33]B. Kateregga and D. Shenk, *Islam and Christianity* (Nairobi, Kenya: Uzima, 1980), pp. 74, 157-63.

[34]Childress and Macquarrie, *Westminster Dictionary of Christian Ethics,* pp. 46, 71, 361, 375, 623.

[35]G. Forell and W. Lazareth, *Corporation Ethics: The Quest of Moral Authority* (Philadelphia: Fortress, 1980), p. 48.

Chapter 8: Honesty and Deception (Part 1)

[1]C. Joseph Pusateri, *A History of American Business,* 2nd ed. (Arlington Heights, Ill: Harlan Davidson, 1988), pp. 281-82.

[2]Anusorn Singhapakdi and Scott Vitell, "Ethical Ideologies of Future Marketers: The Relative Influences of Machiavellianism and Gender," *Journal of Marketing Education,* Spring 1994, pp. 34-36.

[3]Ibid., p. 34.

[4]Steve Stecklow, "Crumbling Pyramid," *Wall Street Journal,* May 16, 1995, p. A1; and Thomas Giles, "Double Your Money Scam Burns Christian Groups," *Christianity Today,* June 19, 1995,

pp. 40-41.

[5]Lewis Smedes, *Mere Morality* (Grand Rapids: Eerdmans, 1983), pp. 222-24.

[6]J. Brooke Hamilton and David Strutton, "Two Practical Guidelines for Resolving Truth-Telling Problems," *Journal of Business Ethics* 13 (1994): 907.

[7]Ibid., p. 908.

[8]Norman Bowie, "Does It Pay to Bluff in Business?" in *Ethical Theory and Business,* ed. T. Beauchamp and N. Bowie, 3rd ed. (Englewood Cliffs, N.J.: Prentice-Hall, 1988), pp. 446-47.

[9]Hamilton and Strutton, "Two Practical Guidelines," p. 907.

[10]Sissela Bok, *Lying: Moral Choice in Public and Private Life* (New York: Vintage, 1979), p. 26.

[11]Ibid., p. 28.

[12]Smedes, *Mere Morality,* p. 223.

[13]David Holley, "A Moral Evaluation of Sales Practices," in *Ethical Theory and Business,* ed. T. Beauchamp and N. Bowie, 4th ed. (Englewood Cliffs, N.J.: Prentice-Hall, 1993), p. 466.

[14]William Lawrence, *Beyond the Bottom Line: Where Faith and Business Meet* (Chicago: Moody Press, 1994), p. 154.

[15]Richard Chewning, *Biblical Principles and Business,* 3 vols. (Colorado Springs: NavPress, 1989), 1:131.

[16]Samuel Johnson in *Selected Essays from the Rambler, Adventurer and Idler,* ed. W. J. Bate (New Haven, Conn.: Yale University Press, 1968), p. 174.

[17]John Emshwiller, "Fraud Charges Prompt Questions on U.S. Trading Rules," *Wall Street Journal,* December 14, 1994, p. C1.

[18]David Clyde Jones, *Biblical Christian Ethics* (Grand Rapids: Baker, 1994), p. 144.

[19]Dante, *The Divine Comedy: Inferno,* trans. Charles S. Singleton (Princeton, N.J.: Princeton University Press, 1940), canto 11, p. 111.

[20]T. Beauchamp and N. Bowie, eds., *Ethical Theory and Business,* 4th ed. (Englewood Cliffs, N.J.: Prentice-Hall, 1993), p. 464.

[21]Jones, *Biblical Christian Ethics,* p. 148.

[22]Bok, *Lying,* p. 224.

[23]Ibid., pp. 24, 32-33.

[24]Jones, *Biblical Christian Ethics,* p. 148.

[25]Smedes, *Mere Morality,* p. 221.

[26]Augustine, "Lying," in *Treatises on Various Subjects,* ed. R. J. Deferrari (New York: Catholic University Press, 1952), vol. 14, chap. 14.

[27]Bok, *Lying,* pp. 82-83, 36.

[28]Smedes, *Mere Morality,* p. 221.

Chapter 9: Honesty and Deception (Part 2)

[1]Lynn Sharp Paine, "Corporate Policy and the Ethics of Competitor Intelligence Gathering," in *Ethical Theory and Business,* ed. T. Beauchamp and N. Bowie, 4th ed. (Englewood Cliffs, N.J.: Prentice-Hall, 1993), p. 491.

[2]"Volvo Drives Smack into the Hall of Shame," *Seattle Post Intelligencer,* December 30, 1990, p. B10.

[3]David Clyde Jones, *Biblical Christian Ethics* (Grand Rapids: Baker, 1994), pp. 150-51.

[4]Sissela Bok, *Lying: Moral Choice in Public and Private Life* (New York: Vintage, 1979), pp. 130-35.

[5]Joel Davis, "Ethics in Advertising Decision Making: Implications for Reducing the Incidence of Deceptive Advertising," *Journal of Consumer Affairs* 28, no. 2 (1994): 387.

[6]Lewis Smedes, *Mere Morality* (Grand Rapids: Eerdmans, 1983), pp. 231-32.

[7]"Volvo," p. B10.

[8]Joan Callahan, *Ethical Issues in Professional Life* (Oxford: Oxford University Press, 1988), p. 112.

[9]Cited in *Federal Trade Commission* v. *Colgate-Palmolive Co.,* 380 U.S. 374 (1964), p. 380.

[10]Tom Beauchamp, "Manipulative Advertising," in *Ethical Theory and Business,* ed. T. Beauchamp and N. Bowie, 3rd ed. (Englewood Cliffs, N.J.: Prentice-Hall, 1988), pp. 426-27.

[11]Peter Kreeft, *Making Choices* (Ann Arbor, Mich.: Servant, 1990), p. 141.

[12]Richard Lippke, "Advertising and the Social Conditions of Autonomy," *Business and Professional Ethics Journal* 8, no. 4 (Winter 1989): 43-47.

Chapter 10: Concealment and Disclosure

[1]Sissela Bok, *Secrets: On the Ethics of Concealment and Revelation* (New York: Pantheon, 1982), p. 6.

[2]George Orwell, *1984* (New York: New American Library of World Literature, 1956).

[3]Derk Boddle and Clarence Morris, *Law in Imperial China* (Cambridge, Mass.: Harvard University Press, 1967), p. 40.

[4]Rami Grunbaum, "Physio, Heartstream Face Off in Legal Tiff," *The Puget Sound Business Journal,* November 24-30, 1995, p. 1.

[5]Sissela Bok, *Lying: Moral Choices in Public and Private Life* (New York: Vintage, 1979), pp. 156-57.

[6]Ibid., p. 145.

[7]John Greenwald, "The Spy Who Cried," *Time,* August 28, 1995, pp. 48-49.

[8]Bok, *Lying,* p. 58.

[9]Steve Stecklow, "Universities Face Trouble for Enhancing Guide Data," *Wall Street Journal,* October 12, 1995, p. B1.

[10]"Internal Memo Reveals Conflict in Outplacement Firm's Loyalties," *Wall Street Journal,* January 27, 1995, p. B1.

[11]Raju Narisetti, "Extra Bites: Intelligent Electronics Made Much of Its Profit at Suppliers' Expense," *Wall Street Journal,* December 6, 1994, p. A1.

[12]Robert Tomsho, "Greyhound Says SEC Is Investigating Possible Violations of Securities Law," *Wall Street Journal,* January 26, 1995, p. A4.

[13]Alix Freedman, "Impact Booster: Tobacco Firm Shows How Ammonia Spurs Delivery of Nicotine," *Wall Street Journal,* October 18, 1995, p. A1.

[14]David Holley, "A Moral Evaluation of Sales Practices," in *Ethical Theory in Business,* ed. T. Beauchamp and N. Bowie, 4th ed. (Englewood Cliffs, N.J.: Prentice-Hall, 1993), pp. 466-67.

[15]Ibid., p. 474.

[16]Neela Banerjee, "Fleeing Civil Wars, Refugees Seek Safety Outside Chernobyl," *Wall Street Journal,* November 8, 1995, p. A1.

[17]Thomas Garrett and Richard Klonoski, *Business Ethics* (Englewood Cliffs, N.J.: Prentice-Hall, 1986), p. 91.

[18]Julie Marquis, "Nurse Tried to Warn About Embryo Swaps," *Seattle Times* (from the *Los Angeles Times*), June 15, 1995, p. A3.

[19]James Roche, "The Competitive System to Work," *Vital Speeches of the Day,* May 1971, p. 445.

[20]Bok, *Lying,* p. 218.

[21]Norman Bowie, *Business Ethics* (Englewood Cliffs, N.J.: Prentice-Hall, 1982), pp. 140-41.

[22]Natalie Dandekar, "Can Whistleblowing Be Fully Legitimated?" *Business and Professional Ethics Journal* 10, no. 1 (Spring 1991): 93.

[23]Myron Glazer and Penina Glazer, *The Whistleblowers* (New York: Basic Books, 1989), cited

by Mike Martin in "Whistleblowing: Professionalism, Personal Life and Shared Responsibility for Safety in Engineering," *Business and Professional Ethics Journal* 6, no. 1 (Summer 1991): 23-24.

[24]Michael Lewis, "The Good Rat," *New York Times Magazine,* October 28, 1995, pp. 26-27.

[25]James Woehlke, "Tax Currents," *The Tax Adviser,* February 1992, p. 123.

[26]Robert Foss, "Independence," minicase for *Arthur Anderson's Business Ethics Series* (St. Charles, Ill.: Arthur Anderson, 1992).

[27]C. Joseph Pusateri, *A History of American Business,* 2nd ed. (Arlington Heights, Ill.: Harlan Davidson, 1988), p. 284.

Chapter 11: Employer-Employee Relations

[1]Adam Smith, *The Wealth of Nations* (1776; reprint Chicago: University of Chicago Press, 1976), bks. 1, 4.

[2]Daniel Boorstin, *The Americans: The Democratic Experience* (New York: Vintage, 1974), p. 363.

[3]Ibid., pp. 364, 368.

[4]Ibid., pp. 363, 368-69.

[5]Ibid.

[6]David Brown, *Choices: Ethics and the Christian* (Oxford: Blackwell, 1983), p. 59.

[7]Boorstin, *The Americans,* p. 369.

[8]John Haggai, "Biblical Principles Applied to Organizational Behavior," in *Biblical Principles and Business,* ed. Richard Chewning, 3 vols. (Colorado Springs: NavPress, 1990), 3:131.

[9]Tony Horwitz, "Mr. Edens Profits from Watching His Workers' Every Move," *Wall Street Journal,* December 1, 1994, p. A11.

[10]Stephen Robbins and Mary Coulter, *Management,* 5th ed. (Upper Saddle River, N.J.: Prentice-Hall, 1996), pp. 532-33.

[11]Ibid., p. 533.

[12]Edward Betof, "Raising Personal Empowerment," *Training and Development,* September 1992, p. 32.

[13]Ibid., p. 32.

[14]Myron Augsburger, "The New Testament Ethic Superseded the Old Testament Ethic," in *Biblical Principles and Business,* ed. Richard Chewning, 3 vols. (Colorado Springs: NavPress, 1989), 1:67-68.

[15]Earnest Huband, "Developing Effective Management Skills," *Management Accounting,* July 1992, p. 45.

[16]Richard Chewning, John Eby and Shirley Roels, *Business Through the Eyes of Faith* (San Francisco: Harper & Row, 1990), p. 39.

[17]Boorstin, *The Americans,* p. 369.

[18]Karl Marx and Friedrich Engels, *The Communist Manifesto,* trans. Samuel Moore (New York: Washington Square, 1934).

[19]Horwitz, "Mr. Edens," p. A1.

[20]Ibid., p. A11.

[21]Lynn Sharp Paine, "Managing for Organizational Integrity," *Harvard Business Review,* March 1994, pp. 107-8.

[22]Alexander Hill, "Colossians, Philemon and the Practice of Business," *Crux* 30, no. 2 (June 1994): 32.

[23]Ibid.

[24]Max De Pree, *Leadership Is an Art* (East Lansing: Michigan State University Press, 1987), pp. xi-xxiii.

[25]Vernon Grounds, "Responsibility and Subjectivity: Applying Biblical Principles in Business," in *Biblical Principles and Business*, ed. Richard Chewning, 3 vols. (Colorado Springs: NavPress, 1989), 1:126.

[26]Paine, "Managing for Integrity," pp. 115-16.

[27]Ibid., p. 122.

[28]De Pree, *Leadership*, pp. 15, 37, 55.

[29]Mindy Cameron, "Boeing Pact's Big Benefit Is Its Long-Term Stability," *Seattle Times*, December 15, 1995, p. B6.

[30]Patricia Werhane, "Employee and Employer Rights in an Institutional Context," in *Ethical Theory and Business*, ed. T. Beauchamp and N. Bowie, 3rd ed. (Englewood Cliffs, N.J.: Prentice-Hall, 1988), p. 271.

[31]De Pree, *Leadership*, p. 12.

[32]Patrick Murphy and George Enderle, "Managerial Ethical Leadership: Examples Do Matter," *Business Ethics Quarterly* 5, no. 1 (1995): 117.

[33]De Pree, *Leadership*, pp. 9, 16.

[34]Ibid., p. 11.

Chapter 12: Employee Rights in Termination and Privacy

[1]*Wagenseller* v. *Scottsdale Memorial Hospital*, Arizona Supreme Court, 710 P. 2d 1025 (1985). Cited in John Allison and Robert Prentice, *The Legal Environment of Business*, 4th ed. (Orlando, Fla.: Dryden, 1992), p. 513.

[2]Ibid., p. 309.

[3]Gillian Flynn, "Take the Fear out of Termination," *Personnel Journal*, January 1995, p. 123.

[4]Ian Maitland, "Rights in the Workplace: A Nozickian Argument," in *Taking Sides: Clashing Views on Controversial Issues in Business Ethics*, ed. Lisa Newton and Maureen Ford (Guilford, Conn.: Dushkin, 1990), pp. 33-37.

[5]Patricia Werhane, *Persons, Rights and Corporations* (Englewood Cliffs, N.J.: Prentice-Hall, 1985), p. 122.

[6]Ibid., p. 127.

[7]Allison and Prentice, *Legal Environment*, p. 513.

[8]*Potter* v. *Village Bank of N.J.*, Superior Court of N.J., 543 A.2nd 80 (1985). Cited in T. Beauchamp and N. Bowie, eds., *Ethical Theory and Business*, 4th ed. (Englewood Cliffs, N.J.: Prentice-Hall, 1993), pp. 342-46.

[9]Allison and Prentice, *Legal Environment*, p. 1026.

[10]Flynn, "Take the Fear," p. 125.

[11]Margaret Jacobs, "Brutal Firings Can Backfire, Ending in Court," *Wall Street Journal*, October 24, 1994, p. B1.

[12]For a discussion of privacy issues, see Nancy Kubasek, *The Legal Environment of Business: A Critical Thinking Approach* (Upper Saddle River, N.J.: Prentice-Hall, 1996), pp. 311-12.

[13]Mark Evans, "Chain to Settle for $1.3 Million in Psychscreen Suit," *Seattle Times*, July 11, 1993, p. A5.

[14]Jim Simons, "Victory for Privacy Rights," *Seattle Times*, March 6, 1992, p. A1.

[15]Junda Woo, "Employers Fume over New Legislation Barring Discrimination Against Smokers," *Wall Street Journal*, June 4, 1993, p. B1.

[16]John Hoerr et al., "Privacy," in *Taking Sides: Clashing Views on Controversial Issues in Business Ethics*, ed. Lisa Newton and Maureen Ford (Guilford, Conn.: Dushkin, 1990), p. 75.

[17]Joseph DesJardins and Ronald Duska, "Drug Testing in Employment," *Business and Professional Ethics Journal* 6 (1987). Cited in Beauchamp and Bowie, *Ethical Theory and Business*, pp. 294-305.

[18]*Luedtke* v. *Nabors Alaska Drilling, Inc.,* Superior Court of Alaska, 768 P. 2d 1123 (1989). Cited in Beauchamp and Bowie, *Ethical Theory and Business,* p. 354.

[19]Allison and Prentice, *Legal Environment,* p. 518.

[20]Beauchamp and Bowie, *Ethical Theory and Business,* p. 352.

[21]Hoerr et al., "Privacy," p. 79.

[22]Donald Bloesch, *Freedom for Obedience: Evangelical Ethics in Contemporary Times* (San Francisco: Harper & Row, 1987), p. 183.

Chapter 13: Discrimination and Affirmative Action

[1]John Allison and Robert Prentice, *The Legal Environment of Business,* 4th ed. (New York: Dryden, 1993), p. 587.

[2]Amy Dockser Marcus and Milo Geyelin, "Work Environment Is Hostile," *Wall Street Journal,* April 8, 1991, p. B1.

[3]*Price Waterhouse* v. *Hopkins,* United States Supreme Court, 490 U.S. 228, 109 S. Ct. 1775 (1989).

[4]Brett Pulley, "Culture of Racial Bias at Shoney's," *Wall Street Journal,* December 21, 1992, p. A7.

[5]Joseph Bouce, "Turf War: Struggle over Hospital in Los Angeles Pits Minority vs. Minority," *Wall Street Journal,* April 1, 1991, p. A1.

[6]Laura Purdy, "In Defense of Hiring Apparently Less Qualified Women," *Journal of Social Philosophy* 15 (1984): 26-33.

[7]Roger Crook, *An Introduction to Christian Ethics* (Englewood Cliffs, N.J.: Prentice-Hall, 1990), p. 167.

[8]Timothy Noah, "Job Tests Scored on Racial Curve Stir Controversy," *Wall Street Journal,* May 26, 1991, p. B1.

[9]Lisa Newton in *Taking Sides: Clashing Views on Controversial Issues in Business Ethics,* ed. Lisa Newton and Maureen Ford (Guilford, Conn.: Dushkin, 1990), p. 97.

[10]Thomas Donaldson and Patricia Werhane, *Ethical Issues in Business: A Philosophical Approach,* 4th ed. (Englewood Cliffs, N.J.: Prentice-Hall, 1993), p. 326.

[11]*Local 28 of the Sheet Metal Workers' International Association* v. *Equal Employment Opportunity Commission,* United States Supreme Court, 106 S. Ct. 3019 (1986). Cited in T. Beauchamp and N. Bowie, *Ethical Theory and Business,* 4th ed. (Englewood Cliffs, N.J.: Prentice-Hall, 1993), pp. 420-25.

[12]T. Beauchamp and N. Bowie, *Ethical Theory and Business,* 3rd ed. (Englewood Cliffs, N.J.: Prentice-Hall, 1988), p. 343.

[13]*Automobile Workers* v. *Johnson Controls, Inc.,* 89 U.S. Supreme Court 1215 (1991).

[14]*United Steel Workers and Kaiser Aluminum* v. *Weber,* 443 U.S. 193 (1979).

Chapter 14: The Environment

[1]Lynn White, *The Environmental Handbook,* ed. Garrett De Bell (New York: Ballantine, 1970), pp. 23, 26.

[2]Ibid., p. 20.

[3]Marilyn Chase, "A New Cancer Drug May Extend Lives at the Cost of Rare Trees," *Wall Street Journal,* April 9, 1991, p. A1.

[4]Richard Routley, "Human Chauvinism and Environmental Ethics," in *Environmental Philosophy* (Melbourne: Australian National University, 1980), p. 121.

[5]Martin Krieger, "What's Wrong with Plastic Trees?" *Science* 179 (1973): 451.

[6]Quoted in William Ophuls, "The Scarcity Society," *Harpers,* April 1974. Reprinted in Thomas Donaldson and Patricia Werhane, *Ethical Issues in Business,* 3rd ed. (Englewood Cliffs, N.J.:

Prentice-Hall, 1988), p. 380.

[7]Craig Smith, "China Becomes Industrial Nations' Most Favored Dump," *Wall Street Journal,* October 9, 1995, p. B1.

[8]Nathan Gardels and Marilyn Snell, "Mexico City Is an Omen," *Utne Reader,* January 1993, p. 94.

[9]John Locke, "The Justification of Private Property," in *Second Treatise on Government* (1764; reprint New York: Macmillan, 1956). Reprinted in Donaldson and Werhane, *Ethical Issues in Business,* p. 182.

[10]James Post, "Managing As If the Earth Mattered," *Business Horizons,* July 1991, p. 230.

[11]Sara Ebenreck, "An Earth-Care Ethics," *The Catholic World,* July 1990, p. 154.

[12]Marianne Jennings, *Case Studies in Business Ethics* (Minneapolis: West, 1993), p. 169.

[13]William Booth, "Mega Dose of Iron Might Be the Cure for Global Heat," *Seattle Times,* May 20, 1990, p. A2.

[14]Ebenreck, "An Earth-Care Ethics," p. 153.

[15]David Webster, "The Free Market for Clean Air," *Business and Society Review,* Summer 1994, pp. 34-35.

[16]William Ophuls, "The Scarcity Society," *Harpers,* April 1974. Quoted in Donald and Warhane, *Ethical Issues in Business,* p. 375.

[17]Gardels and Snell, "Mexico City," p. 94.

[18]William Shaw and Vincent Barry, *Moral Issues in Business,* 6th ed. (Belmont, Calif.: Wadsworth, 1995), p. 528.

[19]Paul Steidlmeier, "The Morality of Pollution Permits," *Environmental Ethics,* Summer 1993, p. 136.

[20]Tom Regan, "The Nature and Possibility of an Environmental Ethic," *Environmental Ethics,* Spring 1981, p. 33.

[21]Bill Dietrich, "Earth First Founder Reflects on Life as an Eco-Warrior," *Seattle Times,* March 12, 1991, p. B3.

[22]White, *Environmental Handbook,* pp. 20-21.

[23]Ebenreck, "An Earth-Care Ethics," p. 157.

[24]Todd Connor, "Is the Earth Alive?" *Christianity Today,* January 11, 1993, p. 25.

[25]Ibid., 25.

[26]Ebenreck, "An Earth-Care Ethics," p. 157.

[27]Loren Wilkinson, "How Christian Is the Green Agenda?" *Christianity Today,* January 11, 1993, p. 18.

[28]Connor, "Is the Earth Alive?" p. 25.

[29]Ibid., p. 25.

[30]Roger Crook, *An Introduction to Christian Ethics* (Englewood Cliffs, N.J.: Prentice-Hall, 1990), p. 238.

[31]See Genesis 2 for Adam's interaction with the animals and garden.

[32]Francis Schaeffer, *Pollution and the Death of Man: The Christian View of Ecology* (Grand Rapids: Eerdmans, 1970), pp. 55-56.

[33]Ibid., pp. 53-54.

[34]White, *Environmental Handbook,* pp. 24-25.

[35]Richard Higginson, *Dilemmas: A Christian Approach to Decision-Making* (Louisville, Ky.: Westminster Press, 1988), p. 220. See also Bernard Haring, *Christian Renewal in a Changing World* (Louisville, Ky.: Desclee, 1964), pp. 50-90.

[36]Higginson, *Dilemmas,* p. 221.

[37]See Schaeffer, *Pollution,* p. 49.

[38]Ibid., p. 57

[39]David Woodruff, "Herman Miller: How Green Is My Factory," *Business Week,* September 16, 1991, p. 55.

[40]Issues regarding the theory of evolution (other forms of life preceding human life) are beyond the scope of this chapter.

[41]Ibid., p. 55.

[42]Kenneth Sheets, "Business' Green Revolution," *U.S. News & World Report,* February 19, 1990, p. 45.

[43]Case taken from George Steiner and John Steiner, *Business, Government and Society,* 4th ed. (New York, Random House, 1985), pp. 434-36.

Chapter 15: Property
[1]Richard Foster, *Money, Sex and Power* (San Francisco: Harper & Row, 1985), pp. 22-23.

[2]Robert Nisbet, *The Present Age* (San Francisco: Harper & Row, 1988), pp. 75-76.

[3]Jacques Ellul, *Money and Power* (Downers Grove, Ill.: InterVarsity Press, 1984), p. 35.

[4]Foster, *Money, Sex and Power,* pp. 19-23.

[5]Brian Griffiths, *The Creation of Wealth* (Downers Grove, Ill.: InterVarsity Press, 1984), pp. 50, 60.

[6]Note also the riches of Solomon's descendant Hezekiah in 2 Chronicles 32:27-29 and the "wealth of the nations" promised in Isaiah 60:11.

[7]Ellul, *Money and Power,* pp. 62-72.

[8]Rick Bragg, "From a Life's Work, a Legacy Is Built," *New York Times,* August 13, 1995, p. 1.

[9]Laurel Touby, "In the Company of Thieves," *Journal of Business Strategy,* November 1993, p. 27.

[10]Foster, *Money, Sex and Power,* pp. 25, 28.

[11]Ellul, *Money and Power,* pp. 76-77.

[12]Milo Geyelin, "Attorney Pleads Guilty to Bilking Firm," *Wall Street Journal,* December 20, 1994, p. B6.

[13]William D. Lawrence, *Beyond the Bottom Line: Where Faith and Business Meet* (Chicago: Moody Press, 1994), p. 27.

[14]Cited in Max Weber, *The Protestant Ethic and the Spirit of Capitalism* (New York: Scribner's, 1958), p. 175.

[15]Touby, "In the Company of Thieves," p. 35.

[16]Mark Robichaux, "Dart and Ronald Haft Reach Pact Seeking End to Bitter Legal Feud," *Wall Street Journal,* October 9, 1995, p. B4.

[17]Foster, *Money, Sex and Power,* p. 29.

[18]Ibid., p. 26.

[19]Jim Mann, "Come Visit the Other Asia: One of Gold As Well As Death," *Seattle Times,* October 31, 1995, p. A3.

[20]Brian Griffiths, *Morality and the Market Place* (London: Hodder & Stoughton, 1982), p. 92

[21]Touby, "In the Company of Thieves," pp. 25-26.

[22]Ibid., p. 25.

[23]Wilma Randle, "When Employees Lie, Cheat or Steal," *Working Woman,* January 1995, p. 56.

[24]David Parker, *Business Competitor Intelligence* (New York: Wiley, 1984), p. 299.

[25]Glenn Simpson, "A 90's Espionage Tale Stars Software Rivals, E-Mail Spying," *Wall Street Journal,* October 25, 1995, p. B5.

[26]Del Jones, "With Internet Surfing, Loafing on the Job Now Easier Than Ever," *Seattle Times,* December 9, 1995, p. A3.

[27]David Stires, "Beyond Crime and Punishment—Restitution," *Wall Street Journal,* September 20, 1995, A17

[28]Lewis Smedes, "Persons and Property," *The Reformed Journal*, April, 1965, pp. 217-18.

[29]Griffiths, *Morality and the Market Place*, p. 95.

[30]Ellul, *Money and Power*, p. 110.

[31]Foster, *Money, Sex and Power*, p. 46.

[32]Anthony Boadle, "Film Exposes Black Market in Body Parts from Humans," *Seattle Times*, November 12, 1993, p. A14.

[33]John McClenahen, "What to Do About the Lone Ranger?" *Industry Week*, February 20, 1995, p. 60.

[34]Bob Herbert, "U.S. Bears Responsibility for Industrial Exploitation," *Seattle Post Intelligencer*, December 29, 1994, p. A13.

[35]Case adapted from Robert Stivers, *Christian Ethics* (Maryknoll, N.Y.: Orbis, 1989), pp. 15-18.